Walter McElreath

Walter McElreath

An Autobiography

edited by
Albert B. Saye

MERCER

ISBN 0-086554-146-9

Walter McElreath: An Autobiography
Copyright © 1984
Mercer University Press
All rights reserved
Printed in the United States of America

All books published by Mercer University Press are produced
on acid-free paper that exceeds the minimum standards set by the
National Historical Publications and Records Commission.

Library of Congress Cataloging in Publication Data
McElreath, Walter, 1867-1951.
Walter McElreath: an autobiography.

1. McElreath, Walter, 1867-1951.   2. Atlanta (Ga.)—
Biography.   3. Cobb County (Ga.)—Biography.   I. Saye,
Albert Berry.   II. Title.
F294.A853M385   1984   975.8'231'040924 [B]   84-20542
ISBN 0-86554-146-9 (alk. paper)

Contents

Introduction

by Albert B. Saye
Richard B. Russell Professor Emeritus
The University of Georgia

Walter McElreath is best remembered as the founder of the Atlanta Historical Society and the first president of the Atlanta Federal Savings and Loan Association. The principal building of the Atlanta Historical Society on Andrews Drive is called McElreath Hall in his honor. His autobiography, written in 1940-1941, is reproduced here. It contains a moving account of his personal life and is also a source par excellence for the history of the period in which he lived.

Walter McElreath (17 July 1867—6 December 1951), the elder son of William Anderson McElreath and his wife, née Matilda Jane McEachern, was born in a log house on a farm near Lost Mountain, in Cobb County, Georgia. His parents were both children of immigrants who had come to northwest Georgia when the area was opened to white settlers by the removal of the Cherokee Indians in 1836.

Walter's father was only 20 years old when the Civil War began. A company of volunteers was organized at what was then known as Powder Springs Camp Ground. William Anderson McElreath was one of the first to join this company, which was mustered into service on 19 May 1861. He served in half of the major battles of the war. Miraculously, he was never wounded. He was at Appomattox when Lee surrendered. With two or three army companions, he walked back to Georgia, and settled in the Lost Mountain area. In 1866 he purchased a small farm, and in that same year he married Jane McEachern. Ten months later their first son, Walter, was born. At intervals of approximately two years, four other sons and four daughters were born to William and Jane McElreath.

As soon as he was big enough, Walter became a laborer on his father's farm. The hours of plowing and hoeing were long, and the work was hard. An economic depression gripped all farmers in the South. Walter's father moved several times in an effort to improve his economic circumstances. In this effort he had little success. After a few years he purchased a portion of the land that had constituted his grandfather's farm near Lost Mountain.

Walter's parents had had little formal education, but they both enjoyed reading. They owned a small collection of books of history, philosophy, and literature.

The first school that Walter McElreath attended was held in a small log cabin at Midway Church, about a mile from his home. The school was conducted by Miss Hattie Fitten for about five months during the year. Each pupil paid as tuition a few cents per day. The pupils were of all ages, from six to sixty. There were no grades and no courses of study. Each student studied what he pleased. The principal subjects studied were spelling, reading, writing, arithmetic, geography, and English grammar. The students studied on their own, and went to the teacher for aid when they encountered a problem. She gave no lectures; she heard recitations and corrected errors. At age twelve Walter McElreath began attending a school at Lost Mountain, and continued for three years. The teacher for the first year was John Mable, who had been a schoolmate of Walter's mother.

Walter's parents were members of the Methodist Church at Powder Springs. Services were held at this church only on the second Sunday of each month. The McElreaths attended a Sunday School that met every Sunday afternoon at the Midway Presbyterian Church. They also occasionally attended camp meetings in adjoining counties. Many participants stayed overnight in tents. These meetings were times of great spiritual revival.

When he was fifteen years old, Walter joined a debating society organized at Midway for the boys and young men of the community. Public speaking was difficult for Walter, and participation in this debating society proved helpful to him. By this time he had already decided that he would become a lawyer.

Walter continued to work on his father's farm and to attend school a few months each year until he was eighteen years old. In 1885, with the assistance of one of his uncles, Walter became the teacher at Piney Bower Academy in Cherokee County. In preparation for this undertaking, in July he attended a teacher's institute in Atlanta, sponsored by Gustavus J. Orr, State School Commissioner. While in Atlanta he boarded in the home of his uncle, Robert McEachern. He was gratified with the results of his efforts as a teacher. Some of his pupils made encouraging progress. He returned to his father's farm at the end of the school year with $130 in his pocket, by far the greatest sum he had ever possessed.

During the next three years Walter taught in other local schools, including Lost Mountain Academy. In the spring of 1890 he announced that in September he would enter Washington and Lee University. His parents were proud of Walter and pleased with his decision. But to his great sorrow, his mother died that June.

In September, at age 23, Walter went by train to Lexington, Virginia, to enter Washington and Lee University. Registration was held the day after Walter's arrival. He registered for Latin, Greek, mathematics, and ancient history. By his request, he was assigned to the Latin class for the junior class and found lesson assignments in that course to be long and difficult. His studies occupied his time fully, but he did manage to take an active part in one of the two debating societies functioning on the campus.

When he returned home for the summer Walter secured a position as teacher in Due West, a local school located about three miles from Lost Mountain. This school closed the first week in September, and a week later Walter was back in Lexington.

The courses of study for which Walter registered the second year were Latin, mathematics, moral philosophy, surveying, and astronomy. He continued to participate in the Washington Literary Society. At the end of the school year, he received certificates of distinction in all of the subjects he had studied, except mathematics.

He did not take the final examination in mathematics because of illness.

Walter spent the years 1892 to 1894 teaching in schools in his home area, largely at Powder Springs High School. During the second year he began to study law at night, reading such books as *Blackstone's Commentaries* and the *Code of Georgia*. In the fall he went to Marietta and studied in the office of R. N. Holland. On 23 November 1894, he was admitted to the bar.

Walter chose Atlanta as the place to begin his practice of law. One influence on this decision was the fact that John N. McEachern, his uncle, lived there and offered to help him get established. Walter went to Atlanta in December 1894. He and his uncle roomed in the home of a Mrs. Washington at the corner of Forsyth and Mitchell streets. By occupying a room jointly, Walter and his uncle reduced their room rent to $3 each per week.

Walter rented an office in the Gate City Bank Building, but he had very little practice. He earned less than $100 during the first year. Much of his time was spent studying the Georgia Code. In August he became ill and returned to his father's home. After a few months he returned to Atlanta. This time he rented an office in the Temple Court Building where King and Spalding and other leading law firms were located. After his income rose to around sixty dollars per month, he married Bessie Anderson on 26 November 1896. Miss Anderson was a native of his home community in Cobb County who had recently been teaching music at Centenary Female College in Cleveland, Tennessee. The income that she earned from giving private music lessons was a great help during the early years of their marriage.

In 1898 the McElreaths moved to a home on East Avenue on Atlanta's north side. The following year they joined the Grace Methodist Church. Mrs. McElreath helped with the church's musical program, and Mr. McElreath was elected to the church's board of stewards in 1903. He soon became chairman of this board and held that position for 19 years.

In 1908 Mr. McElreath was elected as a representative from Fulton County to the General Assembly of Georgia. In 1910 he was reelected, and during his second term he served as chairman of the

Appropriations Committee of the House of Representatives. In his
bid for reelection in 1912, he was defeated.

In 1912 the Harrison Company of Atlanta published a large volume entitled *McElreath on the Constitution of Georgia.* The volume was
well received by the legal profession and by historians.

In 1928 Mr. and Mrs. McElreath moved into a large new home,
"Braebiggen," on Piedmont Road. Their life there was a very happy
one, but seven years later, on 20 November 1935, Mrs. McElreath
died. After a little more than two years, Mr. McElreath married
Mildred Dickey, daughter of William Dickey of Toccoa.

Mr. McElreath was a leading figure in the early history of the
Atlanta Federal Savings and Loan Association. This, Georgia's
largest financial institution, was an outgrowth of the Atlanta Building and Loan Association, founded in 1928 by a group of business
and professional men who often had lunch together each day at
Mrs. Blackburn's tea room in downtown Atlanta. McElreath was
president of the Building Association when, on 26 August 1935, its
application was approved and it became the Atlanta Federal Savings and Loan Association. He continued as president until 1950
when he was succeeded by W. O. DuVall, an attorney who had
served as legal advisor and secretary of the loan association from
its early days and as general manager after 1940. I am indebted to
Mr. DuVall and to Francis M. Bird and Judson C. Ward for encouragement in publishing Mr. McElreath's autobiography.

Perhaps through modesty, Mr. McElreath wrote practically
nothing in his autobiography about his financial activities. Thomas
Hal Clarke, a prominent lawyer and close associate of Mr. Mc-
Elreath, contributed the sketch on Mr. McElreath's part in the
early history of the Atlanta Federal Savings and Loan Association.
The same modesty seems to have led Mr. McElreath to gloss over
his part in the founding of the Atlanta Historical Society. Franklin
Garrett, Atlanta's foremost historian, has kindly written the statement that follows on that subject.

I wish to thank Dr. James W. Alexander for checking the Latin
phrases scattered through the autobiography (in general, he found
them to be correct as written by Mr. McElreath), Mrs. Jeannine
Hall for typing the manuscript, and Ruth, my wife, for reading the
galley proofs. I also wish to thank Georgia Federal and the Atlanta

Historical Society for financial aid that made this publication possible.

Walter McElreath
and the
Atlanta Historical Society
by Franklin M. Garrett
Editor Emeritus, *Atlanta Historical Journal*

In his autobiography Walter McElreath makes short shrift of his connection with the Atlanta Historical Society. Yet through the years it will probably stand as his most tangible memorial.

Early in life Mr. McElreath developed an interest in history and most particularly that of the areas with which he was associated. Indeed, he celebrated New Year's Day in 1895 by settling permanently in Atlanta and promptly hung out his shingle as a practitioner of the law.

Mr. McElreath spent his first couple of decades in Atlanta building up his law practice. At the same time his interest in the colorful history of his adopted city was occupying more of his time and thought. The more he thought about it the more distressed he became that Atlanta had no local historical society. Finally in 1926 he took action. By that time he was fifty-nine and had built up a successful law practice. As the catalyst, he and a group of noted citizens petitioned the Fulton County Superior Court for a charter for an Atlanta Historical Society. The group joining Mr. McElreath in the petition included Joel Hunter, James L. Mayson, Wm. Rawson Collier, E. C. Kontz, Eugene M. Mitchell, Thomas W. Connally, Joseph Jacobs, Henry C. Peeples, Mrs. R. K. Rambo, Miss Ruth Blair, Edgar Watkins, and A. A. Meyer, all of Fulton County, and John M. Graham, of Cobb County. The petition was acted upon favorably and a charter was issued on 30 June 1926 by W. D. Ellis, judge of the Superior Court, Atlanta Circuit.

The purpose of the Atlanta Historical Society, as stated in its charter—its guiding star for fifty-six years—is "To promote the preservation of sources of information concerning the history of the City of Atlanta and the State of Georgia; the investigation, study and dissemination of such history, and to arouse in the friends and citizens of Atlanta an interest in its history."

The original officers of the Society were Walter McElreath, president; Joel Hunter, vice-president; Miss Ruth Blair, secretary and treasurer; and Miss Tommie Dora Barker, librarian. Mr. McElreath also served, for the first couple of years, as acting editor. The first Board of Curators (now Trustees), in addition to the original petitioners, was composed of Forrest Adair, Dr. Phinizy Calhoun, Clark Howell, Charles W. Hubner, Wm. Cole Jones, H. A. Maier, Wilmer L. Moore, J. B. Nevin, Mrs. J. K. Ottley, Edward C. Peters, Mrs. John M. Slaton, Hoke Smith, and W. D. Thomson.

With a limited membership, the Society began to function. It held occasional meetings, usually in homes of members, and at irregular times published bulletins of interest and merit. During this early period the Society began a modest collection of historical items. It was limited in scope by lack of space and because the Society had no salaried custodian or curator to solicit and care for it.

Even so, interest in the Society continued, and in the fall of 1936, under the leadership of lawyer Jack J. Spalding and Mr. McElreath, it was reorganized. Indeed Mr. McElreath had already concluded that income from regular dues alone would not enable the Society to grow or to fulfill the functions he visualized. Miss Ruth Blair, then state historian and director of the Georgia Department of Archives and History, was employed as full-time executive secretary. Rented quarters were established on the ground floor of the Biltmore Hotel. By 1943 these quarters were outgrown and the Society moved to a Peachtree Street location in the Erlanger Theater Building, just south of North Avenue, where more space was available.

Walter McElreath had long realized that what the Society needed, above all else, was a home of its own. To this end a vacant lot at the southwest corner of Peachtree and Sixteenth streets was purchased in 1940 from Frank M. Inman. The Society intended to build its headquarters there but World War II brought an end to that idea. So the Society sold the lot and bought a house. Fortunately for the Society, the handsome Georgian home of the late Dr. and Mrs. Willis B. Jones, designed by architect Neel Reid and erected during 1922 and 1923 at the southeast corner of Peachtree and Huntington roads, was available. It was purchased from the Jones heirs for $60,000, and Mr. McElreath personally advanced a large part of the purchase money. The building was occupied by the Society in January 1947. The Jones property was completely paid for by 1950 and the building was named appropriately McElreath Hall.

The financial basis upon which Spalding and McElreath placed the Society in early 1937 served its time and purpose well. Both men solicited the aid of certain well-to-do citizens and secured a number of $250 annual pledges, each pledge to run five years. In addition to regular dues and periodic membership campaigns, these funds carried the Society along for several years. Among the five-year donors were, in addition to Spalding and McElreath, James J. Haverty, J. Bulow Campbell, Robert W. Woodruff, Mrs. John K. Ottley, Morris Brandon, Harold Hirsch, R. DeWitt King, Thomas K. Glenn, Robert F. Maddox, Thomas H. Morgan, John W. Grant, Robert C. Alston, and James D. Robinson.

Until the Society moved into its own home at Peachtree and Huntington in early 1947, it managed with one salaried staff member, Ruth Blair. Since her employment a decade before, the capable and energetic Miss Blair had concentrated on building up the Society's collection of photographs and pictures. In this effort she was notably successful. Indeed, by the time of her retirement on 1 April 1956, the collection numbered several thousand items and formed the nucleus of the present collection of approximately 10,000. During the spring of 1948 a second paid employee was added, primarily to catalog the growing book collection.

Meanwhile, Walter McElreath, who died in 1951, had sown the seeds for the Society's future prosperity. By the terms of his will, made in 1950, he provided that his entire estate, except for some minor bequests, was to come to the Society as residuary legatee following the deaths of certain persons named in the will. So it was that in 1965, following the death of the last heir, the Atlanta Historical Society became one of the best endowed local historical societies in the country. The estate, the bulk of which was in Life Insurance Company of Georgia stock, was worth approximately $5,000,000.

In 1976, the Atlanta Historical Society observed its fiftieth anniversary. Throughout this half century and since, it has been collecting, preserving, and distributing facts and artifacts about the history of Atlanta, the State of Georgia, and the South.

Mr. McElreath would be proud, indeed, of the Society's physical plant—the former Edward H. Inman estate on Andrews Drive. Its principal building and the site of its operations is named in his honor. Indeed, the objectives envisioned by the founder and his associates back in 1926 are being fulfilled today.

Walter McElreath
and the
Atlanta Federal Savings and Loan Association
by Thomas Hal Clarke
Mitchell, Clarke, Pate, Anderson & Wimberly

By 1928 Walter McElreath was not only one of Atlanta's most respected lawyers, but he had become increasingly active in the business and civic affairs of the city. His association with the Life of Georgia had prospered; he was still serving as general counsel for that growing company, having first been elected attorney for the then tiny and struggling Southern Industrial Aid Society in 1897.

So it is not surprising that following the happy custom of that time he would meet daily with about fifteen friends at Mrs. Blackburn's Tea Room, a popular downtown lunch spot. The group included men from divergent interests—businessmen, engineers, lawyers, old Atlantans, and even some Yankee émigrés. Before he died in 1950, Mr. McElreath reminisced about this group in an unpublished manuscript tracing the history of the Atlanta Federal Savings and Loan Association.

At these daily luncheons, every conceivable question: professional, religious, political and economic, was discussed with as many opinions as participants in the discussions. Upon one question, however, there was unanimous agreement, that was, that the economy of the South was being bled white by the exportation of money in insurance premiums and interest payments to non-resident corporations, while local savings were on

deposit in the local banks at a rate of interest, at that time, much less than
the rate paid on mortgage loans.

To us today, basking in the relatively promising position of the Sun-
belt, that statement may seem hard to understand. But even in the
affluent 1920s the states of the former Confederacy were still in an
unfavorable financial position. Debts run up by the packed state
legislatures of the Reconstruction era were still being paid. The Atlanta Freight Bureau, formed in 1902, was making a little progress
in the question of discriminatory freight rates, but it still cost a
good bit more to ship the same goods North than South. And the
major part of the financial business in the United States was still
centered in the Northeast.

Another difference between 1928 and the last quarter of this
century was the rural mind-set of business and professional people.
Almost everybody had grown up on a farm or in a small town and
the ideas of independence, help, and working together for the common good were an integral part of their upbringing. An understanding of this fact explains Mr. McElreath's next statement:

> This naturally led to a consideration of the building and loan plan and
> the public benefit which would accrue to the community by the estab-
> lishment and successful operation of such associations.

At this time the "building society" format was still regarded
with suspicion in Atlanta. While the plan itself was a good one, several badly managed local associations had folded in the 1893 panic
(along with many others throughout the United States) and this
had left the concept in bad repute for the next twenty or thirty
years.

So after a lot of talk and consideration the "lunch group" decided to organize a building society, and Rawson Collier, R. W.
Davis, R. N. Reed, Edgar Watkins, Sr. and Jr., M. H. George, J.
B. Roberts, R. Kennon Berry, O. F. Kauffman, E. N. Claughton,
and Walter McElreath met formally on 25 March 1928 to constitute
themselves a temporary Board of Directors. Walter McElreath was
named Temporary Chairman, Edgar Watkins, Jr., Temporary Sec-

retary and Treasurer, and E. N. Claughton was authorized to solicit preorganizing subscriptions. So was born the Atlanta Building and Loan Association, and application was made to the Fulton Superior Court for an order of incorporation.

This organization was, in its purpose and makeup, much closer to a building society such as those still found in Britain and some parts of Europe than to the present United States system of savings and loans. Although it was a mutual association, shares were sold to individuals—often on a time basis. There was a membership fee of $3.00 per share—the idea being that the members (that is, share-holders) put money *into* the association in order to have the privilege of later borrowing from it—a privilege open only to members. Unlike a credit union, the borrowing was solely on improved real estate in Fulton County or on the shares of the Association, and shareholders could only borrow up to the sum they already had invested in the Association.

Fortunate both in the number and quality of the founders who were willing to work without remuneration of any kind to put their idea into effect, and also in the timing of its inception—1928—the young organization prospered. Walter McElreath was later to remark that if the organizers had waited a year or so, the effort would never have been made. The stock market crash in 1929 foreshadowed years in which the whole nation was plunged into depression and every section suffered as parts of the South had suffered during Reconstruction. Certainly the small Atlanta Building and Loan barely managed to hang on. The officers went without any recompense until the year 1937. In 1930, because capital was so scarce, the offices were moved to less expensive quarters, reducing the rent from $125 per month to $50 per month for the first year and $75 for the second!

During this period two incidents occurred that well illustrate Walter McElreath's own personal integrity and business philosophy as well as that of his friends. One of the original backers and investors in the fledgling Building Society was E. N. Claughton. He was known to his friends and associates as, in Mr. McElreath's words, "an exceedingly energetic promoter and high-powered salesman and it was apprehended that he might use high pressure methods in selling shares, but it was thought that the Executive

Committee might be able to put a brake on the use of such methods, if necessary, and that Mr. Claughton's energy and ability as a salesman might be profitably utilized."

Consequently, on 10 March 1928 the Executive Committee entered into a contract with E. N. Claughton to sell the first million dollars of Class A shares issued by the Association. Mr. Claughton was to receive $2.00 of the $3.00 membership fee of each share subject to two conditions: (1) approval of the Georgia Securities Commission and (2) approval of Mr. Claughton's conduct as a salesman by the Building Society's Executive Committee, which could at any time cancel his contract.

The uneasiness of the Executive Committee over Mr. Claughton's zeal seems to have been well founded, because in 1929—and especially as the economy slowed down—purchasers of membership certificates expressed more and more dissatisfaction. Many "thought or claimed to think that their membership certificate entitled them to participate, without further investment, in the earnings of the Association or to withdraw the amount paid for them." Although the officers of the small Association did not have to do anything about this grumbling and, indeed, could not legally redeem the certificates in question with the funds of other shareholders, they went out of their way to help disaffected shareholders sell their holdings. This, of course, worked against the Association as time was thus spent in finding buyers for "old" shares which could have been used to promote "new" sales.

The second evidence of the board's character and integrity occurred in 1933 when many banks over the United States went "bust" and President Roosevelt ordered banks closed to prevent the runs that were occurring everywhere. Building and Loans did not have to close as banks did, so shareholders flocked to the Association office to make withdrawals. Naturally there was not enough cash on hand to pay all who came. The directors hastily waived the withdrawal rule and ordered the cashiers to pay a little cash to each person who applied. This bolstered public confidence. After the banks were reopened, the withdrawal rule was strictly applied again and half of the gross collections were set aside to pay withdrawals in the order of application made. The directors borrowed $25,000 from the Federal Home Loan Bank Board, which they had joined in 1932, and completely paid outstanding debts to the local bank, enabling Atlanta Building and Loan to make a limited number of new loans and to pay a dividend of seven percent. This was a phenomenal record at the nadir of the Depression.

The next major step in Mr. McElreath's direction of the Atlanta Building and Loan occurred in 1935 when the Board decided to make application for "federalization," the process whereby the old Atlanta Building and Loan Association would become the Atlanta Federal Savings and Loan Association. This was accomplished on 28 August 1935, when the institution as it was to function for the rest of Mr. McElreath's life came into being. Shortly afterwards Atlanta Federal moved to 22 Marietta Street, which remains its headquarters today. Mr. McElreath remained as president, accepting a salary for the first time in 1937. But he continued his insistence that a strong reserve was absolutely necessary to the strength of Atlanta Federal, and this reserve policy has continued to be a first priority.

Wise in business, civic minded in support of his community, Walter McElreath was also a patriot. He and his fellow officers considered it a duty that Atlanta Federal should support America's war effort in the 1940s, and so much of the institution's assets were invested in government bonds that the total finally reached $8,000,000, an amount so great that some funds had to be sold — happily, at a profit! — to bring the final amount into line with prudent management. It was typical of Mr. McElreath's ideas of management that the profit was immediately assigned to reserves.

When peace finally came, the Association was at the threshold of really large loans. In accordance with its president's ideas of civic responsibility, these loans were made to churches, to returning GIs, and to the black community, as well as to the more usual home applicants. Nowhere has this philosophy been better expressed than in Mr. McElreath's own history of the Atlanta Federal Savings and Loan Association.

But the mere size of this or any other financial institution cannot be taken as the sole criterion by which its true success can be measured. The true criterion is the measure of benefit which it has been, and which it can continue to be, to the community in which it operates. As was stated in the beginning, the motivating purpose of the organization was to gar-

ner the funds of local savers and to lend them locally, and thus improve
the local economy by keeping the interest paid on loans in the community
whose funds produced it.

Walter McElreath believed this credo, and under his direction as
president and then chairman to his death in 1951, Atlanta Federal
was an expression of its truth.

Walter McElreath
and the
Industrial Life and Health Insurance Company
by Walter McElreath°

*In the year following his marriage Mr. McElreath was elected attorney for a
struggling young life insurance company. The company had been founded in 1892
by John N. McEachern, Mr. McElreath's uncle, and three associates. In the years
ahead Mr. McElreath was to become the guiding light of this company, originally
named the Industrial Aid Association. Something of his work in the company can
be gleaned from the paragraphs quoted here from the history of the insurance company that Mr. McElreath wrote and the company had printed in 1935.*

The history of the Industrial Life and Health Insurance Company is more than the history of a successful business enterprise. It
is a chapter in the social history of the times. Its organization and
promotion was a step forward in the practical development of the
social principle of cooperation and mutual aid in tempering the privations consequent upon sickness and the financial distress too
often attending death in families of small means. . . .

By the last quarter of the nineteenth century the social value of
mutual aid by voluntary associations, supervised by law, had become so apparent that there was a movement all over Europe to give
legal sanction and support to organizations with this beneficial purpose. . . .

°From Walter McElreath, *History of the Industrial Life and Health Insurance
Company* (Atlanta: Industrial Life and Health Insurance Co., 1935).

From the fact that this form of insurance was provided for people engaged in industry, it became known as "Industrial Insurance," a name which persists, although it now applies to the plan of collecting the premiums and to the character of benefits paid rather than to the class to which the insured belongs. . . .

In America, organized mutual aid was first practiced by such great fraternal orders as the Freemasons, the Knights of Pythias and the Odd Fellows. These great secret orders put the emphasis on the enjoyment of mystic symbols and ceremonies and their moral, educational and social purposes and gave relief as an incidental benevolence. Imitating, to some degree, the secret ceremonies of these great orders, other societies sprang up in large numbers with greater emphasis on the benefits provided for the members in cases of accident, sickness and death, some of them being substantially insurance companies in the form of fraternal orders. Typical of this class were the Royal Arcanum, the Knights of the Maccabees and the Knights of Honor. In 1892, at about the time of the organization of the Industrial Life and Health Insurance Company, thirty-one orders of this class in America had 1,187,168 members and $2,387,061,039 of insurance in force.

Numerous as were the members of these fraternal orders and vast as was the amount of insurance in force and the benefits paid, such orders were not adapted to supply the social need of mutual aid. Their membership was restricted to such individuals, races and classes of individuals as were socially, racially and morally acceptable to these fraternal orders and the millions of people most in the need of protection could not join them. To adequately meet the social necessity for mutual aid, it was necessary that companies should be organized on a purely business basis in which any person needing this class of protection could get it with no other qualification except sound health and the payment of the necessary premiums. The first successful organization in America on this plan was the Prudential Friendly Society, later the Prudential Insurance Company of America, which was organized in Newark, New Jersey, in 1875.

As soon as it was demonstrated that the Prudential Company had been organized on a successful basis, a vast number of similar companies were organized, among them, the Home Friendly Society of Baltimore, which opened an office in Atlanta some time in the 1880's and soon had a successful business. . . .

The lottery of life is constantly turning up fortunate cards upon which the successful stake their future. Such was the friendship which began with an acquaintance formed by John Newton McEachern and Isham M. Sheffield by a chance meeting at a boarding house on Mitchell Street in the year 1889, and which lasted until the death of Mr. McEachern in 1928. Few friendships have ever been so constant and of greater mutual advantages. . . .

In 1891, when he was about twenty-one years of age, Mr. Sheffield was approached by two friends, D. F. Owen and J. J. Carleton, who persuaded him to use his savings in the organization of an industrial insurance company with which Mr. McEachern was to become connected when the new company had become established. . . .

No copy of the first policy of the company can be located now, but a copy of the original By-Laws contains the main provisions of the policy. It was a combination sick-benefit and death-benefit policy, the premium being the same for all ages with the sick and death benefits proportional to the amount of the premium. For a weekly premium of five cents, a weekly sick benefit of one dollar was paid and a death benefit of ten dollars. For a larger weekly premium the sick and death benefits were correspondingly increased. The maximum sick benefit paid was five dollars and the maximum death benefit was fifty dollars.

Policies were written almost exclusively among the negroes and, it being impracticable to have medical examination of the risks, the policy contained rather stringent, but absolutely necessary, limitations upon the amount of benefits which could be claimed and the conditions under which they would be allowed. The insurable age was from four to sixty-five years. All premiums were required to be paid weekly and no benefits were payable if the insured was more than four weeks in arrears; sick benefits were allowed only after seven days of total disability and not more than twenty weeks' sick benefits were allowable in one year; women were allowed only two weeks' sick benefits for childbirth; sickness from consumption and rheumatism were allowed only one-half benefits and no benefits were allowed for diseases contracted before the date of the application, or for drunkenness, or immoral causes. Full sick benefits were paid from the date of the policy. One-fourth death benefits were paid for the first six months, one-half after six months, and full benefits after the policy had been in force for one year. From time to time the policy was liberalized. . . .

Mr. McEachern . . . frequently talked about the fact that the charter under which the Industrial Aid Association was operated was not a satisfactory and adequate foundation upon which to build the company which it was his ambition to develop, and he frequently expressed the wish that he had a charter like that of the Southern Industrial Aid Society, under which to organize the Industrial Aid Association.

In the summer of 1897 the business of the Southern Industrial Aid Society had dwindled to almost nothing and Dr. Julian P. Thomas, the president of the Southern Industrial Aid Society, who was then operating a medical institute where the present Carnegie Library now stands in Atlanta, proposed to the attorney of the Industrial Aid Association a sale of the business and charter of the Southern Industrial Aid Society to the organizers of the Industrial Aid Association. This proposition was taken up with Mr. McEachern, who accepted.

Accordingly, on the first Tuesday in August, 1897, a meeting of the Southern Industrial Aid Society was held and a new board of directors of the society was elected, consisting of J. N. McEachern, I. M. Sheffield, S. C. McEachern, J. D. Middlebrooks, and Snowden Sheffield, all of whom were then connected with the Industrial Aid Association, except Dr. Middlebrooks. The new board of directors met and elected officers. J. N. McEachern was elected president, I. M. Sheffield, secretary and treasurer, and Walter McElreath, attorney for the society.

At this meeting by-laws were adopted, and a resolution passed authorizing the attorney to take the necessary legal steps to secure an amendment to the charter of the Southern Industrial Aid Society changing its name to the Industrial Aid Association of Georgia. On September 4, 1897, this amendment of the charter was granted by the Secretary of State. The Industrial Aid Association of Georgia then assumed all the liability of the Industrial Aid Association of Alabama on all outstanding policies in force and whatever assets the Industrial Aid Association of Alabama had were transferred to the Industrial Aid Association of Georgia.

Thus, the company became established under a legislative charter granting it the full right to engage in the business of insurance in Georgia upon the plan and under the limitations set out in the legislative act incorporating the Southern Industrial Aid Society.

When the company had been reorganized under its new charter the officers and directors proceeded with new energy and vigor to extend the operations of the company. Offices were opened in new territories, the company proceeding cautiously, however, so as not to impair the solvency of the company by undue haste in expansion. . . .

The directors soon began to realize that the name of the company, the "Industrial Aid Association," did not give the company the right prestige in the field, the impression being that the company was a mere mutual aid association. On May 26, 1903, a resolution was adopted to the effect that it would be to the best interest of the association to have a name which would indicate that it was doing an insurance business, and it was resolved that the name be changed from "Industrial Aid Association" to "Industrial Life & Health Insurance Company." Application, accordingly, was made to the Secretary of State for this change of name and, on June 26, 1903, the amendment applied for was granted. . . .

At the . . . annual meeting of the policyholders, held in August, 1914, it was reported that the plan to change to a stock company had been temporarily abandoned. However, the ultimate purpose to transform the company into a stock company was not abandoned, and the General Counsel was instructed to investigate the method of making such change. The question which gave him the most concern was how to deal with the assets of the mutual company which belonged to the policyholders. After much study he decided that the protection of the mutual policyholders could be accomplished and that the change was feasible.

At a regular annual meeting of the policyholders held on the first Tuesday in August, 1918, the directors who had served during the preceding term were reelected. In the preceding year, (1917), the receipts of the company had passed the one-million-dollar-mark, the gross income for that year having been $1,035,863.55. It was, therefore, decided at this meeting to immediately carry out the long contemplated plan of changing from the mutual to the stock plan. . . .

The strong financial condition of the company is clearly illustrated in the following excerpts from the annual statement as of December 31, 1933, verified in detail and approved by examiners from the Insurance Department of the state of Georgia.

Total Income, 1933 . . . . $2,581,019.12
Total Disbursements, 1933 . . . . $2,433,353.97
Total Admitted Assets $1,464,203.47
Total Liabilities $821,481.34
Legal Reserve $743,068.06
Capital Stock $260,000.00
Surplus Above All Liabilities $382,722.13
Surplus to Policyholders $642,722.13
Number of Policies Issued During 1933 730,336
Number of Claims Paid During 1933 153,872
Number of Policies Issued Since Organization 8,832,792
Number of Claims Paid Since Organization 4,340,467
Total Paid to Policyholders Since Organization $23,517,243.92
Insurance in Force December 31, 1933 . . . . $41,883,704.00

A McElreath Album*

*Photographs courtesy of the Atlanta Historical Society.

Walter and Bessie McElreath in 1900, four years into the "desperate enterprise" of their marriage. "Reared tenderly and in plenty," Mr. McElreath wrote of his wife, "she married me when I was poor as a church mouse. . . . Through poverty and weariness and ill health, she never complained. She was my inspiration, my guide, my friend and helpmate. As I climbed from poverty to competence, and from obscurity to public notice, I had her encouragement and help; but I knew that if I had failed she would have shared the failure without a murmur."

The "very handsome brick church" built by Grace Methodist Church in 1906 at the corner of Highland Avenue and Boulevard. Mr. McElreath was by then a member of the congregation's Board of Stewards, and when this building burned to the ground in 1917, he was instrumental in reorganizing the church and in the construction of a new, "pure Gothic-type" structure.

Walter McElreath around the turn of the century, when he was practicing law with his brother Emmett in Atlanta.

Members of the Burns Club of Atlanta pose for a portrait in the early 1920s, with Walter McElreath seated in the center of the front row. Pictured on the front row, from left, are Chief Justice Richard B. Russell, Joseph Jacobs, John M. Graham, Mr. McElreath, Joseph W. Humphries, Dr. John Osman, and Arthur E. Craig. On the back row, from left, are Dave Buchan, James Carlisle, Dr. W. F. Melton, Alex Taylor, Dr. J. W. Beeson, Alex A. Meyer, and Herbert Reid. Mr. McElreath helped raise the money for the Burns Cottage, where this photograph was taken, and "was a constant attendant upon the meetings of the club."

Life of Georgia headquarters at the northeast corner of Linden Avenue and West Peachtree Street in Atlanta, in a photograph taken in 1967. Walter McElreath became attorney for the struggling Southern Industrial Aid Society headed by his uncle, John Newton McEachern, in 1897. By 1903 the firm had become the Industrial Life & Health Insurance Company with Mr. McElreath as its general counsel, and in time the flourishing corporation became the Life Insurance Company of Georgia.

This mansion at 1753 Peachtree Street, N.E., in Atlanta, built in 1925 for Dr. Willis B. Jones, became the first permanent home of the Atlanta Historical Society in 1946, when Walter McElreath advanced a large part of the purchase price of $60,000. In 1950, during the annual meeting of the Southern Historical Association, the building was officially named McElreath Hall at a ceremony in his honor.

McElreath Hall, the present-day headquarters of the Atlanta Historical Society at 3101 Andrews Drive, NW, in Atlanta.

Walter McElreath in a photograph by Thurston Hatcher of Atlanta about 1935. It was in 1935 that Bessie McElreath died, and her husband, on the advice of a friend, plunged himself into his work, "absorbingly and unremittingly."

I

My Country

I was born on July 17, 1867, in a log house about two miles southeast of Lost Mountain, in Cobb County, Georgia.

Prior to May 23, 1836, when the treaty between the State of Georgia and the Cherokee Indians was ratified, all of that portion of Georgia lying north and west of the Chattahoochee River and north of the old boundary of the Creek lands running west from that river was the property of the Cherokee Indians. That large, fertile, and surpassingly beautiful region remained an island of aboriginal occupation long after the current of white occupation had flowed all around it and west of it to the Mississippi. No picture of this region will ever surpass the description of Bancroft who thus describes the homes of the Cherokees:

> Their homes were encircled by blue hills rising beyond hills, of which the lofty peaks would kindle with the early light, and the overshadowing ridges envelop the valley like a mass of clouds. There the rocky cliffs, rising in naked grandeur, defy the lightning, and mock the loudest peals of

the thunder-storm; there the gentler slopes are covered with magnolias and flowering forest-trees, decorated with roving climbers, and ring with the perpetual note of the whip-poor-will; there the wholesome water gushes profusely from the earth in transparent springs; snow-white cascades glitter on the hillsides; and the rivers, shallow, but pleasant to the eye, rush through narrow vales, which the abundant strawberry crimsons, and coppices of rhododendron and flaming azalea adorn.

This description is a prose poem in which no poetic license is used. Although the destructive hands of civilization have wrought for nearly a hundred years to destroy the natural beauty of this region, everything described by Bancroft in his idyllic picture of the land of the Cherokees can still be found in North Georgia. True, the streams which once meandered, clear and sparkling, over the valleys, have been drawn from their errant and leisurely courses and sent racing down ditches carrying their burden of erosion, and the oaks and chestnuts have been cut from all the arable lands; but the blue mountains still spread the azure canvas of their wooded slopes upon which morning beams and evening rays still paint their ever-changing pictures in as much loveliness as when Nacoochee was wooed in the shadow of Yonah; upon the mountain sides the cataracts still gleam; the gorges are still choked with rhododendron, and the azalea still flames on the hillsides.

Bancroft's idyllic description of the land of the Cherokees refers more particularly, of course, to the mountain regions further north; but Cobb County in its primitive state, with its rugged terrain, its hills and dales, its isolated mountain peaks, was a region of a less grand, but of a rare and gentler beauty, all of which has not been completely effaced. There are yet glens on its mountain sides and among the hills bordering the Chattahoochee in which cascades sing their merry tunes, and where the azalea, the honeysuckle, and the laurel still bloom, and the far vistas from the high hilltops of the county are of great beauty.

Cobb County is the southernmost of the counties of the Cherokee country. Its southern boundary is the Chattahoochee and its northern line runs only a league south of the Allatoona Heights. There are no mountain ranges in the county, but the terrain consists of great rolling hills, with a few lone mountain peaks standing like pickets south of the long line of the Blue Ridge. Near the north-eastern corner of the county is Brushy Mountain; near the center stand the twin peaks of the Kennesaws; a little to the northwest is Pine Mountain; and on the western border stands Lost Mountain, solitary and lovely in its loneliness. In less than thirty years from the time the Cherokee removed his wigwam from their shadows, these mountains had become known wherever American history is read and military strategy is studied. These mountains are the con-ning towers on the watershed between the valleys which to the north feed the Etowah, whose waters flow into the Coosa, thence into the Alabama, and thence into the Tombigbee and south into the Gulf, and the valleys which feed the Chattahoochee. From these mountains, the long line of the Blue Ridge can be seen.

Along the watershed westward from Marietta, the highway runs across the field of the Battle of Kennesaw Mountain and on until it winds around the lower slopes of Lost Mountain, and thence westward to New Hope and Dallas. From this road, as it winds around the foot of the mountain, there is a view of surpassing beauty. It is not a scene of rugged and awful grandeur such as can be seen in the Rockies or in the mountains of North Carolina, but it is a scene of soft, gentle, and peaceful beauty. Ten miles to the eastward rise the blue peaks of the Kennesaws; on a clear day Stone Mountain can be seen standing grey against the southeastern ho-rizon; on the south the hills beyond the valley of the Sweetwater meet the horizon like the rim of a blue bowl; and far to the south-west can be seen the gold hills of Villa Rica. The intermediate coun-try lies spread out in a panorama patterned out in woodland and field. In this country lie the graves of my people — two great-grand-fathers; all of my grandparents; my father and my mother; and hundreds of the friends of my youth. To me this is God's country.

The Constitution of the United States conferred upon the Fed-eral Congress the right, "To regulate commerce with foreign na-tions, and among the several states and with the Indian tribes." Very soon after the adoption of the Constitution in 1789, agitation began in Georgia for the acquisition by the State of Georgia of the title of the Indian tribes within the state; and in 1802, when the lands west of the present boundaries of the state were ceded to the United States, it was made a condition of the cession that the

United States were bound to extinguish "at their own expense, for the use of Georgia, the Indian title to all lands within the State of Georgia." By 1825, the title to all of the lands owned by the Creek Indians had been extinguished, and in a few years these lands filled up with white settlers. But the Cherokees still held the country north of the Chattahoochee. Georgia demanded with greater and greater force and insistence that the United States perform its agreement to acquire, for the State of Georgia, the Cherokee lands. During the controversy between the State of Georgia and the Federal Government over the subject, the United States claimed the right of enforcing the intercourse laws for the government of the Indian tribes which prohibited any person from settling on Indian territory, or trading in any article whatever with an Indian without a special license from the proper Federal authority. This was before the day when the supremacy of the Federal Government over the state power had become an accomplished fact by the judicial interpretation of John Marshall and the guns of Mr. Lincoln. The Cherokees had their own printed constitution and code of laws and had declared themselves into a separate state entitled under treaty stipulations to the guaranties of the United States to be protected in the peaceful and quiet possession of the country occupied by them, to them and to their heirs forever. They had accordingly passed a law that no person should settle on their lands, or trade with their people, without a permit from their authorities. Georgia had extended her criminal jurisdiction to the Cherokee country, and in 1831 the Legislature authorized the Cherokee lands to be surveyed. The Governor ordered the survey to be made and it was made accordingly. In 1832 the Cherokee country was divided into counties; a lottery was held, and the successful drawers or persons who had acquired their grants began to move in. On the 16th day of September, 1833, the first Superior Court was held at Marietta. The survey of these lands of the Cherokee Indians, the granting of them to the citizens of the state, and the erection of county governments in a territory recognized by the Federal Government as a foreign nation before the Indian title was extinguished, was an unparalleled assertion on the part of the State of Georgia of the doctrine of state sovereignty.

On the 29th day of December, 1835, a treaty was concluded between the United States and the Cherokee nation by which the
Cherokee relinquished all their claims to their lands in the State of
Georgia. This treaty was ratified on May 23, 1836, and Georgia
took formal possession under the terms of the treaty in May, 1838,
and then the tide of immigration into the Cherokee country which
had begun in 1833 swelled to its flood.

The treatment of the Cherokee Indians by the United States
and by the people of Georgia is a subject not pleasant to contem-
plate. For ages this mild and peaceful race had loved the mountains
and the streams of their beautiful country and wooed them with
soft and liquid names which still cling to them. They were not a sav-
age race. They had demonstrated sufficient aptitude for learning to
support a newspaper published in their own language, thousands
of whom were able to read. They had adopted a written constitution
and had made the beginnings of organized constitutional government under it. The Statue of Sequoya, the inventor of the Cherokee
syllabary, stands beside the highway near the town of Calhoun, in
Gordon County, and his effigy is upon the walls of the Library of
Congress along with that of Cadmus, the Phoenician.

The character of the population which moved into Cobb
County in the first few years after the Cherokee lands were granted
was very high. Of course, some of the first settlers were shiftless
people such as move into any new country to secure a few acres of
cheap land and to live by hunting and fishing. Some were poor people, not of the shiftless class, but who had been unsuccessful in the
older sections of Georgia and of the neighboring states, and who
hoped to make a fresh start in a new country. There were few of the
wealthier class of large slave holders. These had large plantations
in eastern Georgia from which they had no reason for removing,
with social ties too strong to break. However, some of the aristocratic element of the state's population came to the county in its
early years; indeed, for a new and raw country, the number of the
class was relatively large. The main body of the early settlers were
of the higher bourgeoisie class, predominantly Scotch-Irish people
from eastern Georgia and from North and South Carolina. Among
these were the McAfees, Reids, Andersons, Masseys, Stricklands,
Bensons, Winns, Groveses, Mayeses, Gobers, Lemmons, Robert-

sons, McCleskys, Orrs, Mannings, McLains, Wards, Lindleys, McEacherns, and McElreaths, whose descendants are still among the most prominent and respected people of the county. These families all acquired large tracts of the best lands, their farms ranging from three or four hundred acres to a thousand or more. On most of these farms well-constructed frame houses were built, many of them large, commodious, two-story houses tightly ceiled and painted white. Considering the scarcity of machinery in that day and the slow process of sawing lumber and making shingles, it is remarkable how comfortable some of these homes were. Near the houses were great barnyards, with barns, cribs, corn houses, stables and granaries built of logs. On many of these places there was a gin house driven by horse power and, standing by it, a great cotton press with a screw made from the trunk of a great tree which was driven down upon the lint in the press box by horses hitched to the long sloping arms attached at one end to the screw as they traveled round and round the press. Each of these farmers owned great herds of cows, flocks of sheep, and droves of hogs which ran at large in the forests and found abundant pasturage. Around the farm houses and the barnyards, there were great flocks of geese, turkeys, chickens and guineas. The smokehouses were filled with hams hung to the rafters and cured with the sweet smoke of the hickory. There was always a springhouse where butter and milk were cooled in pools into which a constant supply of fresh water ran. The bees from a long row of hives gathered honey from wild flowers and from the sap exuded from the leaves of the tulip. In the yards and gardens around these houses the boxwood, arborvitae, and crepe myrtle grew. Jonquils, hollyhocks, tiger lilies and perennial roses bloomed in profusion. The wisteria and climbing rose clambered over gateways and bowers. There was, always, a great orchard of apples, peaches, and grapes. What a banquet was thus spread for the hungry hordes of Johnston and Sherman!

Every farmstead such as we have described was a place of domestic manufacture. There was, at many such places, a vat for the tanning of the hides taken from the animals slaughtered on the place. The anvil rang at the forge where the farmer sharpened his plows. The hum of the spinning wheel and the rhythmic beat of the weaver's beam were the music of feminine industry. The writer has gathered the bark of the maple and oak and the berries of the sumac to dye the cloth woven at the domestic loom, and has worn homespun woven, dyed, and made into clothes at his home. Quilting bees were social affairs, just as entertaining and as profitable as the meetings of the Wednesday Morning Study Club to settle the fate of the Balkans and to celebrate the millennium of the *Althing*.

Most of the people belonging to the class above described owned few slaves, and many of them owned none. In fact, Cobb County had only a relatively small slave population. In 1850 the white population of Cobb County was 11,571 and the slave population 2,272, or one slave to about five free persons. In the same year, Greene County had a free population of 4,082 and a slave population of 8,266. Hancock County had a free population of 4,272 with 7,306 slaves. Wilkes County had 3,825 free people and 8,281 slaves. Thus, it is seen that in the seventeen years from 1833 to 1850, the population of Cobb County had become greater than that of Greene, Hancock, or Wilkes, although the youngest of these was formed before the year 1800.

Not all the people in the county had homes of the kind which have been described. Some of the most substantial people had homes built of great hewn logs, well joined, and with such open spaces as there were between the logs tightly sealed with mortar. My grandfather McEachern had such a house which is still standing. His first home was a large, commodious frame building, which was accidentally burned about the beginning of the war. On account of the difficulty of obtaining lumber during the war, his next home was built of logs. Several years after the war, it was covered with weather boarding on the outside and plastered on the inside and made into a very nice building. Many of the homes were roughly built and some were mere cabins. But notwithstanding the simplicity of many of the homes, there was a certain air of neatness about most of them, and despite the wind which sifted through the cracks, there was cheerfulness about the great stone fireplace filled with logs of hickory and oak, and there was sweet sleep in the featherbeds under the thick quilted comforts. For two years in my childhood, my father lived on a new farm, in such a house, while he was building a new home; and the memory of the snug warmth of such a bed on a winter's night when the snow sifted in under the boards of the roof is a memory of a comfort which an aging man cannot feel, even in a home caulked and sealed with weather strip and heated by an oil-fed furnace regulated by a thermostat.

The houses of the people were vastly superior to their churches and schoolhouses. In the country the churches were comparatively small, square buildings, unceiled, unheated, and often without glass in the windows. The church to which my father and mother belonged was such a building, and I have sat through a two-hours service with the temperature around freezing, and after service ridden home in an open wagon.

The country schoolhouses were usually log buildings, with an open fireplace at one end and furnished with benches without backs. My school life began in such a building. The curriculum, in many of these schools, consisted of the study of Webster's *Blueback Speller*, Davies' *Arithmetic*, McGuffey's *Readers*, Cornell's *Geography*, Smith's *Grammar*, and writing from a copy set by the teacher. In some of the communities there were better schools taught by highly qualified men of a classic education. Such a teacher who taught the generation just before me was an Irishman by the name of P. B. Wheelan, who had been educated for the priesthood in the old country, but loved liquor better than holy orders, and who taught in various parts of the country. In his school, Latin, Greek and the higher branches of mathematics were taught; but for the most part, education in the country schools consisted only of the meagerest instruction in the elementary branches of an English education. However, it was considered a disgrace not to be able to read and write, and, in my youth, I knew practically no white illiterates.

The dress of the people presented striking incongruities. On week days and on ordinary occasions, most of the men wore homespun jeans in the winter, and homedyed cotton in the summer. Their shoes were brogans made at home, or by the community shoemaker. On Sundays the men of the most prosperous families managed somehow to be dressed in broadcloth, calfskin boots, and a beaver hat. This was possible because such a suit was worn only on Sundays and special occasions, and would last a lifetime. This might be described as the "bee-gum" age. Some of these suits and hats survived the War Between the States and came down to the time of my childhood and youth. And the ladies—there were no

women in those days—that is, there were no women among the
genteel classes—they were all ladies. On Sundays and at weddings
and other special occasions, the ladies wore black, shiny silk
dresses, the kind that made a swishing sound when their wearers
walked. As a boy I did not think any woman was "quality folks"
unless her skirts rustled in that manner. All of the ladies of this class
wore heavy earrings or earbobs of gold, a large breast pin, brace-
lets, and a heavy chain with a locket, all of gold. These were usually
heirlooms. If you wonder how the farmers afforded these things in
that day, remember that it was before Mr. Henry Ford; that they
bought no tires or gasoline or radios, and that the installment plan
had not been invented. Their wheat did not come from Minnesota;
their meat did not come from Chicago; their clothes were not made
by Hart, Schaffner and Marx. It was not the age of the pasteboard
carton and the tin can. A little money went a long way.

There was variety in that day. There were homespun and silk,
coonskin caps and beavers, ox-carts and carriages, cabins and
mansions.

In addition to the class of citizenry above described, there were
in Cobb County in the days immediately preceding the Civil War a
number of the real aristocracy of the Old South. Before 1850, Roswell King, a native of Connecticut, but coming to Cobb County
from Darien, established a large factory at Roswell, the place
named in honor of him, and built one of the stateliest homes in
Georgia. Soon Major James Stephen Bulloch, son of Governor
Archibald Bulloch, came and built Bulloch Hall in which his
daughter, the mother of President Theodore Roosevelt, was married. And about the same time the Dunwoodys built Mimosa Hall,
which with its great oaks, its flagstone walks, its stately pillared
porticos, its flower gardens, its rose-lined pathways and its
hundreds of mimosas, is one of the most perfect survivals of the
grand old days remaining in Georgia. If you doubt the stories you
have heard of the elegance of the old days, go to Roswell when the
mimosas are in bloom and go to the gardens of Mimosa Hall.

The most distinguished of the Roswell colony was Francis R.
Goulding. The date of his removal to Cobb County is not known to
the writer. It was probably some years after the time of which we
are writing. He was, in all probability, attracted to that community

by the high class of people who had settled there, and his choosing Roswell for his home illustrates the character of the people who made up this attractive group. He is said to have preceded Howe in the invention of the sewing machine and made the first practical device for mechanical needlework ever used in this country. He was the author of *The Young Marooners*, which takes rank with *Robinson Crusoe* and *The Swiss Family Robinson*. It is said to have been the inspiration of Stevenson's *Treasure Island* and the organization of the Boy Scouts. His grave is in the Presbyterian cemetery at Roswell.

Charles J. McDonald, Governor and afterwards a justice of the Supreme Court, made his home during the late years of his life near Marietta, to which place he was followed later by his son-in-law, Col. Alexander S. Atkinson, who took for his residence the old home in which William G. McAdoo was born.

One of the greatest places in the county was "Rockdale," the plantation of Dr. William Alston, which adjoined the farm of my grandfather McElreath. Dr. Alston was a member of the distinguished South Carolina family of that name. After receiving the usual education of an antebellum Southern gentleman, he was graduated in medicine at the Jefferson Medical College at Philadelphia, but he did not practice his profession. He married a wealthy Charleston girl who had been educated in Paris, and purchased "Rockdale," built his mansion house, and removed there with his sixty-five slaves. The farm consisted of about six hundred and fifty acres lying at the foot of Lost Mountain. Not all of the farm was cleared, and it will be seen that he had a slave for every ten acres of his farm. It can be imagined that a state of improvement and cultivation was possible with this force of labor. He built a large stone house for the domestic servants and small houses further away from the mansion for the others, great barns, granaries and other buildings. The land was cleared, ditched, and the stones hauled off, and the whole farm brought to the highest state of cultivation. Visitors from Charleston made merry parties on frequent visits to the mansion house built in the old classic style, white with pillared porticos and surrounded with spacious gardens in which the old-fashioned flowers grew. What an opportunity was this grand old mansion for the pyromaniacs of Sherman! They did not miss it. The author now owns that portion of this estate upon which the mansion house stood.

The society of Cobb County seventy-five years ago was a mass of unassimilated social elements—a few aristocrats, a great body of independent, proud, self-conscious bourgeoisie, and a less number of dwellers in the log cabins. If I were the conventional writer about antebellum society in the South, I would designate the latter class as "poor white trash," but as I have never come in contact with such a class, I cannot use the term. I have known poor people that were white and lived in the South, and have known some of them that were sorry and trashy; but so far as I have ever been able to discover, no such distinct class of white people ever existed in Georgia—certainly not in North Georgia. This was a term invented by the slaves on the great estates, proud of the prestige of their masters and their families, by which such slaves with a sort of mental swagger sought to find some comfort in their servitude by a grandiose African assumption of superiority over the white man who did not own slaves. It did not follow that the people of the South who were poor and who owned no slaves were trash. This is a delusion only of the ignorant and of the half-baked candidates for a doctor's degree in some Northern college who write academic treatises on antebellum social conditions in the South. In 1860 there were only 304,000 slave owners in the South out of a total population of 8,000,000. Four out of five families in the South owned no slaves. Four out of five soldiers in Lee's army came from families in which no slaves were owned. They ought to have convinced the world that rather good soldiers can be made out of poor white people, and if they were trash, that trash is a good material out of which to make heroes.

The country has its slums just like the cities. There were a few pine barrens and swamps into which the shiftless and vicious drifted where there was an inferior class; but those no more represent a social order distinctively Southern than Decatur Street is representative of Atlanta, or the Bowery of New York. The Anglo-Saxon and the Scotch-Irish of the mountains of North Georgia, or of North Carolina or of Kentucky or of Virginia, represent just as much of native inherent worth as is to be found anywhere on earth. From among this class, Abraham Lincoln mauled his way to the

White House; Andrew Johnson pricked his way with a tailor's needle to the Presidency; Joseph E. Brown drove his ox team to the United States Senate; and Stonewall Jackson carved his way with his sword to immortality. "Poor White Trash" as a designation of a social class large enough to be distinctive in the South is a term known only to anaemic, academic snobs.

The social psychology of the people of Cobb County before and for a few years after the war was unfortunate in that it was pervaded with too much individual self-consciousness and pride. The people who came from South Carolina and from eastern Georgia brought their social pride and class consciousness with them. In the short time before the war, they never got themselves consciously adjusted to each other. Every family felt itself better than the next family, or inferior, or suspected the next family of thinking itself superior. If a family was not "quality folks," you could not visit the young ladies of the family without losing social caste. This ever-present appraisement instinctively made when one made a new acquaintance, by which one felt a little patronizing towards the new acquaintance, or a little inferior in his presence, persisted during all of my youth. Being timid and poor, I usually felt inferior.

Such was the country in which I was born and reared. If it be said that the period of which I have written was before my day, it must be remembered that the breaking out of the war arrested development for years. Cobb County suffered as perhaps no other county in Georgia suffered except Fulton. The armies of Sherman and Johnston remained in the county for weeks. The great Battle of Kennesaw Mountain was fought there. The livestock was stolen, the fences burned, and the country drained of food. The slaves were freed. The young men all went to the war and many of them never returned. As late as 1874, when I was seven years old and can distinctly remember, there was not a new house of any consequence in the part of the country in which I lived, and scarcely a new cleared field. I therefore remember and have described the country in the condition in which it was twenty-eight years after the first white people settled in the county.

II

My Childhood

My father was William Anderson McElreath, and my mother was Matilda Jane McEachern. They were married on the 13th day of September, 1866. The first year after their marriage, 1867, they lived on a rented farm; and at the end of that year, when I was six months old, they removed to an adjoining farm which my father had bought, where they remained for the next four years. My earliest recollections are of life at this place. What portion of that period is beyond the time of conscious recollection, I cannot definitely determine. The first event which I can recall with certainty occurred when I was a little more than two-and-a-half years of age. A little brother came at that time who lived only a few hours. During the night of his birth, I had been taken to my grandfather's. The next morning one of my aunts brought me home. I recall my mother lying pale in her bed, two or three women sitting by the fire, myself sitting on the floor trying to force a nail through a crack in the floor, something lying on a table with a white cloth over it, some men coming with a little black box, and my father and some other men going away with the little box in a wagon.

Another event of which I have a distinct recollection occurred the same year, of which the approximate date is uncertain. One night in the early fall my father was sitting in a chair leaned back against the jamb of the fireplace reading a newspaper by the light of a brightly blazing fire. My mother took off my day clothes and put on my night shirt. My father laid aside his paper and called me to him and took me in his lap and talked for a long time to my mother about General Lee, the account of whose death he had just been reading.

After the incident first related, my recollection of what happened during the next two years we lived at the place seems to me to be as clear and distinct as my memory of any other period of my life. I have a clear and distinct recollection of the appearance of the farm, the buildings, the homes of the neighbors and of the country.

The dwelling house on this farm consisted of one large room built of logs, with a great stone fireplace in one end. On the back side of the house there was a shed room which served as kitchen and dining room, and one end of this shed room was partitioned off into an extra bedroom. There was a smokehouse near the dwelling, and across the road a large barnyard, or "lot" as it was called in that day, in which there was a corn crib; there was a barn, with a fodder loft in the top story; and there were stables for the cows and horses, and a wagon house, all built of logs. A hundred yards or so from the dwelling house there was a cabin in which the colored hired man, George Glenn, and his wife, Letitia, called "Tishie," lived with their two little black girls.

The furniture of the home was scant. In the main room there was a large bed in which my father and mother slept, and a low trundle bed on which I slept. At night it was rolled out into the middle of the room, and in the daytime it was rolled under the big bed. The bed clothing was really exquisite. The quilts were made of scraps of cloth of different colors arranged in regular designs, the colors being beautifully matched. There were woolen coverlets woven in a beautiful pattern, and snow-white fringed counterpanes. But the piece of bed clothing of the greatest utility was the "yankee" quilt, so called because it was made of discarded Federal

uniforms left on the battlefields. Thickly padded with wool and
lined with Confederate grey, it was protection from the coldest
night. After there were several children in the family, every bitter
night provoked a quarrel as to who should sleep under the "yankee"
quilt. The chairs were straight chairs with split bottoms, the only
rocking chair in the house being a little red chair which was my es-
pecial property. There was a side table, some trunks and shelves. A
picture of General Lee, surrounded by his generals, hung on the
wall, and a similar picture of Stonewall Jackson. In the room in
which I am now writing, a large number of photographs and other
pictures of these two men are hung about the walls. When my consciousness dawned, these two men looked down upon me; and
when, at last, consciousness finally fades, they will still be looking
at me.

From the description of the home of my infancy, it will be seen
that my father and mother were poor. But poverty is a relative term
and theirs was not a poverty that embarrassed them in the least. All
young couples were poor in Cobb County in that day. Little wealth
had been accumulated in that part of the country before the war.
Profits had been invested in slaves and in the clearing of the lands
and the building of homes. Such wealth as had been accumulated
had been swept away by the war, and little besides the land itself
was left. Youth, peace, love, a cozy log house and the future was the
only wealth the average young man, just returned from the Confederate army to begin life in the path of Sherman, could hope for
until his own hands wrought for him a greater fortune.

Notwithstanding the simpleness of my surroundings, my childhood was very happy. What do riches mean to a child? Childhood
is a section of human life exempted from the curse of Adam — a
short period of innocence and play, preceding moral responsibility
and the long subjection to duty and toil which is to follow. No
healthy child, however much it may suffer from neglect or cruelty,
is wholly without happiness. If it did not receive some kindness, it
would not survive. No child who has warmth and sufficient food is
poor. Where father and mother are is home, and "be it ever so humble, there's no place like home." If the home be plain, even squalid
and ugly, the child will find interest and its imagination create
beauty. Into its dawning consciousness the world puts a new won-

der and surprise with every hour. No social distinction afflicts a child with "complexes," inferior or superior. In the democracy of childhood, the son of a king will play in the sand, if allowed, with the son of the hostler, and enjoy it just as well as if his playmate were the son of a duke. Poverty is a state of mind which is not acquired in childhood. A little girl with a rag doll gets just as much joy out of it as the child of the millionaire gets from her more expensive doll, at least until she sees the more expensive toy.

As a child, I was rich. My estate consisted of a little horse mounted on wheels, a rooster on a little box, which when pressed down made a crowing sound, a pair of corduroy breeches which one of my uncles gave me, and a little red tin bucket with a lid which I used as a savings bank. Into this little bucket I placed the coins given me by my grandparents and my uncles and aunts, and I never failed to give the hint to a visitor that the bank needed additions. I kept this little hoard until it had grown to about four dollars and a half; and when I started to school at the age of seven years, it was used to buy my school books. Besides this material wealth, I had two friends. One was a great shaggy dog named Thad. Old Thad was not a particularly amiable creature with everybody. As a watchdog he was vigilant and effective. Strangers had to get a passport before entering the yard. With me he was watchful, patient and kind. I could pull his tail, beat him in play with a stick, ride him like a horse, and he would never resent anything I did. If I was playing about the yard, he seemed to understand that he was my guardian, and never let me get out of his sight. One warm spring day my mother missed me and became alarmed, and seeing Old Thad, she called him; but he would not come to her. Going to where he was, she found me asleep in the dead leaves by a log with Old Thad standing guard.

My other friend was little Fanny Glenn, the little child of George and Tishie Glenn. Fanny was just my age, and difference of race, color, or previous condition of servitude did not set up any social bar between us at play. I remember her very distinctly through having acquired from her an infestation of those interesting little animals, one of which, seen by Robert Burns disporting himself on a lady's bonnet at church, inspired one of his best-known poems. This caused me to lose the long curls which dangled round my shoulders and gave me a never-to-be-forgotten experience with that instrument of torture, a fine tooth comb.

On the 4th of March, 1871, my brother Emmett was born. I do not know whether he was crying or not, as I was not present. I do know, however, that if he was not born exercising that vocation, he soon adopted it, and pursued it with diligence and attained a marked degree of efficiency. Most of my time from that time on for several months was spent sitting in one end of a cradle rocking away in an effort to prevent the overexercise of his talents.

Prior to my brother's birth, I was the only grandchild in the McElreath or McEachern families and, naturally, I was the object of much interest on the part of grandparents, uncles and aunts. I was often carried to the house of my grandfather McEachern, and there I had many adventures. One of my uncles who drove the horses hitched to the levers that turned the shaft with a great cog wheel on top and furnished power to run the gin made me a seat on one of the levers, and I rode round and round as the horses walked in a circle around the shaft. He took me into the lint room where the lint was blown by the gin brush like eddying snow in a storm. One day I ventured into the fowl yard and an old turkey gobbler, resenting the intrusion, attacked me and beat me with his wings. On another occasion, I ventured too close to a mother goose which had a brood. She ran at me and poked out her long neck and hissed until I started to run, and when I turned she took a pinch out of the most vulnerable portion of my body which was exposed to her.

My mother was the most devoted of parents, and my father was always devoted to children. I thought my father was the greatest man in the world, and I wished to be like him. When plowing in the field he wore a pair of trousers with a patch on the seat. My mother made me a pair of trousers of the same material. One day I crawled under the house and made the sleepers ring with loud lamentations. My mother heard me crying and came out to investigate. When she asked me what I was crying about, I told her that my trousers did not have a patch on them like my father's.

At the end of the year 1871, we removed to a farm which my father had bought in Milton County near a place called Freemansville. My aunt, Amanda McElreath, had married A. L. Smith, "Uncle Lee" as we called him, and their home was in the same community. My uncle Pink McElreath who had married my mother's sister also took up his residence near Freemansville, and my uncle John J. McElreath was teaching school near there; and so a sort of family colony was formed at that place. Why any of the family should have gone to Milton County at that time, I have never been able to learn.

There are many good people in Milton County, perhaps as good as there are anywhere, and there were many such in the county at that time; but the county as a whole was backward. It had no railroads and no towns of any size. When the people went to market they went out of their own county to Gainesville, Canton, or Marietta, and drove back into a land of secluded forests and hills into which the outside world seldom entered. This was the natural environment of the "moonshine" still. The people around Freemansville were both skilled in the art of making "moonshine" and capable in its consumption. On one occasion my father carried me to Freemansville, which was a post office and a voting precinct, to an election for justice of the peace. The friends of the opposing candidates and, perhaps, the candidates themselves, were well supplied with campaign funds in the form of "moonshine," raw and efficacious. The day was warm, and by the middle of the afternoon dozens of men were vomiting, or lying dead drunk under the trees.

On another occasion, at the same place, I witnessed a survival of the "gander pulling" days of Longstreet's *Georgia Scenes* — a shooting match. A chicken was tied to a stake at a distance of about one hundred and fifty yards, and each of the contestants gave ten cents a shot at it with a long squirrel rifle, the first man to hit the chicken to have it. If the first man hit the chicken, the owner had sold it for ten cents. His profit depended on the poor marksmanship of the shooters. It took ten shots to hit it; he had sold the chicken for a dollar. Next a turkey was tied to a stake at a shorter distance, the rules in the turkey contest being that it must be hit in the head. Then there was a contest for a cow. The cow was not shot at, but the shooting was at a target, the person making the best score to get the cow. The price of entering this contest was a dollar, and as I recall there was no match unless ten shots were paid for. Those who did not shoot kept up their spirits by frequent visits to a little brown jug from which drinks were retailed in a tin cup.

One day when my father was away from home, two or three buggies loaded with men in a howling state of intoxication came along a road which ran through the farm. The men were shouting, cursing and quarreling. A few hundred yards before they got to the house they stopped, got out, and decided to shoot it out. My mother ran and opened the farm gate through which they had to pass so that they would not stop when they came to it, and came back and closed and barricaded the doors. Two of the men stepped off a few paces, got out their guns and blazed away until pistols were emptied. Too much "moonshine" interfered with their marksmanship and no harm was done. After the duel was over they got back into their buggies and came on through the gates past the house, apparently in a good humor.

After we left Milton County, my father took me with him to Marietta one day, and after the business on which we went was attended to, he took me to the county jail to visit one of his old Milton County friends who had received a surprise visit from a revenue officer. The jailer having some business in town locked the jail and left. When we got ready to go, there was nobody to let us out. Finally, we raised a window looking out onto the platform at the head of the outside stairway and climbed through and escaped. This is the only time I ever broke jail.

Our Milton County home was a very nice and comfortable two-story dwelling with a fine grove of large trees in front, a great orchard back of it, and almost surrounded by a garden of old-fashioned flowers. I never saw so many hollyhocks at any other place. Forty-eight years after we moved away, I went back to the old place. The great oak trees had died and the house stood bleak and bare; but when I went around the house to where the flower garden had been, there stood in the same place a group of hollyhocks, the descendants, I suppose, of those which had stood there in my childhood. The kitchen and dining room were in a separate building from the big house, with a flagstone walk between the two buildings. Beyond the kitchen was a fine spring.

While living there, I took my first chew of tobacco. Several years later, I tried another. The second was my last. My uncle Sam McElreath lived with us the first year we lived in Milton, and helped my father make a crop. He was always my favorite uncle, and was very fond of me. He chewed tobacco and I was always begging him to give me a chew. Finally, he cut off a piece about the size of a pea and gave it to me. I tried to chew it like he did and spit red, but accidentally swallowed it. In a few minutes, I turned white, the perspiration started out all over me, and I fell over limp as a rag. He took me in his arms, carried me into the house, and laid me on a pallet where I suffered more nausea than is involved in all the seasickness that Neptune has been able to conjure up since Saturn was dethroned and the sea was awarded to Neptune in the division of Saturn's empire.

While living on this place, my father went to Marietta and came back with what was then a novelty, at least in that county—a cooking stove. Before that, my mother had baked the bread in an oven, fried the meat in a skillet, boiled the vegetables in a pot, and roasted the potatoes in the ashes. No other method has ever been invented to cook bread as good as corn light-bread cooked in an oven, with the hot coals of oak bark under the bottom and on the lid. It was my regular job to pull the bark from fence rails and deadened trees in the new ground to get fuel to heat the oven.

I have never been able to recall where we attended church while living in Milton, but I have a vivid recollection of two camp meetings, one at Holbrook Camp Ground and the other at Big Spring, in Cherokee County. At the Holbrook camp meeting we were tenters; that is, we had a log cabin, called a tent, on the grounds in which we spent the night. Before we went to the meeting, my father killed a calf and we had veal; and he killed and my mother cooked a little pig not much more than a foot long. It was roasted whole to a nice brown, and the skin of its back was cut into little checks. There may not have been anything else good about that camp meeting, but that pig was *good*. The religious exercises at this camp meeting were attended with a great deal of fervor. After dinner the bugle blew at three o'clock, calling the people to the big shed, or arbor, as it was called. An aged preacher named McClure, with a sentimental nature and an appealing voice, preached a sermon on Heaven; the congregation sang "We Have Fathers Over Yonder," and then the shouting began. No doubt some of those who shouted were experts in the manufacture of "moonshine" and its largest consumers at elections and shooting matches, but this is no impeachment of religion or of the camp meeting as a method of calling rough and primitive men to a better life. There is no place in Georgia now where such scenes can be seen as some of those described in this chapter. It was the voice of devoted preachers crying in the wilderness that has stamped out in large part the gross sensuality of the backwoods.

Milton County, in the days of which we are writing, was primitive, making "moonshine" was a common occupation, and drinking it was habitual; but there were some fine people around Freemansville while we lived there. Cicero Maddox was the postmaster and had a large country store at Freemansville. He was a fine citizen, sober, and a businessman of great ability. His descendants are among the most respected citizens and best businessmen of Atlanta today. There were several other families of high character and respectability who lived in the community, but the proportion of people of refined habits was too small to make a desirable society.

After two years my father sold his Milton County farm, purchased a portion of the old McElreath farm near Lost Mountain, and moved back to Cobb County. I well remember the day we left Milton. The day before, two or three wagons loaded with farm implements, provender, and furniture had gone on ahead. My father took the last load, which consisted of bedding and other furniture, my mother, my little brother Emmett, and my baby sister Cora, who was born in Milton County; and Old Thad ran along beside the wagon. Slowly over rough, narrow and hilly roads we winded our way until noontime, when we stopped for dinner at the foot of Brushy Mountain. At nightfall we reached Sandy Plains, about four miles from Marietta; where we spent the night in the schoolhouse. The next morning while my mother was preparing breakfast at the fireplace of the schoolhouse, I heard the whistle of a locomotive passing on the Western and Atlantic Railroad and heard the rhythmic exhaust of the engine. My father told me what it was and that I would see the cars in a few hours. This sent a cold chill up and down my spine.

The next morning we went on our way through Marietta where I first saw a railroad train, and the next night we reached our new home and a new era in my childhood began.

III

My Early School Days

The new farm on which we took up our residence was the western portion of my paternal grandfather's farm, near Lost Mountain, on which my father had spent his boyhood. On the west it adjoined "Rockdale," the estate of Dr. William Alston, already described.

The house into which we moved and in which we lived for two or three years while the materials were being gotten together for the building of a better home was a three-room log house previously used as a tenant house. Although the home was poor, the building of a new home was not of first importance. There were only a few acres of cleared land on the farm, and the thing of most immediate importance was to get enough land cleared to make a living on the farm and to plant an orchard. The latter task was one of the first and the wisest things done. The large orchard planted around the little home and only a few hundred feet from the site chosen for the later house quickly came into bearing. The varieties of fruits planted were so chosen that the peaches and apples matured successively, and consequently there were peaches from late May until early October, and apples from the early June apples until the Yates and Shockleys in the late fall. There are no such peaches now grown, at least in Georgia, as those that grew in that orchard—the great red-meated Indian peaches, the white English, and the large yellow clingstones.

As soon as we had become settled in our new home, my father employed George Glenn, the colored man who had formerly worked for him, at the princely wage of fifty cents a day, and they set about the clearing of additional lands. There was no eight-hour day in force in that day, and certainly not on that farm. We arose of a morning while it was still dark, had breakfast at daylight, and by sunup my father was in the woods cutting out the bushes and sap-lings, cutting the trees of a suitable size into logs for the building of a barn, splitting rails, riving boards, and building fences, while George Glenn was cutting ditches in the newly cleared bottom lands. After breakfast my mother would milk the cows, wash the dishes, "redd up" the house, churn, and, when they were in season, gather the vegetables for dinner, prepare the noonday meal, and blow a horn announcing that dinner was ready. After dinner she would wash the dishes, and during the afternoon, spin, sew and weave until late in the afternoon when she would milk the cows and prepare the supper which was served about dark, my father coming in from feeding the stock just in time for the evening meal. After supper my mother would wash the dishes and then sew or knit till bedtime. It was such labor as this that made the women on the farm old at forty, wrinkled and bent at fifty, and spent at sixty. It was such labor as this that gnarled the hands of the men, stooped their shoulders, and left them stiff and decrepit at an age when men in other occupations were still in their prime. When planting time came, clearing ceased until the crop was laid by, and then the farmer had a few weeks between "laying by time" and fodder pull-ing to rest and to go to protracted meetings, and the Lord knows he deserved the one and needed the other. The wife did not have this respite, but her labor went on unceasingly. During the years of which we are now writing, my father, as soon as the crops were laid by, went back into the woods, cutting timber and hauling it to the sawmill, splitting rails and riving boards for the new home and the out-buildings. Sometimes, now, in this luncheon-club age, I hear some white-collared savant solve the agricultural problem by advising the farmer to go to work. The trouble with the farmer, from the days of my childhood until now, is not that he has not worked, but that too many people have worked on him.

During the first six months at our new house, there was no school in our community and I was, of course, too young to do any work except light chores about the house. I carried in stovewood, gathered dead bark for the ovens, and watched the younger children while my mother milked the cows. On good days I spent as much time as possible with my father in the woods and fields. There, like Hiawatha, I

> *Learned of every bird its language,*
> *Learned their names and all their secrets,*
> *How they built their nests in summer*
> *Where they hid themselves in Winter.*

I watched the wild geese drive wedges through the sky, the flocks of wild pigeons camp in the treetops, the droves of robins forage in the forests as they paused in their springtime migration, the Indian hens wing their lazy, loping flight, heard the cardinals and the thrushes sing in the apple trees, watched the woodpecker wield his hammer and chisel, heard the turtledove croon his love song, listened to the plaintive notes of the whippoorwill in the twilight, and the eerie cry of the screech owl, and ran with Old Thad after the scampering rabbit.

On the first Monday in July school opened at Midway Church, about a mile from where we lived. The morning I was to start to this school, my father gave me a lecture at the breakfast table. He said,

> Now you are about to start to school. I want you to be a man, behave yourself, mind your teacher, and learn your lessons. Don't be quarrelsome on the playground, don't raise a fuss with any other boy and get into a fight. If you do, I will give you a whipping when you get home, but don't let anybody impose on you. If anybody tries to run over you and impose on you and you don't fight, I will give you a licking when I find it out.

I had already dressed for school, my attire consisting of a three-piece suit, a hat, a white shirt, and a pair of homespun trousers, worn according to the style of that day with homemade suspenders. Soon after breakfast I started away upon the great adventure, carrying my dinner in a little tin bucket and my one book under my arm—a copy of Webster's *Blueback Speller*. That old book has become a relic of bygone days, but millions of boys and girls of the yesteryears were inspired by the picture on the front inside cover of Minerva pointing the young lad to the temple of knowledge and fame. Any man today who knows all there is in that little book is not an ignorant man.

The teacher was Miss Hattie Fitten. The schoolhouse in which she taught was a small log building about twenty by thirty feet, furnished with benches, some without backs. Along the sides of the room were shelves which served as writing desks. The pupils were all ages from children six years to grown young men and women. There was no course of study, everybody pursuing just such studies as he pleased, and there were no grades. The subjects taught were the most elementary. The only subjects taught, as far as I can recall, were spelling, reading, writing, arithmetic, geography—and there was, perhaps, a class in Smith's *English Grammar*. Every morning a chapter was read from the New Testament, all of the pupils who were far enough advanced participating in the reading. The reading went round the room, each pupil in his or her turn reading a verse. There was also a class in history, the textbook being Alexander H. Stephens' *History of the United States*. There were two or three classes in spelling, graded according to their progress through the *Blueback Speller*. There was a class which had progressed through the monosyllables and reached "baker," another which could wrestle with "cinnamon," and another which had reached the polysyllabic stage and could spell such words as "incomprehensibility" and the hard words in the back of the book. The *Blueback Speller* was used as a reader until the pupils could read the *Third Reader*. I do not remember seeing any of those simple books with pictures and Mother Goose Rhymes, such as are now used. Below the grades of those who could spell "by heart" were the beginners. The alphabetic system was used, the phonetic folly of the present day never having been thought of. The first thing a child had to learn was his ABC's, and "a" was just plan "a" and no "ah." The manner in which the child was taught his letters was to have him come up to the teacher's chair and lay the book, open at the alphabet, on the teacher's knee, where she would point from one letter to another until the child could tell the name of all of the letters. When the alphabet was learned, then the phonic significance of the letters was learned by spelling and pronouncing such combinations as *ba, be, bi, bo, bu*, and *by*. On the third page of the *Blueback* short sentences consisting of one syllable appeared, and the child began to read as soon as he learned to spell. The teacher gave no lectures and told no stories. She merely heard recitations and corrected mistakes. While the pupils were studying their lessons, if one of them came to a word which he could not pronounce, he would put his finger just under it to point it out and carry the open book to the teacher who would give the correct pronunciation. If a pupil could not solve a problem in arithmetic, he would take the problem to the teacher who would work it for him. This school was a rather poor school for that day, but it fairly represents the method of instruction in the country schools of that time. The method of teaching was crude, but it had one virtue: the child had to depend upon himself. The emphasis was ever upon learning by the pupil rather than instruction by the teacher. Progress was slower at the start, but a stronger fiber of mentality was developed. In later years, when I became a teacher, I adopted many of the modern methods, but, after giving a pupil a start in a subject and showing him how to study it, I never helped except when he could not help himself. Modern methods of public education in the grammar school grades have all of the advantages and all of the disadvantages of modern mass production.

When I was a child I was shy and bashful to a painful degree. If I was scolded, it scared me almost to death; and if anyone spoke derisively to me or of me in my presence, I suffered pangs of mortification. I suffered from that most unfortunate handicap, somewhat, but not quite, overcome in later years, of being afraid of people. I have always been proud of the courage my father is said to have exhibited at the Battle of First Manassas, but I really do not think he went into a more terrifying situation than I did when I started to school. When the teacher would call on me to recite I would tremble, and it was only by the most supreme effort that I could conquer the disposition to cry. After I had been at school about two weeks, one day when I had finished my recitation, I had a sudden accession of boldness and said in a voice loud enough to be heard all over the little schoolroom, "I am seven years old today." The whole schoolroom burst into a laugh, and all the world went dark for me.

The Fitten family lived about a half mile from our house and consisted of Mr. Isaiah Fitten, his wife, and their daughter, Miss Hattie, my teacher. Before the war he was, it was said, a wealthy planter, and, as I recall, lived near Montgomery, Alabama. He was reduced to poverty by the war, and after it was over purchased a small tract of eleven acres of rough, hilly land adjoining the Mc-Elreath farm, built a modest home, planted a large garden and orchard, and cleared about five acres of ground. On these few acres he made a living for himself and family, doing all the work himself. He was a very dignified, devout man. He was an old man when he came to Lost Mountain to spend the last years of life in hard toil. It was a sad sight to see this old gentleman, who had spent his earlier years in plenty, reduced to toil with the axe, the hoe, and the plow for the bare necessities of life; but with what he made on his few rocky acres, supplemented by the few dollars Miss Hattie earned in teaching her small school for four or five months a year, the family lived in eminent respectability. Miss Hattie continued to teach at the same place for two or three years, during which time I attended her school for about three months in each year.

From seven to ten years of age, I was put to work at such tasks as I was able to perform. Idleness was not a vice in which I was permitted to indulge during any part of my life when my father had control of me, that is, when he was in sight. In the winter when I was not in school, I piled brush and chunked the fire about the log heaps which were burned in the new grounds; hoed, as much as I was able, after crop time came; and in the fall picked cotton. One of my weekly tasks was to go on Friday afternoon to the post office at Lost Mountain to get the mail. On one of these trips I saw a sight which terrified me and still comes into my recollection with horror. On the road between our home and the post office there lived a man who had killed his brother. I do not know what the facts about this homicide were, but I presume the killing was justifiable as nothing was done about it; but the knowledge that he had killed a man made me dread to be about him. When I passed his house I always walked on the other side of the road and got by as quickly as possible. One day when I was passing the house, he drove up in a two-horse wagon, having in his hand a lacey leather horse whip with a lash on the end. He stopped the wagon and called his little boy, almost my age, that is, about ten years old, and when the boy got within reach, he began beating the boy with this whip. The long lash would whistle through the air and wrap itself around the little fellow's shoulders and around his body and his bare legs. The little fellow screamed and pleaded as the cruel lash stung and cut him until he fell upon the ground to better escape the blows. I do not know what the child had done, but I suppose he had been guilty of some childish disobedience. Several years later this same man killed a neighbor and spent a year in jail awaiting trial, and upon his trial was acquitted. Corporal punishment of children at home and in school was commonly practiced in that day, but I never saw or heard of anything equal to this, and only one or two cases approaching it in cruelty. This extreme case is cited as an illustration of the sternness of parental government in that day, happily now outgrown.

After my first two terms at school, I had learned to read and I read voraciously. I hardly did anything but read when I was not at work. Reading as much as I did, I learned very rapidly, and soon could read the newspapers. I think it was about 1876, when I was nine years of age, that Joel Chandler Harris began publishing "The Romance of Rockville" in the *Atlanta Weekly Constitution* as a serial story, each installment of which I devoured as it came out. About this time Samuel W. Small, who later became one of my friends, began to publish his "Old Si" stories in Negro dialect, and a little later Joel Chandler Harris began his series of "Uncle Remus" stories. I could hardly wait for the *Weekly Constitution* to come, and when it arrived, I could scarcely eat or sleep until I had read everything in it except the editorial page. Editorials are like lager beer and olives — a taste for them has to be cultivated, a very keen taste which I have not acquired even at my present age.

I not only read the newspapers, at the age about which I am now writing, but also every kind of book I could get my hands on.

I cared a great deal more about reading than I did about work, a partiality which has not entirely left me.

My first interest in politics began at the age of nine. The year 1876 was the year of the contest for the presidency between Rutherford B. Hayes and Samuel J. Tilden. The people talked about the race at church, at the post office, at log rollings, and wherever two people met. I listened and, of course, was an intense Democrat. When the Electoral Commission seated Hayes, I was intensely disappointed and felt personally cheated.

About the time I was ten years of age, my father hit upon a bright idea and bought me a small boy's axe exactly like the one he used, except in size. I was very proud of my bright new axe, and I soon learned to chop quite well. In consequence of my zeal to show prowess, I was assigned to penal servitude at the woodpile. One Saturday afternoon my father was cutting the big wood for Sunday while I was chopping away at the smaller sticks. Even my light axe began to feel heavy, and finally I sat down and said that I could not cut any more. My father saw that I was sick and told me to go into the house. After getting into the house I had a hard chill. My mother filled a foot-tub with hot water and bathed my feet, and wrapped me in a hot blanket and put me to bed. During the night, I was delirious, and the next day I had a severe pain in my side. The doctor was sent for, but he did not come until night. When he came he looked at my tongue, counted my pulse, took my temperature, and listened to my breathing with a stethoscope. Then he ordered a fly blister to be put on my left side. The suffering I underwent from the burning and from the severe pain in my lung was intense. Most of the time I was delirious, and the lessons I was learning at school at that time were running through my fevered brain. One night when the doctor came in I looked up at him and said, "Doctor, which is above the line, the numerator or the denominator?" The disease ran its course in a few days, but it left me emaciated and weak, and my recovery was slow. Before I could hold a book to read, I lay and conned over the lessons in the books which I was then studying. At that time I had progressed to compound quantities in the *Intermediate Arithmetic*. As I recall, there were three of Cornell's *Geographies*, the "First Steps," the "Intermediate," and the "High School Geography." Whatever its designation, I was studying the second of the series. I lay in bed and bounded countries, named rivers and mountain chains, and named the products of the various countries. One question ran me nearly crazy. I asked my father and mother and everybody who came around what country was famous for its pearls and turquoises. Nobody could tell me. One morning I was able to be propped up in bed. I asked that my slate and arithmetic and my geography be given me. I immediately began to search for the country famous for its pearls and turquoises and found that it was Persia. One bright day in March, my father came in at noon and I told him that I wanted to see out of doors. He wrapped me in a blanket and carried me to the door, and held me for a long time while I feasted my eyes on a sea of peach blooms in the orchard surrounding the house. I have seen the flowers in the gardens of Halifax and the slopes of the mountains of Madeira, but no other earthly scene has ever been or will ever be as beautiful to me as the peach blossoms on that spring day.

The year 1876 was the beginning of that stage in the life of a child when his interest is no longer confined to the immediate things which surround him in the home and school room, or the things he immediately sees or experiences, but begins to concern himself with the distant things of which he reads or hears. Besides being the year of the Tilden-Hayes contest, it was the year of the Centennial Exposition at Philadelphia. The descriptions of the exhibits, the buildings, the pageants, and the visits of celebrated people read like stories from fairy tales to me.

In the year 1878 there occurred in the Seventh Congressional District, of which Cobb County was a part, the campaign for Congress between Dr. William H. Felton of Bartow County and Col. George N. Lester of Cobb County. The year 1877 marked the complete wiping out of Reconstruction influence in Georgia, except in the Seventh and Ninth Congressional Districts, and the resumption of political control by the old-time native citizens who regarded the regular Democratic party as the exponent of Southern sentiment. It was in that year that the present Constitution of Georgia was adopted, doing away with the Constitution of 1868, which had been adopted largely by Reconstruction, carpetbag influences. The last stronghold of the old Union influence was in North Georgia. In that part of the state some of the counties had been strongly Union before and lukewarm during the war, and after the war voted the Republican ticket. Indeed, some of the counties in the Seventh District go Republican in national elections to the present day. For a few years after the war, the Republicans in the Seventh and Ninth Districts combined with the old Union Democrats, and candidates ran in those districts calling themselves Independent Democrats and received the support of the Republicans and the old Union Democrats. After the adoption of the Constitution of 1877, it was determined to stamp out independentism in the two north Georgia congressional districts. Emory Speer was the Independent Democratic candidate in the Ninth and Dr. Felton in the Seventh. Col. George N. Lester, the regular Democratic candidate in the Seventh District, was an old Confederate soldier, who had lost his right arm in the service. He was a fine lawyer, an eloquent speaker, and a man of magnetic personality. Dr. Felton was a farmer, a profound scholar, and a man of great ability, a splendid debater, a master of sarcasm and of caustic wit. During the race in the Seventh District, political feeling was aroused to a pitch to which it was never aroused in Georgia before or since. People talked of nothing else. Brothers fell out and would not speak to each other; the women quarreled at quilting parties; and boys fought on the schoolyards. I was an intense Lester man, and thought a Republican to be a pariah and unclean. A farmers' club meeting was held at Lost Mountain. Both the candidates were invited to be present and speak — with the understanding that neither was to refer to politics, but was to talk on legislation in the interest of the farmer, and that there was to be no demonstration of preference by the crowd. Dr. Felton spoke first and dealt with financial legislation, dealing with the subject of "greenback" or first money. At the conclusion of the Doctor's speech, his supporters could not restrain themselves, and a great demonstration broke out led by Greer Ward, an enthusiastic supporter of the Doctor. In the afternoon Col. Lester spoke, but his supporters, who were perhaps in the majority, gave him only the usual applause. At the close of the day, Park Ward, a rabid supporter of Col. Lester, and a brother of Greer Ward who had led the cheering for Dr. Felton in the morning, jumped to the speaker's stand and said, "We had a demonstration here this morning for Dr. Felton; now I propose three cheers for Col. Lester." Then the rebel yell rolled out, and there was a near riot. Greer Ward and his brother Park did not speak to each other again for years.

In the summer while this campaign was going on, a great speaking with a free barbecue was arranged at Acworth in the interest of the candidacy of Col. Lester. The people came by the thousands from Cobb, Bartow, and Paulding Counties. Just before the speaking began, the train brought Gen. John B. Gordon. When he alighted from the train, the old soldiers pressed around him. Someone introduced my father to him and said, "General, here is a soldier who never dodged a bullet." The General grasped my father by the hand and made some appreciative remark which I do not now recall. The speaking was in the open air before a vast audience. Gen. Gordon was in his prime, and when he arose to speak with that magnetic presence and began with that appealing voice which never failed to send the cold chills down the spine of his hearers, the demonstration was such that I have never seen equaled but once, and that was on the occasion of the visit of Jefferson Davis to Atlanta in 1886. I remember distinctly a large part of Gen. Gordon's speech on that occasion. There had been leveled at him some very bitter criticism on account of his voice in the United State Senate in support of the finding of the Electoral Commission in deciding the contest of the election of 1876 in favor of Rutherford B. Hayes and against Samuel J. Tilden. He stated that he was moved to support the finding of the Electoral Commission in consideration of the ending of Reconstruction in South Carolina, the restoration of white supremacy in that state, and the seating of Wade Hampton as Governor. Both Dr. Felton and Emory Speer were elected in 1878, and Emory Speer was reelected in 1880. Dr. Felton was defeated in 1880 and Emory Speer in 1882. Since then Georgia has been solidly and regularly Democratic. In such times as these, I passed from childhood into youth.

For the first two or three years of my school life, Miss Hattie Fitten continued to teach in the old log schoolhouse of Midway Church near Lost Mountain, and I attended about three months in each year. It is my recollection that the state's appropriation for free school education was at that time limited to three months in the year, and that the schools which I attended were kept open only during the free school term. During my tenth or eleventh year, my

Uncle John J. McElreath taught at Midway and I went to school
to him. He was an old-time country schoolteacher, but as a teacher
he was very much the superior of Miss Fitten. His education
would, today, be considered very limited, knowing no Latin or
Greek and no mathematics beyond arithmetic; but what he knew,
he knew thoroughly. He wrote a splendid copy-book hand, and
understood and taught bookkeeping. He was a good grammarian
and was gifted with a good literary style. He had been a cripple
from childhood, his left arm being withered and his left leg smaller
and shorter than the other. But despite his physical infirmities, he
was a very handsome man. He was tall and slender, with a fine face
covered with a reddish-brown beard which reached nearly to his
waist. He was of a very kindly disposition, of singular purity of
thought and speech, and he inspired the admiration and respect of
his students from the little child just beginning to learn the alphabet
to the grown young men and women who attended his school. I
loved and admired him more than any other man I knew in my
childhood and youth. He was as itinerant as a Methodist preacher,
rarely teaching at one place more than two years. His frequent
change of location was not because there was any dissatisfaction
with him; but he seemed to grow tired of one location after a year
or two, and there was always some other community that desired
him. It was said that he had taught more pupils than any other man
in North Georgia. Wherever he taught he made friends, both of
pupils and patrons, and I still frequently meet some old man who
went to school to him and who speaks admiringly of him. I cannot
fix the exact date of his teaching at Midway. It was in 1878 or 1879,
but I cannot be certain which of those years.

   The years 1876, 1877 and 1878 were not only the years marking
political transition and the beginning of a new era in the political
life of the people of Georgia, but they also marked a period of economic change. In North Georgia, especially in the path of Sherman's devastation, there was an economic paralysis until about
1876. The freeing of the slaves and the casualties of the war left the
task of restoring the country upon so few hands that it took a decade for the farmers to need new fields. They might, probably, have
reached a time of expanding operations two or three years earlier
had it not been for the panic of 1873 which, of course, affected

country folks situated as the farmers of Cobb County were situated less than it affected the business interests of the country; but it had its effects even upon them. In 1876, a time which I can, of course, clearly remember, the country was in about the same condition it was fifteen years before, at the opening of the war. Vast tracts of the country were still in original forest and there were great uncleared, undrained swamps in the country. The roads were streets of mud, up and down hill, with stretches of corduroy through the swamps. About 1876 new lands began to be cleared, the roads began to be somewhat improved, and new houses built. The initial and most marked period of this new activity of development was from about 1876 to 1880. Considering the age of twelve years as the end of childhood and the beginning of youth, my childhood was spent in a primitive country and in a period of common poverty, and the beginning of my youth was coincident with the period of political and economic transition after the war.

---- IV ----

My Lost Mountain
School Days

The most notable instance of the coming of the new era in that part of the country of which we have been writing was the building at Lost Mountain in 1877 or 1878 of the first real, comfortable schoolhouse ever built in the country in Cobb County, so far as my knowledge goes. The building was small, being of one room about forty feet long and about thirty feet wide. It had a smooth tongue and grooved floor, was tightly ceiled, lighted by glass windows, heated by a large stove in the center, and furnished with a small table and a chair for each student. The rear end of the room had no windows and was finished as a blackboard. In front of the blackboard was a long bench extending the entire width of the room which was used as a recitation bench. Between the bench and the blackboard were the teacher's chair and desk. Such a schoolhouse, perfectly warm in the coldest weather and with comfortable seats and individual desks, was a wonderful thing in a country which had known only log schoolhouses, through the cracks of which the wind howled on cold days, and where children sat on wooden benches, often without backs.

The first teacher in the new schoolhouse was as great an improvement as the schoolhouse itself. He was Professor John Mable, a schoolmate of my mother. I entered on the first day school opened in the new building. At this time I was about twelve years old, either a half year over or a half year under that age.

Professor Mable was a teacher far in advance of his age. In the "old field" schools of that day, it was the custom for the teacher on the first day of school to read a set of rules governing the conduct of the student, any infraction of which laid the offending student liable to corporal punishment, which almost invariably followed, as it was thought that failure to punish would ruin the discipline of the school. A stout hickory switch kept in convenient reach was, in that day, considered to be a necessary pedagogical instrument. The schoolmaster sometimes brought one with him on the first day of school. Our new teacher announced on the first day of school that there would be but one rule in his school—to do right—and that there would be no corporal punishment. This adoption of the honor system was remarkably justified by its results. That was the best behaved school I ever attended, and there was not a single serious case of misconduct on the part of any pupil.

The attendance at this school taxed the capacity of the schoolroom to the utmost, a large number of students coming from a distance and boarding in the community. New and modern textbooks were used, and the subjects taught ran from the alphabet to algebra, geometry, and Latin. Some of the students were grown men and women, and perhaps a third were from fifteen to twenty years of age.

I cannot now recall with certainty all of the studies I pursued. I recall distinctly that I was in a class which was studying the most advanced of the series of geographies—I think, Monteith's—that I was in Sanford's *Common School Arithmetic*, and in a class in either Towne's *Analysis* or Swinton's *Word Book*; but I cannot recall what course of reading I was taking. I was far more advanced than most of the boys of my age and was in classes with the grown young men, though it was difficult for me to keep up with some of them. My pride and eagerness to excel the other students in my classes led me into one instance of intellectual dishonesty that taught me the most valuable lesson I ever learned. One day the teacher placed on the blackboard a long column of figures for addition and said, "Now we will see who can add these figures first and get the correct answer." He took a piece of chalk and wrote down his result. I followed him, and adding the first two columns got the same result that he did, and naturally thinking that his addition of the other columns was likewise correct, I then put down the same figures he had put under the other columns; and after waiting a short time, held up my hand and announced the result in advance of any of the other students. The teacher then took up a pointer and followed up one column after another and found that his answer was incorrect in almost every column, except the first two. He then turned to me and said, "Walter, we seem to have made the same mistakes." I learned my lesson for good, and I have never since then been guilty of any act of intellectual dishonesty.

This school marked a social change which was happening over the whole South—the falling of the old aristocracy from their high position of social prestige. Before this school, the children of the Alston family had never attended school in the community. The boys, before the war, had been taught by private tutors and the girls by governesses. After the war, the older children of the family had taught the younger children. The family attended the Episcopal Church of Marietta, and so there had never been any social contact between the Alston children and the country children. Under the old regime, the Alston family had lived in lordly exclusiveness so far as their country neighbors were concerned, but changed conditions and diminished income had, at last, broken down the barriers of caste, and three of the Alston boys and two of the girls were among the pupils who entered on the day the school opened. I promptly fell in love with Sabine, one of the girls several years my elder, but this was not a matter of embarrassment to her as she never found it out. My only act in pursuit of my youthful passion was to practice writing her name on my slate; but I was careful to conceal the fond inscription and to erase it before it was discovered. Before the school was over she was succeeded by several others who were equally ignorant of the state of my heart. There was Luella Gray, and Sally Cooper, and Ola Pickett, a plump little black-eyed girl with adorable freckles about her nose, who always tried to sit next to me on the recitation bench so that I could whisper the answer to her when she did not know it.

I attribute much of the inspiration to such scholarship as my circumstances and my limited abilities have enabled me to attain to Professor Mable and his school. The one-room school had its disadvantages, but it had certain advantages over the schools in which the different grades are taught in separate rooms. The advantage of the graded school is, of course, that the teacher can give more time to a subject when all the students in the room are in the same class; recitations in concert can be more effectively conducted; and drills can be adjusted to the age and the degree of advancement of the students in a particular grade. One of the disadvantages of the graded school is that the students in a particular grade do not see and hear the instruction given to the higher grades. In Professor Mable's school, I watched the two students of geometry put their diagrams on the blackboard, listened to the demonstrations, and I learned most of the simpler geometric figures. I knew a right angle triangle, and an equilateral, an isosceles, a parallelogram, and a polygon, and I understood some of the simpler theorems. I wondered at the cabalistic use of the x's, y's, and a + b and a − b's in algebra, and learned that there was a language in which "amo" was the equivalent of "I love." This raised in me a keen curiosity about those studies, and fixed in me a purpose some day to pursue them. "The thoughts of youth are long thoughts."

Another disadvantage of the graded school is that each grade is a team whose pace is set by the slowest horse, or at least by the average member of the team, while in the ungraded school in some studies, especially in mathematics, each student can go his own pace, and superior ability is not hindered by mediocrity.

At the end of the first year at Lost Mountain, Professor Mable went to a more remunerative school. The next year the teacher was Miss Margaret Hill, and the following year the school was taught by a young man named Robert Pritchard. They were excellent teachers, but not in the same class with Professor Mable.

After the year of Professor Pritchard's school, we removed to another community, and my life there is another part of the story.

If I had learned nothing except what I learned in school during my Lost Mountain School years, I would have made little progress in mental development. Except in technical courses, nobody gets much learning in school. He may get education—that is, he may learn how to study and think, and must learn certain basic facts, necessary as the formulas of thought—but real learning is self-taught. All that a boy indispensably needs is the taste for learning, a capable mind, a few months' schooling each year, and good books. If a boy has these things, he will do the rest, if there is anything in him. And the fact that a boy lives in the country is not to his disadvantage. He has more time for reading, less distractions, and the boon of being sufficiently alone to ponder over what he reads and make it part of himself.

During the years in the period covered by this chapter—that is, from the time I was twelve until I was almost fifteen years of age—I did a vast amount of reading. The first real poems that ever attracted my attention were "Annabel Lee" and "Lenore." I came across them in some old copies of the *Southern Literary Messenger* which were among the few old books and magazines in our home. The reading of "Annabel Lee" was like the opening of a door into a new world. The measure and the music, the passion and the parting, the longing of the lover as he watched the stars and dreamed of the other half of his soul to which he was eternally bound, swept into my consciousness as a vast surprise. Could man-made words talk that way? I thought surely no other poem in the world could be as good as "Annabel Lee." I have now on my shelves practically every English and American poet, and have read most of them. While I do not now think "Annabel Lee" to be the greatest poem in the world, I would have to consider a long time to pick out the one poem that is its superior.

About the time I was twelve years of age, my father bought a copy of Shakespeare. There was not much else about the house to read which I had not already read a half-dozen times. The volume was large and the text printed in small type and, at first, I thought it was a man's and not a boy's book; but I decided to tackle it. I cannot conceive how I happened to fall upon *The Taming of the Shrew* as the first of the plays to be read, but I did, and enjoyed it very much. I reveled in *Richard III, Henry VIII, Othello, King Lear, Hamlet,* and *Macbeth*, but my favorites were *Coriolanus* and *Titus Andronicus*—plays which are rather below the par of Shakespearean genius. Along about the same time I borrowed a large, leather-bound volume of Longfellow's poems and started in at the first and read all the shorter poems, but could not arouse the slightest interest in them. I thought that it was the dullest book in the world, and then suddenly I ran into the "Forest Primeval" with its "murmuring pines and hemlocks," and I was immediately in fairy land. I read the poem to my mother, and when I came to the final scene where Evangeline found her lover dying of fever in the hospital and pressed Gabriel's head to her bosom and "meekly bowed her own" and said, "Father, I thank thee," my voice choked with tears. This poem and the land of Acadia haunted me through the years so that in 1926, nearly fifty years later, I journeyed to the village of Grand Pré, and while I did not find much of the "Forest Primeval," I saw the "dikes that the hands of the farmers had raised with labor incessant," the Basin of Minas, and the valley of the Gasperau; I saw Blomidon—"and the Forest old," and the mountains upon which "sea fogs piled their tents, and mists from the mighty Atlantic," and I visited the church built upon the spot where the old church stood in which the Acadians were herded for deportation, and Herbert's statue of Evangeline taking her last look at the village from which she was about to be exiled; and I went out in the night and beheld the moon rise and the stars blossom out in the infinite meadows of heaven.

It might be thought that it would have been impossible to procure good books in the country in the days of my youth. It is true that only a very few books were owned by any one family, but taking the community as a whole, many very fine books were owned, and those were exchanged, so that anybody who wished to read could procure from somebody a good book on almost any subject. We had a two-volume diary of Denham and Clapperton, two English army officers who had conducted a journey of exploration in Africa. I read these volumes through and through, and was fascinated with the description of the journey through the Sahara, the journey from Morzouk to Kouka, from Kouka to Lake Tchad, and from Lake Tchad to Khartoum, the descriptions of the houses, and the songs and the customs of the natives. About this time, the accounts of Stanley's trips through Africa were being published, which I read with avidity. No better course in the study of geography could have been devised than such a course of reading.

Before the war there was a young man in the community, Frank Ward, who was said to have been a particularly gifted and fine young man. He was of a scholarly turn of mind, and had made a small collection of very fine books. He had just reached manhood when the war broke out and, like all of the other young men in the community, he volunteered. He was killed in his first fight, the Battle of First Manassas. His brother, William A. Ward, whose farm adjoined ours, had some of these books and lent me a history of England. It was a large and rather formidable book for a boy fourteen or fifteen years of age, but I read it through. I am sure much of it was beyond my capacity to assimilate, but nothing could have been more interesting than such characters as Alfred, Canute, William the Conqueror, and Richard Coeur de Lion, and no incidents more thrilling than the accounts of the battles of Crécy, Agincourt, Poitiers, and the Field of the Cloth of Gold. The prejudice I had conceived against the English on account of the Revolutionary War from my reading of the school histories of the United States was strongly intensified even by the English accounts of their treatment of Joan of Arc. It is needless to say that age and wider reading and better judgment have removed this prejudice. I have since found out that all nations are sinners, more or less, and that there are some dark pages in the history of our own country.

At my grandfather McElreath's I found a little book by Isaac Watts entitled *The Improvement of Human Understanding*. This was one of the best books it has ever been my good fortune to read. It is a book that any man, however mature and learned, can read and re-read with profit. I read it over and over and committed many of its rules to memory, and it has been a great aid to me. Then there was that book, than which a better has never been written—*Pilgrim's Progress*. There was a small library at Midway Presbyterian Church from which good books were borrowed, and although nobody had many books, one who had the taste and inclination could always find something worthwhile to read.

I do not cite the fact of my ability to find some good books to read to prove that the means of literary culture were great or that a high degree of culture existed in the environment of my youth, for such was not the case, but to show that a few books, difficult to obtain, is not an excuse for any boy to grow up in ignorance. A few books rightly read and assimilated are a better means of culture than too many books. It is a saying among lawyers that the man of one book is to be dreaded as an antagonist. The same is true in any branch of learning.

Much knowledge of history and literature was not to be expected in the time and place where my youth was spent, but one was often surprised to find knowledge where it was least to be expected. After I became a teacher, I was one day visiting Cousin Fanny Taylor, an old lady who never had any opportunities of education except in the "old field" schools such as I have described, and such information as she could pick up from the scant supply of books in the community. She astounded me by asking if I knew what was the meaning of the word "Thermopylae" and how far the place was from Athens. I told her that Thermopylae meant "hot springs," and gave her the approximate distance from the city of Athens. She said that she had always thought Thermopylae was a descriptive word and had wanted to know the exact location so as to understand the movements of Leonidas and his band of Spartans in occupying the pass.

In the 1870s the temperance movement which spread over the United States reached Lost Mountain. At that time there was no railroad in North Georgia west of the Western and Atlantic, and the people from Paulding and Haralson Counties bought their supplies and sold their crops in Marietta. In the spring when the farmers were purchasing their supplies and in the fall when they were marketing their crops, the road from Dallas by way of Lost Mountain to Marietta was crowded with wagons so near together that one wagon was hardly out of sight of another. The journey was too long to be made in a day, and when night came the teamsters camped alongside the road. There were then eleven saloons in Marietta, and a jug of whiskey was one of the usual purchases. Often two or three persons accompanied each wagon, and usually several wagons made the return journey together. Long before Lost Mountain was reached, the people in the caravan were in a state of hilarious or belligerent intoxication. They cursed and yelled, often in profane and obscene terms, so that the women of the families who lived on the road were in constant fear. The drinking was not confined to the people who passed through from Paulding and Haralson, but their behavior was worse than that of the people in the Lost Mountain community, possibly because the people from the western counties were farther away from home. There were not, so far as I can remember, any habitual drunkards in the Lost Mountain community, though it was not considered a disgrace to get drunk, and it was the custom for everybody to drink in moderation.

About the time of which we are now writing, a change of sentiment came over the people and temperance societies were organized in every community. A Good Templars Lodge was organized at Midway Church, the Presbyterian Church near Lost Mountain, and a lodge of the Knights of Jericho at the Powder Springs Camp Ground where the Methodist Church to which we belonged was located. With the organization of these temperance societies, a remarkable change of sentiment occurred with reference to the use of intoxicating liquors, and in a few years the sale of intoxicating liquors was abolished in Cobb County. In the part of the county where I lived, the reform was real and practically complete. The drinking of liquor fell under such complete reprehension that for the last fifteen years I lived in the county I did not know of a single case of drunkenness in our part of the county. My father was one of the organizers of the Good Templars Lodge at Midway, and when I was twelve years of age I joined and took the pledge. For years I observed it sacredly, and have only on rare occasions taken a drink, and have never been in the slightest degree intoxicated.

On the second Sunday in each month we attended the services of the Methodist Episcopal Church, South, to which my parents belonged, at Powder Springs Camp Ground, and on the third Sunday in each month we attended the Presbyterian Church at Midway. On Sunday afternoon we attended Sunday school at Midway. This Sunday school was operated as a Union Sunday school, and was held in the afternoon so that the people of other denominations could attend the morning service at their own churches on the Sundays on which the services of their respective churches were held, and all of them could attend Sunday school in the afternoon.

The textbooks used were the Shorter Catechism and the Bible itself. Afterwards, the International Lessons were used. I enjoyed Sunday school very much, and derived much profit from it.

From the regular church services, I am not conscious of having derived any very great amount of intellectual profit. I listened to the preacher because I was taught that it was irreverent not to do so. Except during the revival season, the preaching was doctrinal and dry. The revival season was one of great terror. Even at that age— that is, from twelve to fifteen years—I was radically heretic and militantly unorthodox, but I kept my views to myself.

As a child I was taught that God was the "Good Man" and the devil the "Bad Man." My conception of the "Good Man" was all kindness and love. I could not associate with him the idea of harshness, hate, or the desire to punish. When I became conscious of the doctrine of predestination and election in the Shorter Catechism, I did not believe it; and when I heard Uncle Archie Johnson try to explain it and justify it, I did not believe he knew what he was talking about. When I heard our own Methodist preachers pronounce a doctrine almost as harsh—the doctrine of the original sin of Adam imputed to the whole human race for all time, and the doctrine of total depravity from which no human being could escape except by the atoning sacrifice of Christ—I did not believe that. No infidel literature taught me to disbelieve these doctrines, for I had never read any such literature. It just did not appeal to my reason and sense of justice, and contradicted all of my conceptions of the nature of the "Good Man" to believe that he got mad at one man about an act of disobedience and vowed to himself to harbor that resentment throughout eternity and to punish generations of people who could not help being born. It seemed unlikely that he was persuaded to modify partially his sentence, not by forgiving the human race, but by advising his son that if he would take the punishment himself, he would give the human race a chance to escape. I thoroughly recognized the fact of sin and was conscious of responsibility for any sins I had myself committed, but I did not think that I was responsible for what my grandfather did, much less my ancient ancestor Adam. As to the sins I had myself committed, I did not believe the Lord was very mad at me. I believed that he was sorry for me and that if I would quit and ask forgiveness for anything I had done, I would get it. So when the revivalist got up and preached about the anger of God and hell fire, I had an uneasy feeling, of course; but when he called up mourners and told me in effect that the Lord was so vindictive about it, that if I did not come and kneel down at the altar, he would not pay any attention to me anywhere else, I did not believe that. I thought I could settle the matter with the Lord myself, and I wanted to be let alone about it. I did not object to being preached to, but when some devout brother started down the aisle and I saw him coming after me, I rebelled. I never did join the church until people let me alone about it. I have not changed my ideas very greatly after forty years of church membership.

While I think that the theology of my youth was wrong in many respects and the methods of the church were in many ways repellent rather than attractive and engaging, I still think that the church, in that age and in every other age, has been the one divine, saving influence of society and of humanity. However harsh the doctrine and crude the methods of the church, it has stood for righteousness and faith, and it has made men better, restrained their evil proclivities, and elevated society. It is to the Presbyterian Church at Midway and to the Methodist Church at what was formerly called the Powder Springs Camp Ground, now called McLand, that the remarkable history of the Lost Mountain community for law observance, sobriety, and social purity is to be attributed.

It was at about the age of which I am now writing that I formed the definite desire to acquire a real education. It is my belief that the character, aspirations, and ambitions of a boy are always fixed before he is fifteen years of age, and I know that it was so with me. I noticed that on important public occasions such as Sunday school celebrations, farmers' club meetings, and political rallies where there was public speaking, the speaker was usually some young man who had gone to college and had come back the hero of the people of the county. Among these were George F. Gober, A. S. Clay, and W. R. Power who, after graduation, had been admitted to the bar, and, a little later, there was A. B. Vaughan, a young man of unusual education and talent, who after graduation at Mercer College had entered the ministry. All of these young men had been country boys like myself, and I noted that their education and their professional status made them objects of universal attention, respect, and admiration. I began to study about my future and to wonder why I should not follow their example.

One day when I was about thirteen years of age, I was plowing a contrary horse in a rocky field and I decided that I would someday go to college, get an education, and be a lawyer. I do not know of any greater incentive to the forming of a resolution to go to college, get an education, and become a lawyer than plowing a contrary horse in a rocky field. It is not an incentive to enter the ministry, and I am sure A. B. Vaughan never plowed a contrary horse in a rocky field. A contrary horse and a rocky field are not a means of grace. St. Peter was a fisherman; St. Paul, a tent maker; St. Francis of Assisi, the son of a merchant; John Bunyan, a tinker; and Bishop Alpheus W. Wilson, of the Methodist Church, a tanner; but I never heard of a disciple, or an apostle, or a saint, or a bishop who plowed a contrary horse in a rocky field.

No sooner had I decided to go to college and get an education and be a lawyer than I got a hammer and saw and a jackplane and made me a desk, and put it up in a corner of the house and printed the word "Office" on it, and set about writing speeches. It is one of the calamities of literature, like the burning of the Alexandrian library, that none of these forensic efforts have been preserved. The world will still have to rock along with the speeches of Curran and Erskine.

About the time I was fifteen years old a debating society was organized at Midway to which most of the boys and young men of the community belonged. The society met every two weeks and debated such subjects as, "Resolved, That George Washington was a greater man than Christopher Columbus," or "Resolved, That there is more pleasure in pursuit than in possession." Four debaters to each side were chosen each meeting, and a subject agreed on for the next meeting. Oratory was not conspicuous among my native talents. The experience productive of the most agony during my school days was the Friday afternoon exercises when we all had to "say a speech." My memory went blank, my voice quavered, and what to do with my hands presented an impossible problem. I would have suffered a nervous collapse after each of these Friday afternoon exercises if I had not had Saturday and Sunday for rest and recuperation, and to recover from my mortification. When the debating society was organized, I joined and determined to overcome my natural ineptitude for public speaking. I had heard that Demosthenes had practiced at the seaside with pebbles in his mouth. As I did not have a convenient seaside, I decided to dispense with the rocks; but while plowing, I put a patient horse through an auditory experience that would have brought severe penalties upon me if there had been an agent of the Society for the Prevention of Cruelty to Animals near enough to take cognizance of my case. By dint of much practice, I finally developed sufficient proficiency in debate to be second choice when sides were chosen. With growing confidence I became rash, and one night I attempted to get funny and ridicule my opponent, an older boy with a quick mind and natural wit. He had the conclusion, and when he got through with me, I had acquired a dread of concluding speeches which has been of inestimable profit to me at the bar.

The community around Lost Mountain has been a remarkably fine one from the time of the first settlement of Cobb County. From the early 1840s until a few years ago, some of my people lived there, and I have constantly visited the community and kept informed of what transpired there. Nobody ever made liquor; there was never, to my knowledge, a public social scandal; and I never heard of the commission of a crime of any sort in the community.

The most prominent among the early settlers were Harvey Mayes, Johnson Williams, William A. Ward, Ben Fannin, Dr. William Alston, Russell Sorrels, George Lewis, John McElreath, the Kemps, Pharrs, Pickens, and Robinsons. The land was rich, and all these families were hardworking and prosperous.

Where the public road from Marietta to Dallas crosses the road from Powder Springs to Acworth on the southwestern shoulder of the mountain, there has been a country store and post office since before the war. The first merchants to have a store at Lost Mountain were the Hirsches. Later, the eldest of four brothers, Raphael Hirsch, located at Marietta and was a leading merchant there for many years after the war. Henry and Norris Hirsch, with their younger brother, Joseph, who later joined them, removed to Atlanta, and amassed great fortunes, and their descendants are among the wealthiest and most influential citizens of Atlanta and of Georgia.

At the period of which I am now writing, Lost Mountain was the most important point in Cobb County west of Marietta. Joshua Jackson had a large country store there in which he carried a large stock of general merchandise. There was a Baptist Church, a large blacksmith shop where — in addition to the ordinary work of making and sharpening plows — plow-stocks, wagons, buggies and cradles for harvesting wheat were made. There was a shoeshop where boots, shoes, and harnesses were made and repaired, and there was a large sawmill and gin.

The post office served the people for miles around and, in the summer, after crops were laid by, and at other seasons when work was not pressing, there was always a large crowd at the post office to meet the weekly mail. This was the occasion of the weekly tournament at checkers between Juell Dunton, famous as the originator of the Dunton Yam, and Matt Pickett, as the father of Ola. In these gatherings, stuttering Tom Robinson was usually present. Upon his return from the war he was tried by the Midway Presbyterian Church for profanity uttered while in the army. He admitted the charge and justified himself by saying that a man stole his rations and he said "God damn him," and he thought that a man who would steal a soldier's rations ought to go to hell. He was acquitted, probably because he said he was sorry — and was not — and the members of the session forgave him because they should have reprobated his conduct and did not. Wesley Jackson, a one-legged Confederate soldier, clean, elegant and refined, was usually there. Richmond Johns, the community agnostic with a face and head like Robert Toombs, poured forth his trenchant comments on things in general. Like many men of his type of mind, he made up for his deficiencies of belief by his fair and honest dealings. When he sold seed corn he always gave good measure, heaped up, shaken down, and running over because, as he said, when he went to hell he did not want any accusing empty half bushels standing around to mock him. Russell Sorrells usually came striding up, walking up with a long staff, erect, tall, and lithe as an Indian, despite his seventy-five years. He was the only live Republican in the community, and preserved his life and the respect of his neighbors by his fine character. Sometimes Dr. Alston was present with the simple habits and the quiet, dignified demeanor of the trial aristocrat. At these meetings, the state of the crops, politics, and the news of the community were discussed, and the old soldiers fought over again the battles of the War Between the States. When the mail carrier came, he brought two great mail sacks, one filled with letters and the other with newspapers, packages of government seeds, and catalogues from Portland, Maine, or Lynn, Massachusetts. I usually received a letter or two from some member of my father's or grandfather's family, a copy of the *Home and Farm*, the *Weekly Constitution*, and a sample copy of some magazine for which I had written under the false pretense of wishing to subscribe.

When I was not in school I had to work on the farm, and farm work has never been a cinch in any time or place. The poetry of farming exists chiefly in the mind of the man who looks on rather than in actual experience. Getting up at five o'clock on a cold morning to feed the stock, hauling corn out of bottom land infested with cockleburs and Spanish needles when the piles of corn are covered with frost, and plowing a contrary horse in a rocky field for fourteen hours a day should be used as forms of disciplinary punishment for bankers and Kiwanians who make luncheon addresses on the indolence of the farmer. If I could see one such individual drive a two-horse team with two bales of cotton from Lost Mountain to Marietta over the roads as they were fifty years ago, through the Mud Creek Swamp and up the Joe Green Hill on a cold day in November, and stand around the public square for three hours before getting his cotton cut while the cotton buyer was waiting to get quotations from the New York Cotton Exchange, and then get a bid of six and three-eights cents a pound for it, I would hunt up the graves of Gilbert and Sullivan, dig them out and tell them that I had at last found "the punishment that fits the crime." Cleaning out fence corners in February and March, swinging a scythe in June, and pulling fodder in August are tolerable on the same principle of the Latin poet, *Haec olim meminisse juvabit*. What the farmers think about life in the country is proclaimed by abandoned farms from Vermont to Texas. Millions of deserted farmhouses and dilapidated barns bear testimony to the economic revolution under Abraham Lincoln which freed the Negroes in the South and enslaved the farmers

North and South. The emancipation of the Negroes was a right thing done in a wrong way, and proceeding from hypocritical motives. The War Between the States killed a million men to make the farmers villains and slaves to commerce and an industrial regime.

From what has been said, it might be inferred that my youth was all work and study and that life at Lost Mountain was dull. This is far from true. My reading was not all in English history and Watts's *On Human Understanding*. There was the *Life of Jesse James*, surreptitiously acquired and furtively read. The woods were full of squirrels and rabbits, and the streams, then unditched, were full of fish. I had an old army musket which I used as a shotgun; and on days when it was too wet to work, I spent the time prowling through the woods shooting yellowhammers, woodpeckers, doves, and a squirrel when I could find one, and twisting rabbits out of hollow trees with a split stick. When a rain came in the spring and muddied the streams, my brother Emmett and I lit out to the creek, and usually came back with a long string of cats, perches, and horny heads. The swimming hole in the summer was a social rendezvous for Emmett and me and the boys of the Barnes and Ward families. In the fall there were possum hunts in the dark woods, usually winding up with a feast on raw turnips in a neighbor's turnip patch. Sells Circus came to Marietta, and the flaming posters pasted on the blacksmith shop at Lost Mountain raised anticipation to a high pitch. Emmett and I sat on the benches and saw the bareback riders jump through flaming hoops and heard the clown crack his jokes.

Life at Lost Mountain did not entirely consist of plowing a contrary horse in a rocky field. Youth holds a magic wand which conjures joy out of any circumstance.

V

The Bugg Farm Era

In the fall of 1881 the Lost Mountain farm was sold and another about two miles south, known as the Bugg farm, from the name of a former owner, was purchased. This farm, if eighty acres of sterility can be called a farm, had no house on it fit for a home, and a small adjoining farm was rented on which there was a fairly good house in which the family lived for two years.

The Bugg farm consisted of two landlots of forty acres each, one of which had been cleared many years before, and worn out, and practically abandoned. All except a few acres of this landlot was grown up in broomsedge, briers, and old field pines. On the other lot there was a fresh field of about five acres, and the rest was in original forest. As soon as we had become settled, the old task of clearing new grounds, splitting rails, building fences, and preparing for the building of a new home began all over again. This kept me out of school during all of the year 1882, and all of the year 1883 except for about two and one-half months in the summer. During the first winter I spent every day, when it was not raining too hard, in the woods cutting trees, piling brush, hauling wood from the clearings, rolling logs, and building fences. This work went on notwithstanding the extreme coldness of the winter. On extremely cold days a fire would be built in the woods, and when hands became so numb that the axe could not be wielded, they would be thawed out at the fire. In the early spring, before planting time, I was put to work cutting briers, clearing out fence corners, and digging sassafras and persimmon sprouts out of the old fields. My part in the preparation for planting was to strew the guano. If there is any uninformed Rotarian who thinks strewing guano is a light job for a fifteen-year-old boy, he should take a week off in March and try for a postgraduate degree in agriculture with a twenty-five-pound pouch of guano strapped over his left shoulder, and walk back and forth over a plowed field all day, distributing it through a guano horn evenly in the rows as fast as a man with a plow can open the furrows and another coming on behind can cover it. After the ground was bedded up, my task then was to drop the corn and sow the cottonseed in the rows through a guano horn. After one or two years, mechanical cotton planters came into use which lightened and expedited the planting of cotton by opening the row, dropping the seed, and covering it in one operation. In a week or two after the planting was done, the corn and cotton came up, and the three months' fight with crab grass, Poor Dick, and ragweed began. Among instruments of torture, the gooseneck hoe holds high rank. Few men are strong enough to chop an acre a day of cotton, which was the standard task. While engaged in such a task, the sweetest music ever heard was the sound of the dinner horn calling to an hour's respite, and the joy of eventide was entirely disassociated from any poetic appreciation of the glory of the sunset.

After the crops were laid by in 1882, we went back again to the woods to cut timber to be sawed into lumber for sale and for the building of a new home. There were on the uncleared portion of the Bugg farm a great number of mammoth pine trees, some of them four feet in diameter, and standing seventy-five or eighty feet high, or even higher. I remember one tree that made eight ten-foot cuts large enough to be sawed into lumber. Besides the pines there were many large poplars, oaks, and sweet gums. My father would take one side of a tree and I the other, and we brought the tree down with a crash and a roar. When the trees had been felled, they were sawed into "stocks" with a crosscut saw, one end pulled by my father and the other by me.

Beside the crosscut saw, a contrary horse in a rocky field fades into comparative insignificance. If I had read *Les Miserables* and *Ben Hur* before my experience with the crosscut saw, the labors of the galley slaves would have broken my heart; but after that experience, I was able to read of the tortures of Jean Val Jean and Ben Hur with emotional equanimity. After a summer spent with the crosscut saw, and ticks and red bugs, and a week or two of the delightful diversion of fodder pulling, came cotton-picking time until early winter.

In the fall of 1882 I made my first trip to Atlanta. When I knew, a few days before, that I was to make the visit, anticipation became almost as eager as that preceding my first circus. On the morning of the trip, my father and I arose long before day, and after breakfast started on the drive to Marietta to catch the early morning train. As we drove along through the darkness, the great comet of 1882 rested its head near the Eastern horizon, and spread its long tenuous tail across the sky almost to the Western horizon. When we arrived at Marietta, I boarded my first passenger train, and wondered at its marvelous speed of twenty miles an hour as the landscape flew by. There was a great circus parade on the streets in which Louise Montague, advertised as the Ten Thousand Dollar Beauty, rode a mammoth, gaily caparisoned elephant. I followed my father about the city on various business errands, and late in the afternoon we went to the office of John B. Goodwin, then a young and rising lawyer, who had been reared in our community, for the purpose of placing in his hands a note for collection. Not finding him in his office, we went into the office of General Lucius J. Gartrell and left the note with him. I marveled at the great bookcases holding perhaps one-fourth the number of books now in my own library, and wondered if it was not the largest law library in the world. Atlanta was a village then in comparison with the city of today, but it appeared to me to be a great place.

In the fall of 1882 Robert Bullard and Hansel Baggett located a sawmill on our farm to saw the timber which we had cut in the summer before, and I was assigned the task of driving a team of oxen to a log cart for dragging the logs to the sawmill. This task was the third member of the great trilogy of exasperations, the other two members of which were the contrary horse in a rocky field and the crosscut saw. My first experience in earning money for myself was to earn the princely sum of a dollar and a quarter a week by getting up at four o'clock in the morning and building a fire in the boiler of the sawmill engine so as to have steam up when the mill hands arrived for the day's operation. I held this job until a neighbor underbid me and took the job at seventy-five cents a week.

Farm work in the spring of 1883 reached the high watermark of torture. About ten or fifteen acres of new ground had been prepared for cultivation. Plowing in a new ground where the plowshare strikes a root at an average distance of about every seven feet, causing the plow handles to dig the plowman in the side, is a form of exasperating torture which stands supreme and solitary. At this task I acquired a facility of forcible expression which the circumstances palliated if they did not justify.

The same year that we moved to the Bugg farm, Mr. I. D. Upshaw purchased a farm at the Camp Ground about a mile distant from our farm and opened a country store there. A few weeks later I met his son, Will Upshaw, a boy about a year older than myself. We were attracted to each other and soon became warm friends. Meeting Will Upshaw at that time was one of the most fortunate things that happened to me in my early youth. The Camp Ground community as a whole was an excellent one, in no way inferior to the community around Lost Mountain, but the boys on the farms immediately adjoining the Bugg farm were a tough lot; and if I had had no other associates than our immediate neighbors, the effect on my character and ambitions would have been disastrous. Mr. Upshaw, the father, had been a schoolteacher, had lived in Atlanta, and was a man of fine mind, and a superior, though not a college, education. His boys had had superior opportunities, and Will, especially, was brilliant even at his early age. He had a strong, active, alert and acquisitive mind, a tenacious memory, and was, even at the age when I first met him, as ambitious as Caesar. He had a taste for literature and learning, an ambition to speak and write, and a desire to get on in the world which exactly coincided with my own tastes and ambitions. He was exactly the tonic I needed at that time and for many years thereafter. I have always had a certain innate inertia of action and a disposition to wait and let things happen. Will Upshaw was all aggressiveness. He did not wait for opportunity to come, but rushed out to meet it. During our youth and young manhood, we were constantly together, confided in each other, and laid plans for the future. I did not approve of all of his enthusiasm and self-assertiveness then, as I have not entirely agreed with him in any portion of his brilliant career; but he has always been my true and loyal friend under all circumstances and, consequently, differences of temperament have not interfered with our lifelong friendship.

As stated before, I did not attend school for a year and a half after we moved away from Lost Mountain, but the purpose and effort to obtain an education did not stop. Some time after we moved to the Bugg farm, perhaps, in the late winter of 1883, Mr. Upshaw proposed to teach a free school in English grammar at night at the Camp Ground. A large number of the boys and girls and the young men and young women of the community joined the school, myself among the number. Mr. Upshaw thought that *Webster's Unabridged Dictionary* and *Clark's Grammar* were the two greatest books in the world. He was not far wrong in holding that an exact knowledge of the meaning and the right use of words is the foundation upon which all learning and culture is based. At the grammar school, I noticed the remarkable quickness of perception and facility of expression of my friend Will, and I determined that I would overcome the lead which he had over me by reason of his superior advantages. In the summer of 1883 Mr. Upshaw taught a regular school which I attended for about ten weeks. He was a fine teacher, but a severe disciplinarian, and a hard taskmaster. Obedience to the rules was required to be absolute, and any failure to master a task was visited with some form of disciplinary punishment. Sometimes it was inflicted with the birch; sometimes the punishment was to stand in the floor; and sometimes it was to stay in at recess. I managed to escape all forms of punishment. In fact, I was never punished or even reproved at school except once, under circumstances which will hereafter be related.

The next year, 1884, the school was taught by a most excellent teacher, Miss Joe Wilson, a half sister of Mrs. J. M. High of Atlanta. At this school I finished English grammar, studied English composition, and worked through elementary algebra. I do not recall exactly what other studies I pursued, but I do know that I studied with intense application. After this school closed, I began to study at home systematically and diligently, putting every spare moment into study and systematic reading. I carried on my studies in mathematics, and got hold of some Greek books and tried to learn Greek without a teacher but, naturally, I made little progress beyond learning the alphabet. However, I took an unabridged dictionary and committed to memory the Greek and Latin phrases in the back of the book, with their translations. Afterwards I found them very useful.

In the fall of 1884 the election of Grover Cleveland occurred. As the election approached it became more and more apparent that at last the Democrats had a chance to win. The Mulligan letters and the scandals connected with the Crédit Mobilier caused a disaffection in the North which presaged disaster to the Republican party and raised the hopes of the Southern Democrats to the highest pitch. When the newspapers told of the result of the election in the other states and it was known that the election depended on the result in New York, which was doubtful for a few days, the suspense became painful. Late one afternoon, two or three days after the election, after picking cotton all day, I went down to the post office at Upshaw and heard the news that the election of Cleveland was assured and that there would be a torchlight procession and a celebration at Marietta that night. It was then nearly sundown, but I told Will Upshaw that I would go to Marietta for the celebration if he would go with me. He eagerly agreed. I rushed home, ate supper, saddled a fine young horse which we then owned, and rode down to Upshaw's store where I found Will waiting for me on a mule about sixteen hands high. Off we rushed in a run. We had ten miles to go and less than two hours to make the distance if we were to get there on time. We both had too much knowledge of horses and mules to injure them by pressing them too hard, but we gave them all that they could stand and arrived in Marietta just as the rear of the procession was leaving the street by which we entered. We fell in behind the procession, yelling like Comanches. The procession marched around the public square with banners waving and bands playing, the marchers carrying transparencies on which the Republican rooster was shown vomiting up the Mulligan letters. On the north side of the square a tremendous bonfire had been built and a speaker's platform erected. After the crowd had assembled around the platform the bonfire was lighted, the transparencies were consigned to the flames, and General Pierce M. B. Young of Bartow County delivered a speech which further aroused a crowd already aflame with enthusiasm. After the bonfire had died down and the enthusiasm of the crowd had spent itself, Will and I went over to the office of the *Marietta Journal* and heard Benn Perry, Editor of the *Cherokee Advance*, who had just arrived on the train from Atlanta, tell how Henry Grady had rushed into the hall of the House of Representatives and announced the election of Mr. Cleveland and declared the House adjourned. A few years before Mr. Cleveland's death, I wrote an account of this ride which was published in an Atlanta paper, a copy of which was sent to Mr. Cleveland, who wrote me an autographed letter of acknowledgment in which he said that when he thought of the days of 1884 and what was involved, he was almost overwhelmed with a sense of the responsibility which he assumed.

During the winter months of 1885, I again attended school at Camp Ground, Miss Wilson again being the teacher. It being necessary for her to be absent for a day or two, she put me in charge of the school. It was during this term that I received the only punishment I ever received at school. There was a contemptible boy in the school who disliked me and was always trying to provoke me to a row. I did not think he was worthy of my notice until one day we were sitting around the stove during school hours when he began to make remarks of an aggravating nature. I paid no attention to him until he made a remark so grossly insulting that it put me into an uncontrollable rage. The animus behind his desire to provoke and insult me arose from the fact that Miss Wilson was constantly reproving him for his sorry lessons and general misbehavior, while she clearly indicated that I was her favorite pupil. I told the boy who made the insulting remark that I would whip him after school. The news was whispered around that after school there would be a fight, and when school was dismissed the boys all loitered around the school until the teacher had gone. My antagonist tried to get away, but the other boys forced him to remain. When the coast was clear, I drew my knife and started at him, when one of his relations seized an axe and jumped between us, and raising the axe, stated that if I advanced any further he would split my head open. Now, some things can be braved, but an axe in the hands of a twenty-year-old man six feet high is a bar to advance which a discreet person hesitates about crossing. Thus foiled in my attempt to have it out with the offender, I flew into an uncontrollable rage and began to curse the object of my wrath with all the facility at profanity which long practice in driving an ox-team to a log cart had enabled me to acquire. The longer the scene lasted, the louder and more emphatic my words became, until the people living in the neighboring houses came out to their gates and heard a classic review of all the curse words in the English language, and a few others invented for the occasion.

The morning after my disgraceful exhibition of temper, I went to school expecting to be expelled. When school was called to order, expectation was written on every face. Miss Wilson stated that the father of the boy who was the recipient of my compliments on the afternoon before had been to see her and demanded that I be expelled, or that he would take his boy out of school. She said that she was shocked; that she had thought I was the best student she had ever taught; that I had never failed in a lesson or been guilty of any act meriting reproof; and that she could not have believed what had been told her if the report had not been corroborated. She asked me what I had to say, and I replied that he had offered me an unbearable insult which I was prevented from avenging, and that I was guilty of all that had been told her and was ready to quit the school if it was her desire. She then said that she did not wish me to quit school, that she knew that I had provocation, but that profanity on the school grounds could not be excused, and that I would have to stay in at all recesses to the end of the term. This was a mild sentence, and I was afraid that if I refused to accept the sentence she would expel me, which would disgrace me in the community; and so I agreed to abide by her disposition of the matter. All of the students sympathized with me, not one of them more than Miss Wilson, and none of the students teased me about the matter. I bore my punishment for about three days, and was then in a position to quit school without being expelled; so one day when I was in the room alone with Miss Wilson, I got up and said — "Miss Wilson, I am not going to stand this any longer." She made no reply, and I walked out. I did not stay in any more, and the matter was never referred to again. This episode worked a reformation in my manners. I stopped swearing then and there, and have never been guilty of the practice since.

At this school I developed a certain accuracy and superiority of scholarship over the other students. I was the best mathematician in the school, and all of the other students came to me with their problems. I was the best grammarian, and was always chosen first or second in the spelling matches. This did not indicate that I was any prodigy as I was older than most of the other pupils and their grade of advancement was not very high. About the first of March I quit school to work on the farm, having already formed the resolution to try to get a school and teach the next year and earn money to continue my education; but I realized that I was too young and without sufficient education to secure a position as teacher in any leading community. I had an uncle, A. L. Smith, who lived in Cherokee County on a farm on the Etowah River, about two miles below Canton. He told me that there was a school near his home that he thought I could get, and in April I made him a visit for the purpose of arranging for the school for the next year. There was nothing that could be done about the school at that time, and I arranged to go back in the fall and canvass the patrons for the purpose of obtaining the school.

Having formed the purpose to complete my education, I determined to pursue my studies at home. After working like a slave on the farm all day, I studied at night as long as I could keep my eyes open. I had a table by my bed with a small kerosene lamp on it by which I studied until ten or eleven o'clock, and then I would pile into bed and sleep so soundly that when I awoke it would seem that the night had not been an hour long.

In the early summer of 1885, it was announced that in July there would be conducted in Atlanta a teacher's institute, or normal school, free to all teachers and those intending to teach, admission to the school to be granted on the certificate of the State School Commissioner. I immediately wrote to Hon. Gustavus J. Orr, the

State School Commissioner, who granted me a certificate of admission, and I attended the school during its session of four weeks. The school was attended by leading teachers from all over the state and by some from neighboring states.

The teachers in charge of the school were Dr. Gustavus J. Orr; Prof. B. M. Zettler, Superintendent of Public Schools of Bibb County; Prof. W. H. Baker, of Savannah; Dr. G. M. Phillips of West Chester, Pa.; Dr. J. Harris Chappell, then of Jacksonville, Alabama, later President of the Girls Normal and Industrial School of Milledgeville; Maj. W. F. Slaton, Superintendent of the Public Schools of Atlanta; and Prof. W. A. Bass of the Boys High School of Atlanta. These men lectured generally on pedagogy and methods of teaching specific subjects. Besides these there were lecturers on special subjects, among them Dr. James H. Carlisle of Wofford College who delivered a lecture on Thomas Carlyle; Prof. H. A. Scamp of Emory College who lectured on the Romaic pronunciation of Latin; Dr. H. H. Tucker, Editor of the *Christian Index*, who spoke on poetry; Dr. J. G. Armstong, Rector of St. Phillip's Cathedral, who lectured on Shakespeare; and other noted scholars and educators.

One of the most interesting lecturers of the school was a lady teacher from Ohio who had a set of charts which were to be used in the teaching of reading by the phonetic method, as she called it. Under this system the child was taught to read before he was taught to spell, and before he knew his letters. He was taught that the word "cat" meant the animal pictured on the chart over the sign or symbol "cat"; that the word "hat" meant the thing a man wore on his head; that the word "bat" meant the thing that flew around in the night; and that somehow the child would find out the phonetic difference between b and a and t; and that in some mysterious way, unexplained, he would finally find out the names of these letters. This method was an innovation at that time which has been adopted into the present method of educational incubation. To me it seemed the equivalent of teaching a child to play a sonata, and then letting him find out, by accident, that there was such a thing as a scale; or, to hitch a horse behind a cart to push it instead of in front of it to draw it.

This school was of great profit to me. I was perhaps the youngest person who attended it, certainly the youngest male attendant. I was unused to city people and city ways, and was timid to a painful degree. I listened and took notes, but took no part in answering the questions of the teacher, none of which were directed to me. I was oppressed with a sense of the superiority of the other people attending the school, and did not trust myself to speak out but once. One day Prof. Bass put a large and long example in addition on the blackboard, as an exercise in rapid addition, and asked that the result be announced by everybody as soon as reached. I concentrated with all my power, and was the first to announce the correct result. This was the one feather in my cap during my attendance, and was useful in teaching me that a country boy might think as well as other people.

A few days after the institute began, it was announced that the names of all persons in attendance would be published in the *Atlanta Constitution* the next day, July 29, 1885. The next morning when I came into the center of the city at the point where the Federal Reserve Bank now stands, I met a newsboy selling the *Atlanta Constitution* and saw my name in print for the first time. I now have the clipping in a scrapbook.

The institute was held in Mallon Hall of the old Girls' High School Building, which was located on the lot where the new City Hall of Atlanta stands. The present Capitol of Georgia was under construction. The legislature was in session in the old capitol building at the corner of Forsyth and Marietta streets where the Western Union Building now stands. General Grant died on July 22, 1885, while the institute was in session, and a public funeral which I attended was conducted in the hall of the House of Representatives on the same day as the funeral in New York.

I boarded at the home of my uncle, Robert M. McEachern, on Thurmond Street, which was not the slum section of today, but was a respectable workingman's section. I spent the time when not in attendance at the institute in walking about the city seeing the sights. The city at that time was a wonderfully large place to me, though a small town in comparison with the present metropolis. I went out with a party of young people into an old farm beginning about Mangum Street and extending west to a large tract of woodland. The tallest building on Whitehall Street was the present building occupied by Hirsch Brothers. The streetcars were all horse drawn, and the streets were lighted by gas. The most imposing building in the city was the present Kimball House which had been rebuilt after the original house of the same name was burned in 1883.

The Bugg farm was never profitable in any year, and the year 1885 was a disaster. The crop was poor, and we made only four bales of cotton, which sold for less than six cents a pound. Then poverty, which had been creeping upon us from the time we moved to the place, came in and took his seat. My father lost the farm and was overwhelmed in debt. He had to sell out and become a renter. In that country to live on rented land was a badge of social inferiority. In the country this feeling of inferiority is the most poignant pang of poverty. Poverty there is not a question of sufficient food, or of warm clothing, or of shelter. Everybody, landlords and tenants, had that at the time and in the country of which I am writing; but the sting of poverty was to have to walk while others rode, to wear common clothes while others wore fine ones, and to live on rented land instead of owning it. To the father and mother it was the sense of failure, and to their children the fear of being called "poor folks."

At the end of the year 1885 the family moved to the Hewett Farm, part of which had been rented, and I went to teach at the Piney Bower Academy.

VI

Professor McElreath

At the time about which I am now writing, every male school teacher was a "Professor," most country schools were "Academies," every village school was a "High School," and there were so-called "Colleges" all over the land. The curriculum of an academy usually went as high as the fifth reader; of a high school, through English grammar; and of a college, to Caesar's commentaries and algebra.

The method of securing a school in the country at the time about which I am writing was for the prospective teacher to circulate among the patrons "Articles" for signature by the parents of the children in the community. If he succeeded in securing a sufficient number of signatures to justify him in opening a school, he took possession of the schoolhouse at the time agreed, and opened his school. In the fall of 1885, armed with "Articles" which I had copied from those used by my uncle, John J. McElreath, I went to Cherokee County for the purpose of securing the school which my Uncle Lee Smith had promised to help me to secure. As school articles are now a literary curiosity, I am inserting here a copy of the articles used in obtaining my first school.

Georgia, Cherokee County,

Articles of Agreement between Walter McElreath, party of the first part, and us who have annexed our names to these Articles, parties of the second part, by which said McElreath agrees to teach a school at Piney Bower Academy, to consist of two terms—the first to begin on the first Monday in December, 1885, and to continue four months; the second to begin the second Monday in July, 1886, and to continue two months; and, he agrees to teach Spelling, Reading, Writing and Intermediate Arithmetic at five cents per day; Common School Arithmetic, Grammar and Geography at 7 1/2 cents per day; Higher Arithmetic, History and Algebra at 8 1/3 cents per day; and he further agrees to secure the benefit of the Public School Fund and to give to each patron his or her pro rata share of the same, and to teach and govern said school to the best of his ability. All time lost on the part of the teacher to be made up or deducted.

We, the subscribers, agree to furnish the number of scholars set opposite our names and pay the said McElreath the above named rates of tuition. Money due October 15, 1886. This November 16, 1885.

(Signed)	A. L. Smith	2
	John H. Collins	1
	William Daniel	2
	M. V. Davis	$1\frac{1}{2}$
	William Gunter	1
	J. S. Tucker	1
	Alfred Edwards	2
	J. A. Bruce	$1\frac{1}{2}$
	J. A. Brigeman	1
	T. W. King	2
	N. Brooke	$\frac{1}{2}$
	J. A. Gunter	$1\frac{1}{2}$
	G. W. Canant	1
	J. N. Wilson	1
	J. E. Summer	$1\frac{1}{2}$

As it was understood that each patron expected to send twice the number of children he contracted to send, the signatures reasonably assured a school averaging about forty pupils. As soon as the articles were signed, I returned home to make what arrangements were necessary to take the school.

In order to be properly dressed, I bought a suit of clothes for $4.50, and had $1.25 left. I had no timepiece, and after the school opened I bought a Waterbury watch from one of my pupils for $2.50, and gave him credit on his school bill. My recollection is that I got $2.45 in money during the four months of the first term of school, in addition to the $1.25 which I carried with me, out of which I paid my railroad fare home at the end of the term.

The Piney Bower "Academy" was an exceedingly crude affair, built of logs, with a stick and dirt chimney, and benches made of slabs without backs. It was located in the river hills about three and one-half miles below Canton. The community was regarded as an exceedingly tough one. Half of the people had, at one time or another, been in trouble with the revenue officers, and it was freely predicted that I could not control the school and that the people would not pay for tuition. The school opened the first Monday in December with about twenty pupils. By Christmas I had acquired the goodwill of the pupils, and after Christmas the number went to forty or more. During the next summer the attendance went to about seventy, which was the largest number that had ever attended a school at that place. Many of the pupils were several years older than their teacher, but none of them had advanced further than the fifth-reader class. Some of the nearly grown boys came to school barefoot, and a few of them barely knew their letters. But crude and unlettered as these mountain people were, they had the brightest of minds, and some of them absorbed knowledge like a dry sponge absorbs water. Their minds were fallow ground in which it was only necessary to plant the seeds of learning. I recall one young man in particular who, at the beginning of the summer term, only knew his alphabet, but in two months could read the Third Reader and could write a legible hand. Contrary to prediction, I had not the slightest trouble in controlling the school, and when it closed I collected almost every dollar of the tuition due me.

When the school first opened I was conscious of an air of suspicion on the part of pupils and people, but this suspicion was quickly disarmed by devoting myself strictly to the business of teaching the school and asking no questions. I indulged in no lectures on the evils of intemperance or the crime of illicit distilling. Before I left the community two or three of my patrons asked me if I had ever seen a still in operation, and when I said I had not, they offered to take me to one, but I declined.

While the people were crude and some of them lived in huts, others lived in a lavish plenty which reminded me of Cedric, the Saxon. The Canant children repeatedly asked me to go home with them and spend the night. I had never seen their home and supposed it a poor place, and being reluctant to go, I found one excuse after another until excuses were exhausted; and so I finally consented. The road to their house ran for about two miles through a dense and unbroken forest over hills and through gorges; and as we went further and further, I expected to come at last to a crude mountain home where I might have to sleep on a hard bed with one or two of the boys. The boys were large, brawny fellows who liked to hunt, and sometimes they came to school with the aroma on their clothes of that beautiful little animal which is more famous for its odor than for the beauty of its pelt.

When we arrived at the house I was agreeably surprised. A large and comfortable house was set on a small plateau not far from the river, in a yard swept clean as a parlor. The house was uncarpeted, but the plank floors were scoured clean as a new pin. The beds were covered with white coverlets, and when I retired for the night it was into a feather bed soft as down. The barnyard had two great corn cribs filled to the roof with shucked corn in the ear, and was said to contain more than two thousand bushels. The cow lot was crowded with perhaps thirty cows and yearlings that fed in the forests. There were droves of hogs and flocks of sheep, chickens, geese, guineas and turkeys. The tinkling of the sheep bells, the cackling of the geese, and the lowing of the cows in grateful anticipation of a feast of corn, fodder, and shucks made pleasant music in the gloaming as the boys ran about with baskets of corn and armfuls of fodder and shucks.

The supper I sat down to that night was the greatest feast of which I have ever partaken. Among the sophisticated, it might not have been called a supper, but in the country the name of a meal depends upon the time it is served. There was no such thing as tea

in Cherokee, and nobody ever heard of dinner at night. In this instance it was the meal and not the name of it that counted. There
were biscuits shortened with real lard, loaf-bread, light-bread, and
that prince of all breads—crackling-bread; there were ham and red
gravy, backbone and short ribs, and fried chicken. There were pick-
led peaches, studded with stems of spice, preserved peaches, figs
and pears, blackberry jam and honey. There was sliced potato pie,
potato custard, and fried peach pies. O, you degenerate child of the
twentieth century with your orange marmalade and your salad on
a lettuce leaf, you ought to get a pie made of sun-dried Georgia
peaches, made in the shape of a half moon, and fried in butter until
the crust is crisp!

There was buttermilk and pound cake coated with white icing,
and—well, I knew I would forget something—there was sausage
seasoned with sage and red pepper. You can boast of your paté de
foie gras, your filet mignon, your chocolate éclair, or whatever other
concoction some French chef may have invented, but none of these
compare with the supper at the Canants. After supper we gathered
around a roaring fire in the "big house," and then Mr. Canant told
me that he was particularly interested in me because he was originally from Cobb County and knew my people. His family was
large, and there was a young lady and one or more children of some
deceased relative who lived with his family. Before we retired the
young lady played several old-fashioned melodies on a zither. Life
can be more formal and polished than in such homes, with less real
joy and contentment.

The first term of the Piney Bower school ended the last of
March, and I returned home and immediately began work as a
plow hand. About this time the newspapers announced the plans
for the unveiling in Atlanta on the first day of May of the statue of
Senator Benjamin H. Hill and the expected presence of Jefferson
Davis at the unveiling exercises, and I determined to go. On the
morning of May 1, accompanied by my brother Emmett, and our
cousin Horace McElreath, I walked nine miles to Marietta and
took the train for Atlanta, arriving in the early forenoon. The crowd
around the Union Depot and the Kimball House and in all of the
streets in the center of the city was so dense that it was practically
impossible to pass through it. We attempted to make our way

through the crowd to the statue, where the exercises were to be held, but our efforts brought us no nearer than Five Points. Finding that it would be impossible to reach the statue by way of Peachtree Street, we made a wide detour to Ivy Street where the crowd was less dense, and finally arrived on Peachtree Street just across the street from the platform which had been built just behind the statue. At that time there was on the east side of Peachtree Street a residence set back far from the street, with a wide lawn in front of it, surrounded by an iron fence. In this yard benches had been placed for those having tickets. We did not have tickets, but we felt that a nine-mile walk entitled us to enter the yard; and in the press of those entering we succeeded in getting seats on the front row, directly opposite the speaker's stand. At this vantage point we heard all of the speeches: the opening speech by Henry W. Grady, the oration of the day by Hon. J. C. C. Black, and the remarks by Mr. Davis. The splendor of the uniforms in the long processions, the magnificence of the equipages, the wild enthusiasm of the vast multitude, and the sight of the great man who was the hero of the occasion was worth the walk of eighteen miles to the train and return, and justified the stealing of a reserved seat.

When I contracted to secure the benefit of the public school fund for my patrons, I took a desperate gamble. When I took this school I had never stood a written examination, and when I was notified that an examination to be taken by all persons desiring teacher's licenses would be held at the Etowah Institute in Canton in June, 1886, I was scared in an inch of my life. I had been studying every spare moment in preparation; but never having stood an examination, I did not know very well how to prepare for one.

The examination came at a time when farm work was extremely pressing. I did not have a dollar and a half to pay my way from Marietta to Canton and return, and the old mule which my father owned was not a suitable mount for such a journey. I made arrangements with Uncle Pink McElreath, who lived nearby, to plow with our mule and to lend me his horse. The day before the examination I rode to Canton, a distance of thirty-five miles.

The next day I stood the examination with fifty other applicants for teacher's licenses. The examination was completed about three o'clock in the afternoon. I had no idea at all whether I had passed or not, but a sickening fear that I had not. As I had promised to have the horse back the next day, I walked two miles to where my Uncle Lee Smith lived; and after I had left the house, at five o'clock in the afternoon I started on a night ride of thirty-five miles. I accomplished the journey, arriving about daylight, and worked in the field all of the next day.

It was several weeks before I heard from the examination, during all of which time I was in agonized suspense. When I at last heard from the examination, I learned that only one of those who stood it (a college graduate and a teacher of several years' experience) had received first grade. Five received second grade, of which I was one, and the others received third grade and fourth grade, except thirteen who failed entirely. The teachers in Cherokee County were classified into four groups, their respective grades being determined by the examination just described, and paid according to grade. The fourth-grade teachers received, out of the public fund, as I now recall, but two cents per day for each pupil; the third grade received three cents; the second, four cents; and the first, five cents.

The unexpectedly high grade made by me not only gave me a better opinion of myself, but it materially affected the money I received from my school. If I had been able to obtain only a credit of two cents a day, they would not have been so willing to pay their tuition bills. When I returned home in the fall of 1886, after making my collections for the year and paying my board, I had one hundred and thirty dollars and a new suit of clothes and a hat which I had bought in Marietta on the way home. This suit of clothes cost eighteen or twenty dollars, and was the first decent suit of clothes I ever had. My father thought it was rank and profligate extravagance, his opinion being somewhat biased by a yearning desire, and perhaps a pressing necessity, to borrow all of my money. I lent all except a few dollars of the money I had earned to my father, who repaid it by letting me earn it out of a cotton patch the next year and by giving me a calf which turned out to be a fine little Jersey and sold for a fancy price. I have observed that minor sons frequently have to earn money twice to get it once—if at all.

My mother, in order to get a few things for my little sisters, had opened an account at the country store near us, intending to pay for it with barter, but found it impossible to do so. She came to me, as timid as a child, and told me about it, and said that she had found it impossible to pay the debt, and asked me to pay it for her. I have never been so proud of having money as I was then. I did not wait a minute, but immediately saddled a horse and rode to the store and paid the bill, amounting to four or five dollars. This nearly exhausted my savings, but I hid out a few dollars.

My grandfather, John McElreath, and my grandmother were left alone in 1886 by the removal to Texas of Uncle Doc and Aunt Nannie Griffin who had lived in the house with them. They were both very old, and my grandfather had been totally blind for many years. The understanding, which was carried out at my grandfather's death, was that if my father would take charge of the farm and take care of my grandfather and grandmother, the farm was to be left to my father. This farm included the one from which we had removed a few years before, and placed us back in the old Lost Mountain environment.

I intended to teach again the next year, but was not able to secure a school for the winter months. I could have gone back to Piney Bower, but my uncle had left the community and I did not care to teach there again after he had left. I applied at several places, but they were all taking back the teachers of previous years. A few weeks after Christmas I took measles and was sick for several weeks, and was not in good health during the winter and spring of 1887, but when I had sufficiently recovered, I went to work on the farm and worked until July. I secured a small school for the summer at Crogen School House, and taught for ten weeks in July, August, and September, and made about sixty dollars.

In the fall of 1887 the Piedmont Exposition was held in Atlanta. President Cleveland was to make a great swing around the country, and it had been arranged for him to visit Atlanta and the Exposition. His appearance at the cities on his itinerary was met with the greatest enthusiasm. The newspapers, for weeks, carried accounts of the great receptions accorded him wherever he stopped, and the enthusiasm of the people of Georgia and the South over his visit to Atlanta increased from day to day as his arrival became nearer and nearer. Preparations had been made that Kennesaw Mountain was to be illuminated as he passed it. On the afternoon of October 17th,

my uncle George McElreath and I started to ride to Marietta and
to the mountain to see the illumination and to see the train pass, but
it began to rain so hard when we were about halfway that we
turned back. I could not bear the disappointment, and rode back
home and told my mother to get ready to go to Atlanta the next
morning; that I was going to take her to the Exposition. She was as
excited and pleased as a child. She had never been to Atlanta, and
perhaps never expected to go there. In those days country women
traveled little, and the majority of the women in Cobb County had
never in their lives been further from home than to Marietta. When
we took the train at Powder Springs it was crowded as full as standing room in the aisles would permit. When we arrived in Atlanta,
the city was crowded everywhere. We could not get a streetcar, and
so we walked out to Uncle Robert McEachern's where I left my
mother and rushed back to town. It was announced that the President and Mrs. Cleveland, the former beautiful Frances Folsom,
were to be entertained at the Capital City Club that evening, and
that they would leave the Ladies' Entrance of the Kimball House
on Decatur Street just before eight o'clock. I milled around with
the crowds until near the time for the President to appear. The Silvey Building was then under construction, and there was a large
pile of bricks, perhaps ten feet high, in Decatur Street directly opposite the door of the Kimball House at which the presidential carriage was standing. I attained the top of this pile of bricks in time
to see the President and his wife come out and get into the carriage
and drive away. At a late hour, I arrived back at Uncle Bob's, and
slept on the floor with fourteen others in the same room. People
slept in churches, in hallways, in law offices, and many walked the
streets all night. On the next day we visited the Exposition, and in
the afternoon we saw the President and his wife drive around the
racetrack in the same carriage in which Jefferson Davis had been
driven on his visit to the city the year before. There was a great
show of military forces massed in serried ranks on the hillside over-
looking the racetrack; and after the parade was over, there was a
sham battle. Late in the afternoon, after an exhausting day, my frail
little mother and I boarded the train for Powder Springs, with every
seat taken and every inch of standing room occupied. My mother
was the only woman standing in the coach in which I was riding,

and I approached a damned yankee from Ohio, a big brawny, middle-aged fellow, and asked him to give my mother a seat. He said, "No, I have to ride to Ohio, and am going to keep my seat." There are only ten thousand ninety-six damned yankees in the cemetery at Marietta—I am sorry there are any—but if there had to be that many, there might as well have been ten thousand and ninety-seven.

In the fall of 1887 I entered the Powder Springs High School and attended it for about nine months. This was the first school I ever attended for as much as five months consecutively. The teacher was Joseph G. Camp, a man of superb education, rare magnetism, and great ability as a teacher. He was a graduate of the University of Georgia, and an orator of real and rare eloquence. The scholarship of this school was exceptionally high for a village school of that day. Here I began the study of Latin, geometry, higher algebra, composition, rhetoric, American history and Robinson's *Higher Progressive Arithmetic*. When I began there was a class in Latin already reading Caesar and Sallust, and a class in mathematics which had gone through geometry and plane trigonometry. At the beginning of the term, this class started in to review geometry and university algebra from the beginning. Of course, I could not keep up with the class at first, but I determined to overtake them in the course of the year, and I applied myself so diligently to all of my studies that I became almost hypnotized, and a week would go by so rapidly that at the end of the week it would seem that not more than a day had gone by. At the end of the year I had overtaken the class of the year before, but I was not so skillful in Latin translation as those who had been over the course twice, not having had time to acquire as large a vocabulary; but I had learned the etymology and the syntax of the language well enough to pursue the study of the language to some profit without a teacher.

In the fall of 1888 I applied for the school at Lost Mountain, then known as the Lost Mountain Academy, and was successful in securing it. There was not a prouder young man in the United States than when I took my place as teacher in the schoolroom where Professor Mable had taught when I was his pupil, a few years before. The general level of education in the community was higher than in Professor Mable's day, but there were no pupils in my school quite as far advanced as were a few in his school; but the

Lost Mountain Academy was regarded as one of the best, if not the best, country school in the county. For several years after I taught there, the grade of the school improved until it became a real country academy in which Latin, algebra and geometry were taught. After a few years, it succumbed to the system which has abolished higher education in the country, and is now a mere elementary school. There is no sadder symptom of the decay of country life than the passing of the old country academy from which so many of the great men of the past gained their first impetus to scholarship.

The school was a success from the beginning. There were several boarding pupils, and by the next summer the school was so large that I could not teach it by myself, and employed an assistant. The students were well behaved, easy to control, and most of them extraordinarily diligent in their studies. At the end of the first year I held an "Exhibition," as the closing exercises of a country school were called in that day. This exhibition was attended by people for miles around. The *Marietta Journal* said:

> The closing exercises of the school were attended by a vast audience from all parts of the county. The exercises were chaste and fine and well rendered. The Powder Springs band discoursed sweet music to the delight of all. Miss Sallie Watson won the admiration of all by a very fine song. Professor York also rendered some excellent pieces. On the whole, it was an occasion long to be remembered.

The *Powder Springs Correspondent* said:

> Most of our young folks went up to Professor McElreath's Exhibition at Lost Mountain on Wednesday night of last week. Everything passed off nicely and the students acted their parts well. The Professor deserves credit for the excellent management of his school and the success of his exhibition. The Powder Springs band boys furnished music for the occasion and were given a nice reception by all those pretty girls up there.

At the end of the school I announced that I would teach again the next year, and made no canvass, and took no subscriptions. At last life was brighter. After paying up the few bills which I had made and buying clothes, I had about two hundred and fifty dollars. I paid my father about fifty dollars which I thought was compensation for board, seeing that I worked on the farm during vacation and that two of my brothers and two sisters attended school and were provided all their school books at my expense.

The next year the school was larger than the first year. The spring term ended about the first of April, and by this time I had decided that in September I would enter Washington and Lee University. When I announced my intention, my father and mother were pleased and proud. My mother said that she wanted to help me get the right kind of clothes, and that she wished to knit a lot of socks for me. I had never had a vacation, and I decided that I would do no regular work until school opened in the summer, but spend the vacation in study and reading.

In the latter part of May, one of my mother's sisters became desperately ill, and my mother spent a week waiting on her. She came home pale and weak. One day I saw her at some laborious task, and seeing her feebleness, I went to her and took her in my arms. She looked up at me with a look of unearthly love and said, "I am afraid I won't be with you long." I thought she was weak and tired, and did not suspect that I was hearing expressed a premonition of death. A night or two later my father came running to my room and told me to go to my mother's room and stay with her until he could go for the doctor. I rushed into her room and found her suffering intensely. As soon as I entered the room she said, "Walter, I have never been sick before, but I am going to be very sick this time." For about a week we were desperately anxious, but one morning she seemed much better. Farm work had been neglected during the week, and I decided that I would help out; so I took one of the horses and went to a distant field to plow. About ten o'clock my little brother, Preston, came running to the field and told me to come to the house, that mother was worse. When I got to her room, for the first time in my life the thought came home to me that death, which had entered other homes, might come to mine.

My mother was the one person in the world that I really loved. I loved my father and brothers and sisters, of course, but not as I loved her. No day had ever passed, when I was at home, when I did not find some time to talk to her alone, and when I was away at school or teaching, I yearned for her company. I had never thought of death in connection with her. During the week she had been ill, I was in agony because she was suffering, but I thought, of course, that she would get well. And there she lay gasping in the crisis of pneumonia. When I came in, she said, "Please go and milk me some warm milk and bring it to me." One of the ladies watching by her bedside said, "He cannot milk now, the cows are in the pasture and will not be here till night." She asked what time it was, and when told that it was still morning, she said, "O, Lord, if it's that time of day, I cannot last — I am gone." The doctor came to her bedside and she said, "Doctor, I want to live so bad; I can't die and leave my children." At twilight on the first day of June, 1890, she died, and a darkness crept into my soul with the gathering shadows of that night which has never left it. Her funeral was attended by a vast concourse of people. In the obituary notice written by Rev. Frank S. Hudson, he said:

> She was an obedient daughter, a kind sister, a faithful wife and loving mother. She left an influence on earth that will continue through eternity. Her Christianity endured the tribulations of life, and shone in the darkness as well as in the light. In the chambers of the sick and the suffering, with gentle hands and sympathetic heart, she labored and loved as a ministering angel. Her last illness was of brief duration, was patiently borne, and she died in peace. Hundreds followed her to the grave and took the farewell look on the delicate face of her who was greatly beloved.

Like the good poet Gray,

> *I do not know where his islands lift*
> *Their fronded palms in the air;*
> *I only know I cannot drift*
> *Beyond his love and care.*

Whether this love and care has prepared some Elysian field of conscious pleasure, or whether He takes those who have served His purpose into His arms, like a mother takes a tired child, and gives them surcease of toil, trial and trouble, in an eternal sleep, is beyond mortal power to know. Sometimes when sore with the struggles and toils of life, I have looked upon the possibility of Nirvana with complacent yearning. For this poor, frail woman (who lived her life in the hard years after the Civil War, who bore nine children for whom she toiled, sacrificed, and prayed, who died at the early age of forty-eight years, before her oldest children had reached the age when she could realize her hopes in them and while her youngest children needed a mother's daily care) I hope, if I cannot feel certain, that she has found some place where her tired limbs have been rested, where kind angels wait upon her, where she has the pretty clothes which she never had on earth, and where no harsh word or unkind deed ever wounds her gentle, sensitive soul; and I hope that someday I may walk down some sunny pathway and find her there waiting, and see the lovelight in her eyes as I walk up to her and take her in my arms as I did that day when the first premonition of death came to her.

After she went away the task of running the household fell upon my two older sisters, Cora and Edith, Cora being seventeen years of age and Edith, fifteen. The family consisted of ten people, including my grandfather and grandmother. Grandfather was old and blind, and grandmother was old and not easy to get along with. No harder task ever fell on any young girl than that which fell on Cora; and few girls in similar circumstances ever better performed such a task.

The week after the funeral the neighbors to the number of about twenty appeared with their horses and mules and their hoes, and worked over the entire crop. Such neighborly deeds as that, which it was the custom to perform for a neighbor in trouble or need, are one of the reasons why I love Lost Mountain.

In the summer of 1890 Will Upshaw, who was the correspondent at Upshaw, planned a picnic for all of the county correspondents of the *Marietta Journal*. This paper, published by Neal and Massey, was a fine county paper which gave unusual prominence to the local news from the several communities in the county, contributed by local correspondents. For some time I was the correspondent at Lost Mountain. This picnic was held on August 8, 1890, in the grove in front of the old Camp Ground Church, and was attended by a great crowd from all parts of the county. I was the master of ceremonies and made the opening address. I prepared this address with all the care of which I was capable, and still have the published copy of it. I must confess that it now makes painful reading. If there is anything more painful to read, in late life, than the ornate periods of a speech made when immaturity tried to take the laurels off of the reputation of Sargeant S. Prentiss, I have never discovered it. However, a young man must begin sometime, and if his grandiloquence does not provoke the crowds who hear him to apply the lynch law to him, he may tone himself down to a level where he may be tolerated. There was some excuse for the "curls" which fledgling orators put in their speeches in 1890, for that was the era of Henry W. Grady, John Temple Graves, and Lucian L. Knight. I would advise any man likely to become possessed in later life with the idea that he was a genius in boyhood to preserve some of the ambitious efforts of his early days and read them over occasionally as an antidote.

The summer session of my school at Lost Mountain ended on the first week in September with closing exercises at which several of the students acquitted themselves with great credit. This occasion, which marked the parting with the fine young men and women and boys and girls with whom I had labored for two years, more as a comrade and friend than as master, was a sad occasion for me. The next week I bade goodby to youth and its associations and went away to Washington and Lee University.

VII

Country Life
in My Youth

Having reached the point in my story where I was about to leave the distinctly rural life in which I was born and brought up, the impulse is irresistible to introduce an interlude and to make some observations concerning a period in the life of the community in which my youth was spent which is now gone, and the like of which will never again be seen.

The self-contained, self-sufficient, and self-sustained condition of the country when domestic manufacture was depended upon, and in which the people, in very fact, lived at home, lasted until about 1876, a sufficient time for me to see and remember the country in its pioneer condition; and then it began to change rapidly until the time of which I am now writing (1890) when these old conditions had almost entirely disappeared, and a new earth, if not a new heaven, was being created. This economic revolution was largely the result of the War Between the States, whose real cause, like the cause of all wars, was economic rivalry, through political means, and a fight for markets. The beginning of the "irrepressible conflict" did not arise out of a righteous and disinterested purpose to secure the abolition of slavery. Nullification in South Carolina did not arise out of an effort to abolish slavery, but out of opposition to a tariff thought to discriminate against the agrarian South in favor of the industrial North. As the breach between the sections grew wider and approached a state of armed conflict, partly out of sincerity and partly as propaganda to arouse the people of the Northern states to a fighting pitch for a righteous cause, the war to secure political supremacy, trade advantages, and profitable markets became a holy crusade to abolish slavery. So completely did this "Battle Cry of the Republic" obsess the minds of the North that they came "Marching Through Georgia" with fire and sword "treading out the vintage of the Lord" and making the paths straight for the carpetbagger and the commercial traveler. The slogans of 1861-1865 were perhaps as honest, and no more sincere than our pretense that we entered the world war in 1917 "to make the world safe for democracy."

After the War Between the States was over and the people in the path of Sherman's march had recovered sufficiently to have any purchasing power, a new economic era began. Factory woven textiles took the place of homespun and the domestic loom, the cards and spinning wheels became antiques; machine-made shoes took the place of the old homemade footwear; the community shoemaker forsook his last, and the local tanyards were abandoned; Milburn and Studebaker wagons and Columbus buggies superseded the vehicles made by the local blacksmith and woodworker; the steam engine began to furnish the motive power for the grist mills and the cotton gins; water mills, turned by the overshot wheel which stood upon every stream where there was enough water and sufficient fall, fell into decay; and the kerosene lamp took the place of the tallow candle.

The purchase of all of the things above enumerated and more, needless to mention, took actual cash or credit which ultimately had to be settled in money, or goods readily convertible into money, and cotton — legal tender on the market square — was the only commodity which the farmer could raise which could instantly and at all times be converted into actual cash; consequently, as necessity demanded increased purchases, more and more cotton was raised.

Soon the ground formerly sown to wheat was planted in cotton and flour was bought, thus increasing the necessity for cash. The cornfields began to be encroached upon until there was not enough corn raised to fatten the hogs, and side meat began to be hauled to the farm from the supply houses. More and more cotton was raised, and finally an overproduction of this staple caused a gradual decline in its price until it fell below the cost of production; and then the farmer resorted to the "long loan" and sold himself into slavery by mortgaging his farm.

The country had about reached the condition above described at the period about which I am now writing. Many young men around Lost Mountain married, and left their native community, and went to Sand Mountain, in Alabama, or to Texas where cheaper lands were to be had, and where there were supposed to be better opportunities.

Many of the young men who had attained their majority and were not ready to marry and go west had nothing upon which to make a start in life; and their fathers, themselves fighting a losing game, debt ridden and discouraged, could not help them. These young men started the exodus from the farms to the city. Some of them became lawyers, doctors, or school teachers, while others found jobs as railroad brakemen, clerks, streetcar drivers, and industrial insurance agents. Thus, it will be seen that in the little more than two decades which elapsed from the date of my birth until I left the country, I saw the old order change, yield place to the new, and then saw the new order quickly decay until now, when it is kept alive by the hypodermic treatment of the Agricultural Adjustment Act.

Of course the emigration of the people of the country which has assumed such great proportions in the last generation has not been entirely due to the failure of country life. In every age and in every country, the gregarious instinct, fundamental in human nature, has caused the population to collect into great cities, far beyond what was necessary to carry on the work of the cities, and to the injury of many of those who thus transplanted themselves, and to the detriment of society. It cannot be gainsaid that life in the city with its greater ease and comfort, its allurements and opportunities, is more desirable than life in the country, but what is desired and is easiest and most alluring is not always the best.

While the decay of country life had reached the point where its further and progressive decay was manifest, it had not at that time reached the point where it did not afford compensating joys and advantages for its hardships and disadvantages. The semi-isolation of a country home and the absence of distractions, with the closer companionship among the members of the family, was conducive to a deeper affection between the members of the family than a life where more than half of the time is spent in a crowd where distractions prevail. Among the neighbors there was much actual kinship. Intermarriages among neighboring families well nigh made all of the little community world akin. If there was sickness the neighbors came in, "sat up" with the sick, and helped with the housework; and, if there was prolonged illness in crop time, the neighbors came in and worked out the crop. If a poor man's horse died, the neighbors would chip in and help him to buy another. If his house or his barn burned down, the neighbors met and helped him raise another, insurance premiums being paid in neighborly kindness. The neighbors helped one another at house raisings, log rollings, corn shuckings, and quilting bees, with no charge except a good dinner.

Country life in the days of my childhood and youth was not a dull life. At Christmas an apple, an orange, a bag of raisins, a few sticks of candy, a pack of firecrackers, and a mouth harp in the stocking hung by the fireside gave as much joy as the expensive gifts on a Christmas tree in a city home give to the children of the wealthy. In summer the orchards teemed with fruit so abundant that most of it rotted on the ground; there were the watermelon patches, free for all; there was the millpond in which to swim, and the revival meeting, and the singing school to go to. When the crops were gathered in the fall came corn shuckings and 'possum hunts; but best of all sports was the great rabbit hunt, with perhaps fifty men and boys and half as many dogs, the men led by Anderson Dobbins and the dogs led by old "Loud." And when the nights grew long and cold, word would be sent around among the young people that on a certain night there would be a "party" at some neighbor's house. An engagement, now known as a "date," would be made with some country belle, and there is nothing in modern society which can beat a five-mile ride to a country party on a cold night in a narrow buggy with a pretty country lass snugly wrapped in a warm laprobe, and to come into the hearing of feet swishing on a bare floor to the rhythmic tune of a fiddle.

On long rainy days when it was too wet to go out of doors, the time was delightfully spent in doing much profitable reading. Thus, I read *Pilgrim's Progress*, Watts's *Improvement of Human Understanding*, and the history of England until I felt as if Alfred and Canute and William the Conqueror and the Black Prince were familiar friends; Bourienne and the story of Napoleon's battles until I could see the tumult at Wagram, Marengo, and the Bridge of Lodi. I so read the history of Greece that when I studied ancient history at Washington and Lee University the story of that glorious country was a lesson already half learned. On rainy days and long winter nights I read Shakespeare, Longfellow, Poe, and *The Lady of the Lake*. But not all of my reading was of this high character. I spent many delightful, if not profitable, hours reading surreptitiously the *Life of Jesse James*, which I kept in the barn hidden under the fodder, and such entrancing romances as *A Sailor's Sweetheart* and other literature equally edifying. But try as I would, and did, I never succeeded in getting hold of any of the works of Boccaccio, the perusal of which was supposed to be excelled in wickedness only by the reading of the works of Darwin. Later when I was able to satisfy my sinful longing to read these books, I was disappointed to find the *Decameron* was neither as interesting nor as wicked as I expected, and was surprised to discover that Charles Darwin was not as sinfully heretical as he had been represented. A deck of cards, greasy with much use, also carefully concealed, served to while away many a rainy day, when some of the neighbor boys slipped over for a game of "seven-up" in the barn. When this game was indulged in, preparations were always made for quick concealment in case of sudden surprise; and if my father came unexpectedly to the barn, he always found us innocently engaged in some other diversion.

I have always thought that when Edwin Markham sought to paint a picture of debasing toil, he made a mistake in writing *The Man with the Hoe*. If anybody thinks country life is, or was in my youth, an empty or an ignorant or an uninspiring life, he only needs for his disillusionment to look up a list of the successful men in the business and professional life of any American city and thus discover how many of them were born and reared in the country. Hard labor and the enduring of heat and cold hardened the muscles and the spirit, and built a spirit of courage and independence. A country boy, tough of muscle, is usually tough in courage. The boys around Lost Mountain never learned to turn the other cheek. An insult meant a fight, and a feud was settled with fist and skull.

The dweller in the country acquires an education not found in schools or books. There the countryman

> . . . exempt from public haunt,
> Finds tongues in trees, books in the running
>   brooks,
> Sermons in stones, and good in everything.

The city is a workshop fit only for those who have reached maturity; and one of the most salutary tendencies of the present age is the decentralization of the population of the cities, made possible by modern means of transportation, by the building of houses farther and farther out into the suburbs and closer to nature.

There is not now as much happiness in country life as there was in the days of my youth, but such hardships and privations as there are now in country life are unnecessary, and are the result of laws which discriminate in favor of the industrial, laboring, and financial classes whereby the price of the necessities and luxuries of life are adjusted to their earnings, and are put beyond the purchasing power of those who labor in the fields.

In the present days of complexity, unrest, and unreasoning discontent, the evangels of the "abundant life" are frequently heard ignorantly prating about the "horse and buggy days." To the man who knew the "horse and buggy days" their hardships and privations are forgotten in a yearning nostalgia. Robert Burns, in his incomparable portrayal of the simple life in *The Cotter's Saturday Night*, said that it was from such homes and such scenes that old Scotia's grandeur sprang, and he prayed that his land might be free "from luxury's contagion weak and vile." A life abounding in a mind well cultivated, in noble deeds unselfishly done, and in strenuous labor well performed is the true "abundant life," though it may be a life of poverty and self-denial. The "abundant life" as preached by its modern apostles leans too much in its meaning to an envious desire for material comfort and wealth and leisure. Jesus Christ and St. Paul did not preach a doctrine of epicurean ease and comfort and idleness, but preached and practiced the ethics of stoicism. Labor of muscle or mind six days out of the week was the plan of the Creator of the universe and is the natural condition of man's existence, and when society cannot find that much useful labor for every man able to perform it, just to that extent is a society wrongly organized. No man is entitled to any more leisure than just enough to enable him to better perform his task when he goes back to it. No man can succeed who does not "improve each shining hour" with useful labor. There are drones in every hive, but the workers drive them out and kill them.

In my childhood and youth I was frail, and not strong enough to split rails, rive boards, cut ditches, and keep up with those of greater physical strength; and such was not my forte, anyway. I was not born a genius for anything, as I have abundantly found out, but I was born with a bent for intellectual exercise, learned early to love books, and when I reached the point in life at which I have now arrived in this story, my country life ended and I took the road which has not always been easy, and which has led away from the simple life of my early years into the thorny wilderness of a different and more complex way of life. Being born in the country and reared under the conditions existing was no handicap, and is no excuse for anything in which I have failed.

I have lived to see a new earth, and there is much doubt whether there is a new heaven of more real happiness than in old and simpler days.

VIII

Washington and Lee University

On Monday following the close of the Lost Mountain School I left for Lexington and arrived in Chattanooga in the early night and went to the Read House, as the train north did not leave until the next morning. This was the first time I had ever been outside the state of Georgia, and I was surprised to see that the stars apparently occupied the same positions in the sky as when seen from Lost Mountain. The hotel was crowded and I was given a room with two beds, one of which was occupied by two young men from Mississippi who were going to some Virginia college. The room was lighted with a single electric light. Neither I nor two of my roommates had had any experience with electric lights, and we could not find out how to turn out the light, and so we let it burn all night.

If it seems strange that a young man twenty-three years of age should have felt so far away when a hundred miles from home, it is only necessary to consider the changes that have taken place in the last fifty years in the means of transportation and in the habits of the people. It is safe to say that more people from the Lost Mountain community have been in Chattanooga in the past ten years than had ever been in Douglasville or Dallas in 1890.

The next morning at daylight the train left for Knoxville, Bristol, and Lynchburg. The aspect of the beautiful country from Cleveland to Knoxville and the sight of the mountains from Greenville made the morning journey one of joy and wonder to my untrained eyes.

At noon we arrived at Bristol, and stopped for dinner. Bristol was not then the splendid city of today, but seemed to be a small country town with unpaved streets and scattered houses. Where the station now stands there was a small wooden building which served as a depot. A narrow wooden footbridge led across a ravine to one of the old-fashioned railroad eating houses where the passengers rush out of the train into a dining room to the table already set, gulp down a meal in twenty minutes, and rush back to their places in the train.

A few miles after leaving Bristol we came into the valley country of Southwest Virginia where the wide green meadows, covered with flocks and herds, stretch away to the Blue Ridge on the east and the Cumberland Mountains on the west. The contrast with the red hills of Georgia was so great that I could hardly realize that I was in the same world I had left the day before. At sunset we stopped for a few minutes at Montgomery White Sulphur Springs. It had been raining and the sun shone out just before setting. Long streaks of mist rising from the valleys and climbing around the mountain tops, glowing white in the evening sun, made a scene of extraordinary beauty. I jumped out of the train just for the sake of pressing my feet on the soil of Virginia, made romantic to me by the stories of the Civil War, and by the tales of the fireside. I was just a little ashamed of my enthusiasm, but I had hardly touched the ground when I heard one of my Mississippi friends of the night before exclaim, "Well, this is the first time my feet ever touched the soil of the Old Dominion."

At Lynchburg it was again necessary to lie over for the night, and I went to the Hotel Neville. By this time, my education had progressed so far that I was able to put out the lights; but I spent most of the night getting up to look at my watch to make certain that I would not miss the train the next morning. I left the next morning about daylight for Lexington, fifty miles up the James, and I shall never forget the beauty of that ride. The railroad runs alongside the river, occupying, much of the way, the old tow-path used when canal boats ran up the river. Great dams were built across the river every few miles to make it navigable for the canal boats. On each side of the river were mountains. When the sun began to shine upon the waters, mists began to rise from the surface of the placid waters, and trail away over the meadow lands, and lean against the mountains, and climb higher and higher up their sides until they were floated away as clouds in the autumn sky.

Arriving in Lexington about nine o'clock in the morning, I enquired where I could get breakfast, and was directed to Burke's Restaurant on Main Street, a dingy half barroom and half restaurant affair where greasy food and bad coffee were served by an untidy waiter. This was a poor introduction to the Lexington of which I had dreamed. After breakfast I secured directions to the University, and went down the street with a beating heart. I soon came to the turnstile at the entrance to the grounds, and there lay before me the magnificent campus, with its walks and drives laid out by General Robert E. Lee; and on an eminence stood the stately old buildings of which I had dreamed. Awkwardly and timidly, I approached a building in front of which I saw a group of young men standing, and in which I supposed the office of the University was located. I had had little experience with the class of young men which I supposed made up the student body of that old school, and I imagined I should be embarrassed by their unsympathetic reception, and that I would be a choice victim for their hazing pranks. The first young man I spoke to greeted me cordially, went with me to the office of the clerk of the faculty, and, when I came out, I found him waiting for me. Knowing that I was a stranger, he offered to go with me to my boarding house; but I declined his offer and went to the college dormitory known as the "Blue Hotel" located on the campus, and secured a room. That afternoon the student who had been so kind to me in the morning, in company with two or three other old students, called on me and asked me to take a walk with them about town; but I excused myself upon the ground that I was tired from my long trip and was compelled to rest. The real reason for my declination was that I suspected that they wished to get me off on a snipe hunt, or some similar excursion with which seniors are supposed to entertain freshmen. Late in the afternoon I decided to take a walk uptown to see what sort of place I had come to. In the upper part of the town I saw a large crowd of students collected around a student standing on a goods-box and singing "Darling Chloe" and other Southern songs in one of the sweetest tenor voices I have ever heard. I learned that the singer was Clifford Lanier, nephew of the gifted poet and musician, Sidney Lanier. After supper on the first night the noise of a large band of students was heard coming from uptown to the campus. Thomas F. Farrar, another student who had arrived the same day and had taken a room in the Blue Hotel directly across the hall from me, came into my room in a state of wild apprehension and said, "here they come; what shall we do; how I dread it." I told him they could not afford to kill us, and that there was nothing to do but to take what was coming to us. We sat for an hour or so as the uproar continued, and no hazers appeared; but Farrar and I thought that our day of reckoning was only postponed. The next day we learned that the demonstration we had heard the night before was a "calythump" celebrating the reunion of friends who had returned to college, that a "calythump" was merely a riotous band of students out for innocent college pranks, that it was a tradition of Washington and Lee that no new student was to be hazed or embarrassed, and that it was the part of a gentleman for an old student to show only kindness and helpfulness to a new man.

A striking contrast to this custom of treating new students at Washington and Lee occurred in the death of a cadet at the Virginia Military Institute a few days later. It was the custom there to subject the "rats," as the raw cadets were called, to a process of severe hazing. One of the cadets resisted and fought the hazers, and in the scuffle was hit over the head and died. His body was carried through the Washington and Lee campus, preceded by the V. M. I. band, and followed by the cadets marching in column and by the students of Washington and Lee, commanded by Robert E. Lee, Jr., the son of Rooney Lee and a grandson of General Robert E. Lee. The solemn roll of the muffled drum, the shadows of the night, and the bier of the young cadet who but a few days before had come to Lexington with the ambitions and hope of youth, made a scene of such sadness as never to be forgotten. Among the crowning glories of General Lee, let it never be forgotten that his noble influence abolished hazing forever at Washington and Lee.

The next day after my arrival was opening day. General G. W. C. (Custis) Lee, the President, and the members of the faculty were seated at tables in the reading room of Newcombe Hall, in the University library building. The student desiring to enter the different classes was required to apply to the professor of the particular department he wished to enter, the head of the department determining from the interview what particular class in his department the applicant was entitled to enter. I had a letter of introduction to General Lee from the Hon. A. A. Clay, then Speaker of the House of Representatives of Georgia, and sought him out first. When I told him my name, he stated that someone had written him a letter about me and recommended me to him. He was very cordial, and although he was habitually shy and reticent, and rarely entered into conversation with a student, he never forgot me; and during my stay at the University, I received several marks of his interest and regard.

The first professor to whom I applied was Carter J. Harris, Professor of Latin, affectionately called "Old Nick" by the students. When I told him that I wished to enter the junior class, he asked me about my preparation; and when I told him what it was, he told me that I could not enter the class. I insisted. He said that it would be entirely useless for me to enter that class as I could not do the work required; that I would fail on my examinations and become discouraged, and that it was utterly impossible for him to allow me to enter the class. I told him that I was already twenty-three years old; that I could remain at the University only two years; that I was capable of greater application than he surmised; and insisted that he give me a trial, and let me take the consequences if I failed. He told me that he knew more about the course than I knew, but finally consented to let me take the entrance examination, and said that if I could pass it he would admit me to the class.

The next morning I appeared at Professor Harris's classroom for the examination, with the feeling with which a man faces a firing squad. When I arrived I found several other young men there for

the same purpose. I was most gratified to find that the examination
was to be written instead of oral. The examination was written on
blackboards around the room, and consisted of the conjugation of
irregular verbs, the declension of nouns and adjectives, the rendi-
tion of sentences into oration oblique, and the translation of a passage from the first book of Caesar's *Commentaries*. When I saw the
examination, my heart took a leap for I knew that I would pass it.
I had conjugated Latin verbs and declined nouns at the plow until
I had them down pat. The passage for translation was the twelfth
chapter of the first book of Caesar's *Commentaries*, beginning "Flu-
men est Arar," the smoothest and most rhythmic passage in Caesar,
and I had read and translated it time and again. The next day I was
gratified to find the result of the examination posted up on the bulletin board with my name standing second highest on the list of
those passing.

It did not take me long, however, to find out that "Old Nick," as
the professor was called, had sized up the situation better than I
thought with regard to my preparation and the difficulty of my
keeping up with the class. The first lesson assigned to the junior
class consisted of about twenty pages of Gildersleeve's *Grammar*
and about a page of Cicero's Oration against Cataline, which I had
never read. I decided that he had embarked me on a river that did
not flow as smoothly as the Aras—in fact, it did not seem to flow at
all so far as I was concerned; and I about decided that if it flowed
at all, it would leave me stranded on the rocks by examination time.
I had entered Junior Mathematics, Preparatory Greek, and Ancient History, besides Latin, and the lessons assigned in each
course were so great that I did not see how it was possible for me
to prepare them; but having said I could do the work, I determined
that I would do it. I saw that the methods of study before practiced
would not do, and I set about acquiring a new degree of concentration, so that I would never have to go over a lesson more than one
time. After a few weeks I became so discouraged that I almost died
of the blues. I could not see that I was making any progress whatever. I thought that I had discovered that I was incapable of taking
a higher education, and could not understand how I had succeeded
as a student in the past. The only explanation I could think of with-

out admitting stupidity was that I had undertaken a university course too late in life.

I had too much at stake to fail. I felt that if I could not stand my hand with other young men in college classes, there would be no use for me to enter the profession of law on which I was resolved, nor to try to teach others if I could not learn myself. I therefore strained every faculty into an intensity of application. I made no effort to form any social connections, but studied from early morning until about twelve o'clock at night, with the exception of the two hours from five until seven o'clock in the afternoon. It was a custom in Lexington to take a "constitutional" at five o'clock by a long walk in the crisp air. At that hour all of the students and most of the professors and the citizens of the town were to be seen on the streets or on the country roads; and strange to say, the young ladies of the town chose the same hour for their exercise. Often a party of us Blue Hotel boys would take a sack and visit one of the nearby apple orchards, and come back with it filled with fine old Virginia winesaps. There was no objection on the part of the orchard owners to the students' gathering as many of the windfalls in the orchards as they desired, the windfalls not being marketable. Often I took my walk alone, and went to a cedar grove on a high cliff above the river, and conned over the lesson for the morrow, all the time haunted by the fear that examination time would find me weighed in the balance and found wanting. And I was not alone in my feverish application. There were many others who worked perhaps harder than I worked.

A few years ago Mallory F. Horne, now judge of the Third Judicial District of Florida, who was a law student at Washington and Lee in 1880, told me that when he entered he weighed one hundred and forty pounds, and that when he graduated he weighed less than one hundred. A young student from the state of Oregon would not read his personal mail except on Sunday, fearing that to do so would divert his mind from his studies. Those were the days when poverty compelled many young men to do in one year what they normally would have done in two. But, notwithstanding the hard work, life at Washington and Lee was not without its compensations. Just to live in surroundings so beautiful and inspiring was a joy in itself, aside from the profit gained.

For beauty of campus, buildings, and surrounding scenery, Washington and Lee is unrivalled by any other college in America, with the possible exception of the University of Virginia at Charlottesville. A large green campus, clothed with elms and maples shading walks laid out under the engineering skill of General Lee, with stately academic buildings standing in a long row at the top of a gentle slope, flanked at each end by the homes of the professors with their columned porticos, makes a setting fit, apt, and perfect for the home of the historic old institution. To the east, a few miles away across the beautiful valley, stands the long line of the Blue Ridge. To the west and north are the Alleghenies.

The dominating feature of the scene is House Mountain, a few miles away. One Sunday about the middle of October a party of students from the Blue Hotel decided to walk to the top of this mountain, which we were told was a distance of six miles. The walk was, at first, through green pasture lands, and then along mountain pathways, with occasional stops to fill our pockets with chestnuts, or to pluck wild grapes; and as we went on and on, we caught occasional glimpses of the mountain which, by some natural phenomenon, moved further and further away as we walked towards it until, finally, just before sunset, we stood on its summit. There the scenery was of undescribable grandeur. To the west there were seas and oceans of mountains. To the southeast, sixty miles away, the peaks of Otter stood up against the sky. Below, in the valley, the shadows were gathering dark, while the mountains to the west were aglow; and the lights in Lexington began to glimmer before the sunlight faded where we stood. When the sun had set, we took our bearings and started back to town, disregarding roads and trying to travel a direct course. After walking for what seemed to be a hundred miles, we came to a high road and stopped for a conference. We feared that we had lost our way and had gone far beyond Lexington. Finally we decided to walk on further, and see if we could find a signboard or a house where we could inquire. We walked on for about three miles without finding a house, and then decided to retrace our steps. We walked all the long way back to where our first conference was held, and called a man out of bed and asked him the way to Lexington. He said, "Right straight down the road you are on." And so we went back over the road over which we had walked twice, and about midnight arrived back at the Blue Hotel. After that, the five o'clock constitutional sufficed.

Each of the rooms in the Blue Hotel was occupied by two boys. In drawing a roommate, fate played me a scurvy trick. He was a conceited hayseed from Arkansas who had graduated from a hick college. He thought well of himself for having mastered McGuffey's *Fourth Reader* and having won a medal for oratory for reciting Byron's "Roll on—Thou deep and dark blue ocean—roll!" The only English word whose etymology he perfectly understood was the first personal pronoun, singular; and the only Latin word which he fully understood was "ego" in the form of "egomet." Many a midnight dreary, as I pondered, weak and weary, over the cussed bridge across the Rhine, I had to stop and listen to him descant on his superior intellectual powers, and patronize the effete Virginians in the law class of which he was a member. When he flunked at the end of the term and blubbered like a baby, and accused John Randolph Tucker and Professor Charles A. Graves of discrimination against him—well, I was as sorry as the devil—just exactly that sorry.

I owed a great deal to this amiable creature. One warm afternoon in the early fall I was lying face down on the campus reading over a Greek lesson when he came along and attempted to get funny. Slipping up behind me, he grabbed me by one foot, and started to drag me over the grass. I jumped up and seized him, and we began to wrestle; and as I was about to get the best of him he kicked me on the inside of my right knee and knocked it out of joint. I fell on the campus in agony. At that instant, the class bell rang and he left for class without offering me any assistance. Some of the other boys ran to me, and one of them straightened out my leg and pulled on it, pulling it back into position. They then helped me to my own class where I suffered intensely until the period was over. After the class the boys assisted me to my room. The next morning I could not get out of bed. Sinovitis set in, and it was perhaps two weeks before I could change my clothes, or move my leg without excruciating pain. During all of this time the scoundrel would not do a thing for me. He would go off in the morning and leave me with no one to build fires, or to get me a drink of water. The hostess of the Blue Hotel was all kindness, but she had no other room where she could place me, and, of course, could not render me all the service I needed. There was a young man by the name of Joe M. Dudley who had a room near me who was everything my roommate was not. This is the highest tribute I could pay him. He would come in of a morning and help me bathe, and after doing all he could, would go to his classes; and as soon as he could get away, would come back and look after me with the tenderness of a woman. Joe Dudley was one of nature's noblemen. Until his entrance at Washington and Lee, he had worked as a railroad hand at Clifton Forge, either in the railroad shops or as a brakeman. He was deeply religious, and had desired to enter the Presbyterian ministry, but did not have sufficient money to complete his education, though he had saved enough money to come to Washington and Lee one year. While he was there, a representative of the Railroad YMCA came to Lexington and addressed the students on the needs of YMCA work among railroad men, and Dudley decided that he would enter that work. After spending a year at college, he went back to Clifton Forge and worked for another year, and then entered upon his life-work. He was in charge of the work in Canada for a number of years, with headquarters at Montreal; and during his superintendence of the work in Canada, he secured the erection of fine buildings for the Association in many of the large cities on the lines of the Canadian Pacific Railway system.

The second year I was at Washington and Lee, I was one of the commencement orators, and Joe Dudley came back to hear me speak. For many years I lost sight of him until one day he stepped into an elevator in Atlanta and said, "This is Joe Dudley." He was then Secretary of the RRYMCA of America and Cuba. Among all of the men whom I have ever known, I have never met a finer character than old Joe Dudley.

As soon as it became known about college that I was hurt, Bob Lee sent me a pair of crutches. Bob Lee was another of nature's noblemen by natural endowment, by inheritance, and in his own personal character. Like all of the Lees, he was large, handsome, and clothed with natural dignity and leadership. He was jovial, without hauteur, and friendly — a good mixer without familiarity — a man with whom everybody felt at home and at ease, despite his family prestige and his natural leadership. His social standing was fixed. His circumstances in life were comfortable without the ac-

quisition of personal wealth. A career could add little to his comfort
or standing in the world, and so he took life easy, had a good time,
and radiated good feelings all about him. From college he stepped
easily into political prominence in Virginia, and in a few years was
Speaker of the Virginia House of Delegates. In 1908 he came to
Griffin, Georgia, and delivered the address on Memorial Day. I arranged for him to speak to the Confederate Veterans in Atlanta in
the Hall of Representatives at the State Capitol. His address was
eloquent and masterful. The old Confederates who had followed his
grandfather went almost wild with enthusiasm. He had a remarkable memory of people and never forgot anybody he had once
known. In 1921 I met him on the campus of Washington and Lee.
Although I had only seen him twice in twenty-nine years, he recognized me at a distance and came rushing towards me with his old
boyish enthusiasm. The best description of Bob Lee's personality
can be found in the description of his father, Rooney Lee, in *The
Education of Henry Adams*.

There were two literary societies, the Washington and the Graham-Lee, said to be the oldest college literary societies in America.
They each have, or had, at that time, large society rooms on the
third floor of the main building where weekly meetings were held
on Saturday night. The exercises consisted of speeches, declama-
tions, debates, etc., and business was transacted according to standard rules of order. On Washington's birthday, February 22, the
annual celebration of the society was held in the University Chapel,
at which there was a contest between two declaimers for the de-
claimer's medal and a joint debate among four debaters. To the debater who performed best (in the judgment of a committee selected
by the faculty) was awarded the debater's medal. This celebration
was a great occasion which was attended by the students, the faculty and their families, and by the elite of the town. Perhaps no finer
audience could be assembled in America than the audience which
packed the chapel to the last seat in the gallery. The declaimers and
debaters were elected by the vote of the society, and intense cam-
paigning went on for weeks in advance of the election. Early in the
fall I was visited by a number of the old students who were members of the "Wash" society, as it was called in college parlance, and
asked to allow my name to be proposed as one of the candidates for

debaters. This was a great surprise as I had taken no conspicuous part in the exercises of the Society, but I readily consented. I made no canvass and asked nobody to vote for me, but, to my surprise, I was elected, receiving the highest vote of any of the candidates. After receiving this honor and the responsibility that went with it of upholding the reputation of the Society and of the University, I had the double task of carrying on my regular studies and of preparing a speech.

The subject chosen for debate was "Resolved, that our colleges and universities should not be opened to both sexes." This was one of the worst subjects that could have been chosen, so far as I was concerned. There were no facts illustrating the subject — at least I could find none — and there was no literature available on the subject at that time. The subject, therefore, was one that had to be argued largely upon opinion, sentiment, and personal bias. Not one of the debaters had an opinion on the subject that was worth a moment's consideration. I was at sea as to what sort of speech I should prepare, and finally decided that the nature of the subject was such that all of the debaters would throw in a lot of gallant sentiment and some "curls," and that the debate would, to a large extent, be a contest of orations rather than an argumentative marshaling of definite facts. I, therefore, set about the preparation of a speech into which I tried to put some argument, but my greatest care was to make it as nearly perfect a literary production as I possibly could. This took many, many hours. All of this work had to be carried on under the inspiring companionship of the "Arkansas Traveler" who had made a prisoner of me.

The examinations for the fall term began about ten days before the Christmas holidays. By this time I had some hope of passing in all of my studies, but no idea of winning any distinctions. The results of the examinations in the different classes were announced by a notice posted on the bulletin board at the entrance to the main building. The boys approached this board with the same agitation with which a prisoner hears the reading of the jury's verdict. The first bulletin carrying my name was the class in Latin, and I could hardly believe my eyes when I saw my name with the second highest mark. Then came mathematics with a mark way above eighty — fifty being a pass, and anything above eighty, distinction; then

Greek, and another distinction. The last class for which marks were announced was ancient history. In each department of the University there was an honorary scholarship given to the student reaching the highest mark in any course in that department. There was a very bright man, an old student, in the ancient history class, who was working for leadership of that class and for the scholarship in the Department of History. I had no doubt of his success, but I had determined to make as high a mark as possible. When the marks were posted, my mark was 98; Henderson's was 96, and the others were far below Henderson's. There were two more examinations during the remainder of the term. On the second examination my mark was 100, and on the third and final examination, my mark was between 96 and 100, but I cannot recall exactly what it was. I had led the class in every examination, and my marks were higher than those of any other student in any class of the Department of History, and at Commencement I was awarded the scholarship in the department. At subsequent examinations during that year, I maintained approximately the same standing in all classes.

The success of my first examination was the most fortunate thing that ever happened to me. It destroyed a delusion, under which I had before that time labored, that somewhere among the sons of distinguished and aristocratic families there was a quality of brains with which a common man could not compete. I had gone into the very center of intellectuality among the Lees, Eppses, Cookes, Clays, and McDowells and had held my own with them, and it gave me a confidence in myself which has been of untold benefit to me throughout my whole life. To the "Arkansas Traveler" such success would have been a tragedy. His conceit would have towered like the ash tree, Ygdrasil. In me it raised no delusions of grandeur or superiority. I attributed my success merely to the extraordinary effort I had made. Of course I knew that no effort would have availed if there had not been some intellectual capacity underneath it, but I was well aware that success with me would require the best effort of which I was capable. I have had my full share of faults, but the "big head" has never been one of them.

After the examinations were over, classes were suspended for about ten days, and most of the students who lived near enough went home for the holidays. A few of the Blue Hotel boys remained,

and such a time we had. The intense labor we had undergone made
a few days' rest and relaxation a paradise. One of the boys who remained was a young man from Norfolk named Custon, the son of
a captain in the United States Navy, whose people had sent him a
trunk full of cakes for Christmas. I never saw at one time before or
since so many different kinds of cake. He invited us all to his room
one afternoon to celebrate. When we got there, there were cakes in
front of us, cakes to the right of us, cakes to the left of us, and more
cakes in reserve. There were also two dozen fresh eggs, a gallon or
two of milk, and a jug of rye. The wash bowl was scalded out, the
ingredients were poured in, in the right proportions, and then the
mixture was whipped and beaten until it was right. When it was
finished, it was cake and eggnog, fun and song, until Mrs. Rogers,
the hostess, sent a servant down to stop the "rah-rah." Word was
sent back to go hang herself, but she declined the request and sent
the servant back with another order. Then a bright idea struck our
host. He took a big round cake and filled a pitcher of eggnog and
sent it to the landlady. We heard no more from her, but the vivacity
of her manner at the supper table was evidence that she received
our gift, tried it, and was quite satisfied with its quality.

The library of Washington and Lee at that time consisted of
about forty thousand volumes, part being the collection of the old
Franklin Library, part the gift of W. W. Corcoran, and part the ac-
quisitions of the University by purchase and by other donations.
The librarian was an old gentleman by the name of Benjamin
Franklin Wade, who came to Washington and Lee in 1890, the
same year that I entered. He sat at a high desk at the entrance to
the stack rooms, and kept order in the reading room in front. He
was an old bachelor, and lived in a room upstairs in the library
building, living the life of a recluse, scarcely ever being seen outside
the library building. He sat all day and read, except when he went
to get a book or to return one to the stacks. One day a few weeks
after my entrance he called me to his desk and asked me if I had ever
been to Cassville, Georgia; and when I told him I had been there
many times, he said that when a much younger man he had taught
school at Cassville, and had boarded with Dr. and Mrs. Felton.
After becoming too old to teach, and being without means, he had
secured the position of librarian at Washington and Lee at a small

salary, with nothing before him now but to sit, and read, and smoke his old brier pipe, until some morning when he failed to come down to his desk, someone would go to his room and find the poor old man dead. He advised me not to get into his fix, but to marry and have a family and avoid the loneliness of a bachelor's old age. In 1893, the year after I left college, he died in his lonely room.

A great friendship grew up between me and Mr. Wade, and he allowed me privileges not generally granted to the students. In order to get books, the rule was for the student desiring to take books from the library to file a receipt with the librarian after finding it in the catalogue, and then the librarian would go to the stackroom and bring the book out and deliver it at the desk, and only four books could be had at a time. Soon he gave me permission to visit the stackroom at will, and the right to withdraw as many books as I wished. Sometimes I would spend an hour going over the stacks and reading the titles, and coveting their possession. Much of the Christmas vacation was spent among these friendly volumes.

My three greatest tastes have always been books, flowers, and natural scenery, and the greatest of these is books. I think the happiest times I have ever known have been the hours spent browsing among the book stacks of Washington and Lee, a day in the public gardens at Halifax, and the times when I have stood on some mountain peak and looked out over a sea of mountains with the thin clouds trailing their lacy folds among them.

The speech for the intermediate debate was finished two or three weeks ahead of time. It had been announced that no speech would be considered for the prize which occupied more than twenty minutes in delivery. When the speech was finished, the length of time necessary to deliver it was carefully tested and it was found that it exceeded the length of time allowed by two minutes. It was then pared down by shortening the several sentences where possible to shorten a sentence without omitting it, and by eliminating where preservation by abbreviation was impossible. Finally the speech was cut down to about nineteen minutes, and no further abbreviation seemed possible. It was then committed to memory by being read over and repeated until it seemed impossible to become confused by stage fright and to forget it. Every afternoon I would hobble out through the snow on my crutches to a cedar grove near the river, and it would be declaimed to the trees.

At last the night of February 22nd came, and with it came the greatest triumph of my life. When the master of ceremonies followed by the declaimers and debaters marched down the aisle and took their places on the rostrum, they were confronted by an audience of rare brilliance. The professors of Washington and Lee were there with their families, and the officers of the Virginia Military Institute, brilliant in their smart uniforms. The young ladies of the town, escorted by students or upper classmen of the V. M. I. in military uniforms, and the students, cadets, and leading citizens of the town packed the building to the last seat in the gallery. Back of the rostrum, through an apsis, the marble statue of Robert E. Lee was visible lying above his tomb. On the walls were the portraits of Washington, LaFayette, and a long line of distinguished men. In the audience were General Scott Shipp, Commandant of the V. M. I.; John Randolph Tucker; Mrs. Fitzhugh Lee, the leader of Virginia society; and many other men and women of distinguished lineage and of high social position. The brilliance of the audience, the historical environment, and the critical disposition of university students, than whom there can be none more critical, made the situation appalling. When my time came to speak, I started slowly in order to gain composure, and after a few minutes the audience broke into applause. The applause did not seem to come on account of any particular climax, but it seemed merely to say "The boy is making good." After that I could hardly end a distinct paragraph of the speech without the applause breaking out again. At the end, it was an ovation. The ladies took off their flowers and sent them to me by ushers. During my speech, I watched the two beautiful daughters of General Scott Shipp, and when I sat down one of them tore off her bouquet and sent it to me.

When I finished my speech had occupied twenty-three minutes due to the interruptions by applause. The decision was in favor of one of the other debaters who was a member of a law class and who had taken an A.B. degree at one of the South's leading colleges before coming to Washington and Lee. His speech was perhaps slightly more argumentative than mine, but was prosy and received without enthusiasm by the audience. It was reported by some who heard the deliberations of the committee that I was eliminated for having exceeded the time limit; but this did not satisfy the audience, and the decision was received with disapproval. After the meeting was over a large indignation meeting of students was held on the campus. When I came down to breakfast at the Blue Hotel the next morning, the boys rose and cheered, and every classroom I entered the next day broke into cheers. Waldo Porter Johnson, a gifted student, a poet of rare gifts, and a writer of brilliance, in an account of the debate published in the *Sunny South* said:

> The next morning when he came down to breakfast, the boys rose to a man and the old Blue Hotel rattled with applause. The Professor of Logic, Moral Philosophy and Rhetoric took Mr. McElreath's speech as a text and lectured on it two days to his class in Rhetoric, telling them it was a combination of logic and rhetoric very rare, and that he would have them learn from the style of the young orator from Georgia.

It was the custom for the Society to award a medal to the successful debater, but the word went round that if the matter was brought up in the Society, the motion to award the medal would be defeated, and it was never brought up, and no medal was awarded.

I did not care a cent for the medal. The fact that I had not failed, that I had, without experience or training, won the plaudits of such an audience in such a place was glory enough for me. The high marks I made on my first examinations and the success of my speech established me in the regard of the faculty, the students and the people of the town.

Before the middle of the first year, I had made no social contacts with the people of Lexington. Few of the Blue Hotel boys were in society. The boys who went into society boarded in private families uptown, and lived more expensively than the Blue Hotel boys, but there was no social ostracism of the Blue Hotel boys.

Those old Virginians are a peculiar set. They do not slap you on the back and open their hearts and homes to you until they have had you under observation for a sufficient time to determine that you are worthy of their social recognition, and arriving at this conclusion, the possession of wealth counts for little.

Professor White, head of the Department of Greek at Washington and Lee, was, perhaps, the man of highest dignity and social prestige among the residents of Lexington. He was large, tall, and handsome, with a mien like Jupiter which had earned him the nickname of "Old Zeus" among the students. He lived in a fine old house near the campus. His daughter, Miss Belle, was large and handsome like her father; she sang in the Presbyterian choir with a fine cultivated voice, and moved in society with that serene dignity which came from a natural modesty, and assurance born of an unquestioned social position. To be seen with Miss Belle was the final verdict of social acceptance.

One day about the middle of my first year, Professor White met me on the campus and said, "Mr. McElreath, I wish you to meet me in front of the Presbyterian Church next Sunday after service and walk home with us and be our guest at dinner." I knew then that I had arrived and that he had arranged the matter so that the public would see me walk away from the church with Miss Belle as an announcement of the fact that he had set the seal of his social approval on me. However, social recognition was a comfort of which I was not prepared to make much use. I had little doubt of my ability to observe the usual social conventions. Any innately courteous person of fair intelligence can do that — witness Robert Burns in the drawing rooms of Edinburgh. But Robert Burns was handsome, and before he ventured into Edinburgh society, he had a tailor to make him a fine suit of clothes. I was not handsome, had no fine clothes, and no money with which to get them, and no society manners. I was older at twenty-four than I am at seventy-three. I could sustain myself fairly well in the company of mature and serious-minded men and women, and possibly could have managed fairly well with the sober, quiet, and dignified Miss Belle, but the younger set of ladies who had been from infancy trained in the society of Washington and Lee and the Virginia Military Institute, and who had flirted with students and cadets from the time their skirts met their shoe tops — as they did in that day — was a task for which I knew I was not prepared. A man can make a hundred in ancient history and win applause in a college debate and not be able to interest an eighteen-year-old girl. In the absence of natural proclivity, it takes as much experience to be a successful lounge lizard as it does to master comic sections. I, therefore, sought no social engagements, but such as I made sought me. The last statement I made needs some explanation.

The interest which young ladies take in masculine education, and the troubles which many of them undergo to assist in it, is a remarkable evidence of the self-sacrificing nature of the sex. Knowing that no college commencement could be properly conducted without their presence, many of them came from long distances at much expense of railroad fare and new dresses, to lend the charm of their presence to the commencement occasions. It was a custom of the Lexington families to arrange in advance for an escort to their young lady visitors for each one of the commencement exercises, and favored students had full cards. One of the young ladies who fell to my lot was a young lady from Norfolk, whose name I cannot now recall. She was a tall, slender, spiritual girl who prattled of flowers, poetry and moonlight. She affected ill health, and hovered continually between sentimentality and a swoon, and guarded against the latter by smelling a little bottle chased with silver, the manipulation of which showed to advantage her jeweled hands. She made it plain that she was so delicate that she must have a carriage for her engagements. I managed to date her up for one of the exercises at the college chapel. As the Blue Hotel at which she stopped as a guest of the hostess was on the campus, and the nearest point a carriage could approach to it was the chapel door, I got by without the carriage. Much to my disappointment, she did not faint. I have always felt that this was because I did not meet her social requirements.

Another young lady whom I had the good fortune to escort was a Miss Beverly, the daughter of Judge Beverly, of Richmond, a member of the famous Virginia family of that name. My engagement with her was arranged by her brother-in-law, Professor Henry Alexander White, the professor of ancient history in whose department I had taken the honorary scholarship. Another was a daughter of General Smith of the Confederate Army, but I do not now recall which one of the generals of that name was her father; and another was a sister-in-law of Dr. Forrest J. Prettyman. When I left Lexington the only young lady that shed tears was the eighteen-year-old daughter of the hostess of the Blue Hotel.

The commencement of 1891, like all other commencements at Washington and Lee, was a notable occasion from the standpoint of literary exercises and the social functions connected with it. The commencement sermon was preached by Bishop E. R. Hendrix of the Southern Methodist Church from the text, "Jesus Christ, the Same Yesterday, Today and Forever." The speaker was then in the prime of his great powers, eloquent, handsome in personal appearance, and possessed with the presence and the mien of a great orator. In presenting his theme, he pictured Jesus as a philosophic concept and as a moral force and fact standing against the background of the times in which he lived, and persisting unchanged through the mutations of time and history. He reviewed the political history of the world since his time, and showed how nations and empires had risen, exerted power for a time, and had fallen into decay, and how other nations had arisen with other political organizations and objectives; how philosophic thought had changed, causing men to look at material and spiritual things from a different viewpoint; how dogma had shifted from one emphasis to another, and religion had taken on new forms; but through all the mutations of power, philosophy, and dogma, the essential authority of Jesus Christ was the one constant force (using the word "constant" in the sense in which it is used in higher mathematics). During the delivery of this sermon, my friend William Reynolds Vance and I sat together in the gallery almost hypnotized by the magnificent sweep of the speaker's power. To this day that sermon stands out distinctly in my memory as one of the greatest I have ever heard.

During the commencement week an agent of the Chesapeake and Ohio Railroad made up a party of twenty students to go home by that route, and as an inducement agreed to furnish the party with one of the finest reclining chair cars belonging to the system. I joined the party, buying a ticket as far as Lexington, Kentucky. The car was carried on commencement day to the Greenbrier White Sulphur Springs where it was put on a side track for the night to allow the party to put up at the famous old Greenbrier Hotel, a privilege of which, for financial reasons, only one or two of the party availed themselves.

After looking on for a while at the dance in the large ballroom, we went back to the car to sleep in our chairs. But sleep was a thing denied us. The spirits of the party just released from nine months of grinding labor were too exuberant, and the night was spent in pranks and revelry. The next morning the car was attached to the F. F. V. (Fast-Flying Virginian) and the day's trip was one never to be forgotten. In the party there were several who had finished their courses, and won their diplomas, and were going home to begin their professional careers. Some had spent all their means and would not return to finish their courses. Some expected to return the next year; so with reminiscences, farewells, and plans for another year, it was a party of the greatest human interest, comradeship and hearty goodwill of which it has ever been my fortune to be a member. The trip next day was glorious. It was the second trip of any length I had ever taken, and was my first experience of traveling in the luxury of fine railroad equipment. The scenery was magnificent—high mountains, deep gorges, stretches along the rushing Kanawha, and by the Great Falls—for a few miles beside the Ohio, on which I first saw a steamboat, one of the big palatial boats that at that time plied La Belle Riviere—into the feud lands of eastern Kentucky, and out of the hills into the bluegrass regions, through the wheat and flax fields to Lexington, where we arrived at about three o'clock in the afternoon. There Vance and I left the train, he to take the late night train to his home at Shelbyville, and I to take the night train over the Queen & Crescent, by way of Chattanooga, and the W & A to Atlanta. We spent the afternoon seeing the fine piece of statuary in the county courthouse and visiting the tomb of Henry Clay in Lexington Cemetery. After a fine dinner, I boarded the first electric car I ever saw for the depot where I took the train for home. The next afternoon I was back at Lost Mountain, a very different young man from the one who had left there nine months before.

Several weeks before commencement I had received a letter from Miss Ella Kemp, who had taught a school at Due West during the winter months and was under contract to teach another session in the summer, asking me to join her in teaching the summer session, and to take the place of principal. This invitation came as a Godsend, for it enabled me to earn a considerable sum towards the payment of my expenses at Washington and Lee for the next year.

Due West is the old Gilgal Church, famous in the operations of the armies when Johnston's line stretched from Kennesaw, Pine Mountain, Gilgal Church, and Lost Mountain to New Hope. It is located about three miles northeast of Lost Mountain. The principal people in the community were the Kemps, and Miss Ella was the sister of my Uncle Frank McElreath's wife. She was a fine maiden lady who had had a tragedy in her girlhood. She had been engaged to a young man who was killed by an accident the week before the date set for their marriage. She regarded herself as wedded to her betrothed and with a rare constancy lived in maidenhood wedded to his memory. She had little education, but a lovable nature which made her an effective primary teacher. Many of my old Lost Mountain pupils came to the school which, according to my recollection, reached to over one hundred in number. I boarded with the family of G. W. Pharr, whose wife was a distant cousin of my mother.

The school closed the first week in September, and the next week I was back at Lexington.

The coming back to Lexington was a marvelous contrast to my first appearance there. I had established at least a reasonable reputation for scholarship, acquired friends, overcome that most distressing of all maladies, homesickness, which afflicts a boy leaving home for the first time to live among strangers. When I got back to Lexington and to the Blue Hotel, I felt as if I had returned home. My classes for the next year were Intermediate Latin, Intermediate Mathematics, Surveying and Astronomy, and Senior Moral Philosophy. This was an exceedingly hard course. Intermediate Latin and Mathematics corresponded to Senior Latin and Mathematics in the standard four-year curriculum of that day. Intermediate Latin was a class that required a great deal of work. Besides the regular recitations in grammar and translation, there was an immense amount of parallel reading and exercises. I made this course very much harder than it was to most students by refusing to use "ponies," which I regarded as spurious and dishonest scholarship. While others rode "ponies," I dug. Senior Moral Philosophy was the hardest course in the University. In this class there were six recitations a week. The course was only undertaken by the most mature and advanced students, and it was not required for an A.B. degree, most students quitting the course with the completion of the junior class. I did not take the junior class, but entered senior. The text-books were Hamilton's *Metaphysics*, Bowen's *Logic*, Überweg's *History of Philosophy*, and a prodigious amount of original lecture work by Professor Quarles. Mathematics was never an easy study for me. While no form of mathematics was ever too difficult for me to master if given time, I had no instinctive aptitude for it and more time was necessary for me to prepare a difficult lesson than for some who were more naturally gifted in the science. However, while surveying and mathematical astronomy involved abstruse processes in higher mathematics, I was fascinated with the course and won a distinction, I think, standing second in the class.

I was elected critic of the Washington Literary Society, a position which had, at one time, been held by Thomas Nelson Page, associate editor of the *Southern Collegian*, and one of the Committee on Invitations for the Intermediate Debate. Thus, with an amply gratifying recognition from the student body, I set out on a year of intense labor.

Some years before the period of which I am writing, an association had been organized among some of the leading colleges of the South for the holding of an annual oratorical contest to which the University of Virginia, Washington and Lee, and Vanderbilt University belonged. The contest of 1892 was to be held in the spring of that year at Nashville. When the time approached to select the representative of Washington and Lee for the contest, four students from the University were elected to hold a preliminary contest, the winning student in this contest to be Washington and Lee's representative at the final contest in Nashville. I was among those chosen, another being E. G. Smith of Clarksburg, West Virginia. I do not remember the other two contestants. I prepared a speech, but was not satisfied with it, and wished to discard it and prepare another, but I did not have the time.

At the preliminary contest Mr. Smith's oration was so far superior both as to substance and manner of delivery that he overwhelmingly won the contest. At the final contest at Nashville, he won as easily as he had won in the preliminary contest at Lexington. I had no reason to suspect that he had received help in the preparation of his oration, as he was a man of undoubted ability, but it was a fact that for weeks before the contest at Lexington, he had been under the training of a professional elocutionist.

When the telegram came from Nashville that he had won the contest, a meeting of the student body was held at which it was arranged to give him a royal reception on his return to Lexington. Professor James A. White was selected to represent the faculty and the trustees of the University, and I was selected to represent the student body. On the night of the return, the finest carriage in Lexington was procured to meet the train. I rode in the carriage with Professor White. When the train arrived, Mr. Smith was taken into the carriage, and, preceded by a brass band, was driven through the streets crowded with the people of the town. After parading the streets, we were driven to the campus where the student body was assembled, and Professor [White] made a speech congratulating the hero of the occasion, and I followed speaking on behalf of the literary societies and the students.

My speech on this occasion was one of the best I have ever made, and it taught me a valuable lesson about public speaking. I did not write it, but merely thought out the general line to be followed, and let the words come spontaneously during the delivery. My speech on this occasion resulted in the establishment of cordial relations between me and Professor Nelson of the Department of Mathematics. Professor Nelson was aware of the fact that when I was so crowded for time that I could not make perfect preparation in all of my courses and had to slight some classes, I always eased up on mathematics. He believed mathematics to be the greatest of all studies, and set comparatively little value on language, history, or rhetoric. He said that any intelligent man would acquire all that was useful in those branches by the general course of reading which he would inevitably pursue, and that at college he ought to develop the mathematical faculty as highly as possible under rigid college training. He thought men who pursued the studies of belles lettres at college and neglected mathematics were intellectual weaklings. On account of my high standing in other classes and my medium rank in mathematics, he was not cordial to me, and I did not like him. When I arrived at chapel services the morning after the reception for Mr. Smith, Professor Nelson came to me, grasped my hand, and praised my speech in the highest terms. After this he seemed to respect me much more highly than he had before and our relations grew very cordial.

One feature of commencement was an oratorical contest between two representatives of the Washington Literary Society and the Graham-Lee. Selection as one of these orators was considered a very high collegiate honor, and long in advance of the election active campaigns were carried on in behalf of the candidates for these places. There were several candidates in the Washington Society. I was put forward as a candidate, but I made no effort in my behalf, and as I was considered the strongest candidate, the others began to make all sorts of combinations against me, and I went to the meeting at which the election was to be held expecting to be defeated. When nominations were called for, one of my opponents rose and placed me in nomination, another seconded the nomination, another moved that the nominations close and that the secretary cast the ballot for me. The motion carried, and I was declared unanimously elected as one of the final orators. The contest for the other place was close, finally resulting in the choice of Mr. Fix of Virginia.

The Society having expressed such flattering confidence in me, I set to work to write the best speech of which I was capable. I chose for my subject "The Old Order Changeth," from Tennyson's "The Passing of Arthur," and applied it to the dying influence of the South in literature, statesmanship, business and social ideals. All speeches were required to be submitted to Professor Henry Alexander White, the censor of the orations to be delivered. When he returned my address, he commended my choice of a subject and the address itself, and said that it was not only the best address submitted, but that it was the only one of the addresses of sufficient dignity to be delivered as a final oration. However, it did not receive the medal. Notwithstanding Dr. White's opinion, the subject was unfortunate as an address at Washington and Lee. During the twenty-five years after the war, the peculiar association of Washington and Lee with the lives and memory of Lee and Stonewall Jackson had inspired so many student orations along the Southern lines of thought that the Lexington public was surfeited with speeches on Southern subjects. The medal went to Mr. J. B. Andrews, of Missouri, whose subject was "Thomas Arnold of Rugby."

The judges were college professors who were peculiarly pleased with his glorification of the great teacher, and besides, his speech was good.

Three failures in oratory, if failing to win the prize is a test, convinced me that I might become a good speaker, but not a great orator. This was not a great disappointment, for I did not place the mere orator on the highest pinnacle of intellectual achievement, although that time was an oratorical era. Echoes of the eloquence of Henry Grady were still heard, John Temple Graves was captivating audiences with the wizardry of his lyric sentences, and William Jennings Bryan had captivated the country with his maiden speech in Congress. It was hard for an ambitious young man of that day not to attempt flights too lofty for his wings.

I finished the course which I had pursued for the year with gratifying success. I won a distinction in all examinations in Surveying and Astronomy, and in Senior Moral Philosophy. In the latter class I stood second, the first honor being taken by John W. Davis, whose mark was only two above mine. I passed the distinction mark in two out of three examinations in Latin, but I did not take the final examination in mathematics on account of sickness.

After the close of the session in 1892, I arrived back home with one shirt, one dollar and fifty-five cents, and certificates of distinction in Ancient History, Latin, Surveying and Astronomy, and Moral Philosophy.

IX

Two Years
at Powder Springs

The summer of 1892 was spent in teaching school at the place now known as McLand. Sometime before this school closed, I was called upon by a committee from the Board of Trustees of the Powder Springs High School. They notified me of my election as principal of that school, and requested my acceptance, which was eagerly given.

Powder Springs was a village of between three and four hundred population, consisting mostly of retired farmers and merchants who had amassed sufficient means to live in ease and comfort without work. The surrounding country had always been prosperous; the early settlers were people of the highest class; the social life of the town had always been, and then was, above the average of towns of its size; and the Powder Springs High School was the best school in the county outside of Marietta. Professor Luke Mizell, Dr. A. B. Vaughan, and Professor Joseph G. Camp had set such a high standard of scholarship for the school that it was attended not only by students of the town and the immediate surrounding country, but by many students from other communities who boarded in the town to attend it. Being under the necessity of teaching to acquire the funds to enable me to enter the profession of law, no more gratifying offer could have been made me than to live at Powder Springs and to teach the school at which I had prepared for college.

Among the earliest settlers in and around Powder Springs were the Kisers, a number of whom came early into the community, and built fine houses on good farms near the town. After M. C. and J. F. Kiser, who were in the early days the leading merchants of the town, had outgrown it, they removed to Atlanta, and like the Hirsches, who also began business in Cobb County, became merchant princes. Besides the Kisers, the early settlers of the town and surrounding country who stamped indelibly their character upon the town and community were Dr. Aristides Reynolds, the Andersons, Lindleys, Camps, Butners, and Florences.

The school, which opened for the winter term on the first Monday in November, 1892, opened under promising auspices, with a good enrollment of local and boarding pupils, and with Miss Jimmie Selman, a young woman of the highest qualifications of natural ability, education, and character, as teacher of the elementary grades; but the conditions of the times and other causes prevented the full realization of all of the high hopes entertained when the principalship of the school was accepted.

The entire income of the people of Powder Springs and the surrounding country was from farming and from dealing in farm supplies and products. For several years there had been a steady decline in the price of cotton, the price of a bale having fallen from eighty-five dollars in 1870 to thirty-seven and a half dollars in 1892, and to five cents a pound or twenty-five dollars a bale in 1893. With the fall of agricultural prices, debt and discontent arose. The condition of the farmer was charged to the manufacturers, merchants, bankers, and generally to all professions and occupations other than farmers, all of whom were considered as parasites living upon what the farmers produced. In 1897 the Farmers Alliance was organized. At first it was nonpolitical and attempted to remedy the condition of its members by cooperation in the buying of fertilizers and supplies, and by other forms of cooperation. Cooperative buying not having remedied the situation, the Farmers Alliance was joined in 1889 by the Knights of Labor. A political coalition was thus formed between the farmers and laboring classes which "put a yardstick on candidates for office." In Georgia it elected a farmers' legislature which had hardly a sufficient number of lawyers in it to form a judiciary committee. During the spring of 1892 the discontented elements formed the Populist Party; and during that year and the year following, Thomas E. Watson, with malevolent genius, was sowing the seeds of social and political prejudice all over Georgia, which found fallow ground in the soil of the general discontent. Besides the deplorable condition of the farmer, on account of the low price of his products and of the laboring classes, on account of low wages, there were many unemployed, and in 1894 Jacob Coxey led an army of unemployed to Washington.

The people in the town of Powder Springs were old-line Democrats who did not embrace the philosophy of Watson and Coxey; but around the town there were many, a number of them patrons of the school, who were wrought up to an intense degree of fanaticism. Some of the wildest of these began to incite the country people against sending their children to the Powder Springs High School with the children of "them aristocrats," and taught by "that fellow McElreath, who was not anything but a plow boy who had gone off and got an education and was making five dollars a day." Finally the Populist faction rented a small house on the edge of town and started an opposition school which was popularly known as "Hines Academy" from James K. Hines, who was at that time prominent in the Populist movement.

Besides the political division and prejudice among the patrons of the school, there were factions and family feuds at Powder Springs as in all other communities; but for downright cussedness, one of the factions at Powder Springs outranked anything with which I have ever had experience. It arose out of family jealousy, and found an opportunity for its exercise in the management of the school by the Board of Trustees, and in local and state politics.

I do not think that either faction really had anything against me; but the Populist faction had to fight me to spite the other faction which supported me, and in doing so did and said some things that were so provoking that a street fight resulted between me and the chief of the opposition, Ramsey Sniffles, for which we were both arrested by the town marshal, and fined a dollar each.

Notwithstanding all of this discord and opposition, the school was a reasonable success. We had all of the pupils which two teachers could take care of. The senior department, which I taught, embraced everything usually taught in a high school of that day from English grammar to calculus, and the advancement of some of the pupils is illustrated by the fact that one of them went from Powder Springs High School to the junior class of the University of Georgia, and one to the junior class of one of the female colleges of Staunton, Virginia.

The vacations during the years I spent at Powder Springs were absolutely the only leisure I had ever had up to that time, and I have had little since. The period of which I am writing was before the day of the automobile and the movies, and the only diversions at Powder Springs were an occasional baseball game, a game of chess with the village parson's daughters, an occasional drive with one of the young ladies of the town, and a walk in the late afternoon to the mineral spring.

Among the young ladies of the town was one of approximately my own age whom I had worshiped from afar for several years, but who had circulated beyond my orbit. When I visited the Chautauqua at Lithia Springs, I would peep through the dining room of the Lithia Springs Hotel and see her at the table with her fashionably dressed companions from Atlanta. She then seemed the limit of the unattainable. While I taught at Powder Springs, she was a teacher of music at Centenary Female College at Cleveland, Tennessee, but spent the summer at home with her parents. She had an exquisite voice, highly trained. She had a good literary education, was modest and shy, good looking, with a neat and trim figure, and the most beautiful hands I ever saw. A university education gives confidence and adds to one's social prestige, and I found that I had swung into her orbit. As she will make up a large part of the future story, we will leave her now till we meet her again.

The Populist Party and natural inclination persuaded me that I would be happier in the practice of law than in teaching school. The time had passed when I could afford the time to go to a law school, and money was lacking; and so I set about preparing myself for the bar by private study. I borrowed a *Code of Georgia* from Judge Mathews and studied it at night. I found that the legal mind was, like the taste for lager beer, one to be acquired; but by constant study I acquired some knowledge of statutory law. I borrowed from the Honorable A. S. Clay a set of Blackstone's *Commentaries, Parsons On Contracts*, and *Stephen On Pleading*. I pored over these books at night, and gradually began to discern the faint outlines of the legal principles involved.

The study of law without a teacher is a discouraging task. It brings into play faculties of the mind unused in any other department of learning. The use of terms which have acquired a precise meaning in legal science (in the civil law from the time of Justinian and in the common law from the early days of English history) not usually defined by legal text writers, but assumed to be understood, makes legal literature an abstract science, with little that is concrete for the undisciplined mind to grasp. The use of the case system in recent years has done much to remove this difficulty. I acquired a fair knowledge and understanding of Blackstone's *Commentaries*, *Greenleaf On Evidence*, and the *Code of Georgia*, which were largely committed to memory; but *Parsons On Contracts*, *Chitty On Pleading*, Cooley's *Constitutional Limitations*, and some of the other works which I read passed through my mind like water through a sieve.

When the school closed in the fall of 1894, I went to Marietta and entered the office of the Honorable R. N. Holland, where I had the advantage of the coaching of George D. Anderson and his younger brother, W. D. Anderson.

At that time admission to the bar was upon an examination in open court. The usual practice was for the presiding judge to appoint a committee to examine the applicant on the different branches of the law and to report their recommendation, after which the judge would make such examination as he saw fit; and then, if he was satisfied, he would pass an order admitting the applicant to the bar. The examination in my case was rather perfunctory, both by the committee and by the judge. One of the committee asked me a few questions, and then asked me if I could lend him the sum of three dollars. Under the circumstances, I produced the coin speedily, if not willingly, and he then said that I was unusually proficient in the department of law of which he had examined me.

When the examination in open court came, the judge, the Honorable George F. Gover, admonished me that admission to the bar would not make me a lawyer, but that I would bite the sawdust many times before I would become a real lawyer, a judgment which has found affirmation in many episodes of my professional career.

I was admitted to the bar in Cobb Superior Court on the 23rd day of November, 1894.

--------------------------------- X ---------------------------------

Beginning
the Practice of Law

One of the most important questions in a man's life is where he will locate and perform the work of his life, which is usually decided by circumstance or accident. The accident of birth at a certain place usually fixes the environment in which we will live and work. Like the acorn which falls from the parent tree, he usually takes root in the soil upon which he falls, and grows up with the forest around him. If opportunity were equal in every locality, this would be the ideal thing to do. Every man who tears himself up from the soil in which he first took root and transplants himself into a new environment loses something of the sympathetic relationship with relatives and the friends of his youth which he would have enjoyed in his natural environment.

Naturally, I would have preferred to locate in Marietta and serve the people who had been the inspiration of my youth, and whose love and regard had hovered about me, but my judgment admonished me that such location was not, under all the circumstances, wise. The Marietta bar was, at that time, dominated by the

Honorable A. S. Clay, who had been speaker of the House of Representatives and President of the Senate of Georgia, and his firm, Clay and Blair, had a monopoly on the best legal business in the Blue Ridge Circuit. J. Z. Foster, R. N. Holland, and John E. Mozeley were well established in practice and were still comparatively young men. George D. Anderson and his brother, William D. Anderson, N. A. Morris, and E. P. Green, all bright young men, had begun the practice of law before me. The amount of legal business was limited in Cobb County, and the profession seemed crowded. Besides Cobb County was a strongly political county torn by political factions, and political activity had always been a condition of legal success. I did not wish to become embroiled in factional strife and suffer political animosities. In the state of my finances, Atlanta was the only other possible location, and it seemed well nigh impossible. Operating concurrently with the desire to build my life and reputation upon local acquaintance and in my native environment was the urge to live at the center of things and relate myself to the larger life of the state. The great printing presses from which the news winged its way over the state were located in Atlanta; there was the seat of the government and of commercial power; there the great gatherings were held, where the leaders were heard; and there the great nerve cells of thought were located. Not that the genius of Georgia was located there exclusively, but thought, wherever in Georgia originated, found its best means of expression and distribution through the government, the press, the society, or the commerce of Atlanta. As I rode at night along the highlands around Lost Mountain, a faint glare beckoned alluringly on the southeastern horizon. Thus Rome called to the Latin youth from Lombardy to Apulia and Calabria, thus Paris from the Gironde to the Vosges, and thus London from Caithness to Cornwall. The country has been bled white of its native talent and power, and the pencil of the architect has forgotten its cunning to draw the rural mansion, in learning to design the skyscraper. It is not certain that Cobb County lost anything by my leaving it, or that Atlanta gained much by my coming to it; but my leaving the country for the city illustrates the age-long drift of population, greatly accelerated in America in the past forty years.

A favorite relative, my Uncle John N. McEachern, had lived in Atlanta for a few years and had organized an industrial insurance company which he believed would, properly managed, grow into a highly remunerative business. He came to Powder Springs and told me that he wished me to locate in Atlanta where I could be of legal assistance to him in building up his company, and said that if I would do so he would lend me any necessary financial assistance while acquiring a self-sustaining practice. This assurance on his part decided me to take the risk of trying to establish myself in a large city where I knew practically no one.

I came to Atlanta the last week in December, 1894, rented desk room in an office on the fourth floor of the Kiser Building, and went back to Powder Springs and Lost Mountain for the holidays, returning to begin my legal career on the first of January, 1895. My uncle was living in a boarding house operated by a Mrs. Washington, on the second floor of what was known as the Thrower Building, at the corner of Forsyth and Mitchell streets. Atlanta, at that time, was a place of about ninety thousand inhabitants, and the Thrower House was in a very respectable boarding-house section. The north side of Mitchell Street from Concordia Hall, which stood on the corner west to the railroad, was occupied by substantial old brick residences which were operated as some of the best boarding houses in the city. The block on the south side of Mitchell and the west side of Forsyth was occupied only by the old brick residence of Samuel M. Inman, standing in the midst of a great lawn surrounded by hedges. The Aragon Hotel and the Grand Opera House had just been built and were regarded as the limit of extravagant luxury.

The rate for a room and board at Mrs. Washington's was $4.00 a week with one to the room, or $3.50 a week with two in a room. My uncle and I occupied the same room and thus got the cheap rate. The boarders were all men, and while respectable and well behaved, were mostly clerks, installment furniture collectors, and money sharks. I do not think there was a book in the house. At night after supper the boarders told jokes and played set-back, except on the nights when they indulged themselves in gallery seats at the Grand. Anything more depressing and dreary than life in such a boarding house to a young man like myself who had spent a life in literary pursuits and had had the agreeable social surroundings which obtained at Powder Springs in that day, had never come within my experience.

The only law books I bought in the first few months of my lack of practice were the *Code of Georgia* and Silman and Thompson's *Form Book*. The only opportunity I had of putting either of these books to use was to study the *Code*, which I did earnestly and very thoroughly. A casual reading of the law of liens, with the remedies applicable to each, showed me that a thorough knowledge of the law of liens was essential; so I made a complete digest of the law of liens, and studied the sections of the Code containing this law until I had a complete knowledge of the subject. I employed the same method, so far as possible, to the other chapters of the code, and so fixed the numbers of the sections of the Code of 1882 in my mind that it was years after the Code of 1895 came out before I could use it with any facility.

The winter of 1895 was one of the coldest ever known in Atlanta. Snow fell to the depth of eight or ten inches during the early part of January, and before it had gone another heavy snow fell upon it, and the ground was covered for about six weeks. During this time sleigh bells tinkled in the streets, and business was practically suspended. The clerks in rival stores on Whitehall Street engaged in snow battles, while the clerks from the other stores stood in front of the buildings in which they were employed and looked on. Harry M. Reid, who had not then been elevated to the bench, and who had an office on the same floor of the Kiser Building with mine, came in to see me one day the latter part of February and said that not one person had been in his office during the month. If the weather had been good, it probably would not have brought me any business, but it was awfully depressing to sit all day, day after day, and wait, with rent and board going on.

About the only persons I knew when I came to Atlanta (besides my uncle) were Col. John B. Goodwin, the Mayor, who was a very useful friend to me; W. S. Duncan, a prosperous grain merchant who had formerly lived at Powder Springs; the members of the firm of Camp Brothers, also from Powder Springs; E. A. White, and his wife, formerly Addie Scott, old friends; and W. W. Gaines, Lowndes

Calhoun, and Walter P. Andrews, who had been schoolmates at Washington and Lee, and who were then practicing law in Atlanta.

The first case I ever tried was the defense of a writ for five dollars on a policy of industrial insurance filed by Henry Lincoln Johnson, a colored lawyer, noted as the National Committeeman of the Republican Party for Georgia. I moved to dismiss the action on account of the manner in which the action was brought, and the motion was sustained. I thus had the satisfaction of winning my first case, which I took as a good omen; but the petty nature of the case and the mean and sordid surroundings of the court filled me with disgust.

In 1895 four justice courts had concurrent jurisdiction throughout the limits of the City of Atlanta. The territory north of the railroads comprised the 1234th district, and the territory on the south comprised the 1026th district. There was a justice of the peace and a notary public *ex officio* justice of the peace in each district. In the 1234th district S. H. Landrum was justice of the peace, and on the south side these offices were held respectively by Edgar H. Orr and J. G. Bloodworth. Their court days were, respectively, the first, second, third, and fourth Mondays in each month. The courtrooms were dingy halls, with a back room in which the cheap goods seized upon levies were stored. On Monday of each week in the year, a jam of lawyers stood for perhaps two hours while the dockets were called and the cases assigned. In this crowd of lawyers were most of the younger members of the bar and a few older practitioners whose whole professional life had not carried them beyond the petty litigation of these minor tribunals. Among the most interesting of the justice court specialists were "Peanut" Johnson, A. A. Manning, and Morris Macks. They did not know much law, but they knew every technicality of justice court procedure, and it was woe to the man who made the slightest slip in procedure or proof when they were on the other side. The jurisdiction of justice courts was limited in amount to one hundred dollars. The cases were mostly suits on merchants' accounts, money shark debts, distress warrants, attachments for purchase money, and actions for installment furniture dealers, foreclosures of mortgages on personal property, and garnishments of the salaries of laborers. The petty nature of the actions, and the fact that most of them were against the poor, the unfortunate, and the improvident, made the practice distasteful. However, the experience was valuable, and young lawyers had to serve an apprenticeship in these courts, and were to a large extent dependent upon the meager fees earned in them for subsistence while acquiring a sufficient acquaintance to get business in the Superior Court. Another source of income was from the making of abstracts of title. This work was not quite so irritating as plowing a contrary horse in a rocky field, but for drudgery and torture it takes high rank. The indexes at that time gave only the names of the grantor and the grantee, with no indication of the property conveyed, and it was necessary to examine every deed made by a particular grantee to see whether he had made more than one deed to the same piece of property. John R. Wallace had made more than three thousand deeds, and when his name appeared in the chain of title, it was necessary to pull down every book and examine every deed in which he was indexed, either as grantee or grantor. Sometimes an abstract would take a whole week, and when finished, the usual fee was ten or fifteen dollars. During the first year I did not get a chance to make a fee even at this laborious task. My practice consisted of a few collections and a few justice court cases, my earnings amounting to less than one hundred dollars.

In the latter part of July, or in August, my health completely broke down, and I went back to my father's home at Lost Mountain. I sat around the house a few days, and then had to take to bed. I sent for Dr. W. D. Wright, who lived about a mile away; and when he came, he told me that I had typhoid fever in a very dangerous form. I grew rapidly worse, and in a few days I was desperately ill. The nature of my sickness was what is known as typhoid hemorrhagic fever. Great black spots appeared all over my body, and I had severe hemorrhages. My gums bled so fast that I could hardly expectorate the blood as fast as it collected in my mouth. Dr. Wright quit his other practice and spent his whole time with me. At night he would make a pallet by my bed, and sleep there where he could give me attention at a moment's notice. One day he came to my bedside and told me that he had done all he could for me, and that if I did not take a turn for the better in a short time I would not live. He asked me if I knew of any other physician that I would prefer for him to call. I suggested Dr. R. R. Murray at Powder Springs, and my father went for him. Dr. Murray told my father that he was so much my friend and that my case was so desperate that he did not wish to take the responsibility, and suggested that he get the best physician possible. My father then went to Marietta and told Dr. Malone my condition, and he came at once. After he and Dr. Wright had examined me, they went outside under the trees and held a long consultation. I lay and watched them and knew that it meant life or death. After a while they came back, and Dr. Malone told me that he was giving me a prescription which, if I could take for twenty-four hours, would stop the bleeding, and cautioned me that my life depended on my keeping my nerve for two or three days. One night, about three days later, my heart would palpitate violently for a few minutes and then stop; and I would alternately flush up with a burning fever, and then become cold. I realized that I was in what I had heard referred to as the crisis of fever. During the first part of the night, the doctor and those assisting him would put hot cloths on me when I would have extreme chills, and ice packs when I would flush up with fever. About midnight I fell into a profound sleep, and when I awoke the next morning I looked up at Uncle George McElreath, who had sat all night watching me, and said, "Uncle George, I am well." He said, "I know it; I saw the change come over you while you slept." I had a long convalescence, and was not able to return to Atlanta until the first of November.

Sickness, such as I had, has its compensations. When in good health we sometimes feel that nobody cares for us. While I was sick, practically everybody that I knew in the western part of Cobb County came to see me. Nearly all of my old pupils came. People came from Marietta, Powder Springs, Douglasville, and Atlanta, and my room was banked with flowers. Since then I have loved humanity with a new love, and know that under the seeming indifference of people there is a divine sympathy.

A week or two before I was taken sick, I had visited Miss Anderson at Sweetwater Park Hotel, at Lithia Springs, and found that the friendly regard I had had for her was ripening into a deeper feeling; but I had said nothing of my feeling to her because my circumstances were such that I did not think I could, in fairness, ask any woman to commit herself to me. All of the other young women of my acquaintance had come to see me, and I felt that she might hes-

itate to do so as it might be construed as an advance on her part. I
sent her a note and told her that I would appreciate a visit from her,
and she came immediately.

As was said above, extreme illness has its compensations. These
are not all in the receipt of kindnesses. There is spiritual profit in
coming face to face with death. This came to me. I could see
through the window the physicians in consultation; I read the fears
of friends in their eyes and their countenances; I saw my father
walk away from the doctor, and I heard him sobbing in uncontrollable anguish, before he came and sat down by the bed and said,
"You are the oldest of the children and we have all looked up to you,
and we cannot bear to lose you." When he went out, I was left alone
for a short time and I said to myself aloud, "O Richard, *O mon Roi,
l'universe t' abandonne*" ("Oh, Richard, Oh my King, the world is all
forsaking thee"). The feeling I had was not a feeling of fear, but a
feeling of self-pity that all the work I had done was to go for nothing, and that all the hopes I had cherished were to be frustrated—
that the world was forsaking me. I lay for a long time reviewing my
life, and finally made up my mind that I would not yield to fear; that
I would not lose consciousness; but that I would grimly fight for life
to the last gasp. Dr. Wright afterwards told me that this was all that
saved me; that if I had become excited or had given up, it would
have been impossible for me to get well.

It has been forty-five years since that illness, but everything
connected with it stamped itself so indelibly upon some faculty of
consciousness as to become part of me. I often doze off into semi-
consciousness at night and see that angel of mercy, our neighbor,
Mrs. Martin, whose presence in a sickroom was worth more than
any doctor as she sat watching; and the homely face of Dr. Wright
comes to me at night; and at times on the crowded streets, I smell
the flowers and see the young lady friends of the countryside who
brought them; and I often imagine I hear the screech owls that sang
their eerie songs in the long nights. As I lay awake at nights during
convalescence, I studied and studied about the problems of
whether I could start law again, and considered giving up the law
and returning to teaching. I do not think that there have been six
months since then when I have not dreamed over these same

thoughts, and have waked up with a shock of surprise that it was a dream.

When I went home I carried all the money I had left, and told the family to use it for me and the family. It was well that I had it, for in that day country people had little money in the summertime. When the crops were sold in the fall, a little money was usually kept to buy small items for which cash was paid, but by August it was usually gone. When I got ready to come back to Atlanta, I did not have a cent in the world. My father had sold some cotton, and I borrowed five dollars from him; and with that as my only capital, I came back to Atlanta to make a new start at the age of twenty-eight years. When I got back to Atlanta, I found that my uncle John McEachern had bought a nice new home on Oglethorpe Avenue in West End and had moved his father and my Aunt Lizzie into it, and he asked me to live with them. My grandfather was very old, entirely helpless, and childish with senility. After life at Mrs. Washington's boarding house, to be again at home and with my own people was like heaven to me.

In the spring before I got sick, I rented an office in the old Gate City Bank Building jointly with the spiritual first cousin of the Arkansas Traveler who was my roommate at Washington and Lee. While I was sick the office which he had occupied was taken over for repairs on the building, and my books and desk were moved up to another office. I had a fine roller-top desk. My old officemate had been told that I would not get well; and so he pried open my desk and took my papers out. When I got back he was sitting in my swivel chair, and using my desk as his own. I decided that he and I were not highly congenial; so I rented another office. When I started to move my desk, he demanded ten dollars for rent on it and my books, all of which he had been using for his own convenience and profit, and which the building would have stored for nothing. I paid it. I have been called an unforgiving man; but he lived for several years after that time, and died a natural death.

During the fall of 1895 the great Cotton States and International Exposition was held in Atlanta. The beauty of the buildings and grounds, the wonder of the exhibits, the vast crowds, and the splendor of the illuminations at night made a show such as few of the people of Georgia had ever seen. The railroad yards were jammed every morning with trains that brought enormous crowds. The streets were crowded all day long. Every conceivable kind of fakir bartered his wares. Dime museums flourished on every street. One of these was levied upon, and Judge Orr had several mummies in his storeroom awaiting a bailiff's sale. Vast stucco hotels stood on Fourteenth Street, and there were several in various parts of the city. I had no law practice, and therefore plenty of time to visit the Exposition; and when I was not at the Exposition grounds, I spent a great deal of time on the streets looking at the strange crowds — American Indians, Circassians, Hindus, Japanese, and people from every corner of the globe — who had come as professional midway entertainers or fakirs.

While the Exposition was in progress, a great religious meeting was held in a large tabernacle on Williams Street under the direction of Dwight L. Moody. The structure in which the meeting was held seated possibly six thousand people, and it was filled at each service. The fame of the great preacher made him somewhat of an exhibit, like the attractions of the Exposition itself, many of those attending doing so out of curiosity to hear the great preacher. But there was something about the meeting besides the show; there was certainly much religious sentiment and feeling. I attended the meeting several times and observed and studied the great preacher. He had a strong, but not particularly agreeable voice. He was not an orator, according to any of the usual conceptions of oratory. He was evidently not a man of much education, and in his manner and delivery exhibited few of the graces of culture; but there was about him an earnestness which showed that he was completely absorbed in his work. I saw him frequently on the streets, going from place to place where he held services during the day. He was always alone and carried his limp-backed Bible under his arm, and seemed like a man in a dream. From my observation of him, he impressed me as a perfect example of what a man, although of mediocre natural powers, can do if he is deadly in earnest, has one idea, and is completely absorbed in it.

When I returned to Atlanta after my sickness, I rented an office on the seventh floor of the Temple Court Building, which was at that time the building in which most of the leading law firms of the city had their offices. The principal firms in the building at that time were N. J. and T. A. Hammond, King and Spalding, B. H. and C. D. Hill, Glenn & Rountree, James A. Anderson, Westmoreland Brothers, John B. Goodwin, Mayson & Hill, and many younger lawyers. O. E. and M. C. Horton shared the office with me. O. E. Horton had started practice about the same time I did, and had been engaged by another firm to examine land titles for them. I was pretty soon employed to make an abstract. Horton very kindly aided me in making it, and I soon became one of the toilers of the record room. A little practice began to come, my acquaintances began to grow, and in a few months I was making, perhaps, about twenty-five dollars a month.

In the spring of 1896 I became engaged to Miss Anderson, who was at that time teaching music at Centenary Female College at Cleveland, Tennessee. This contract at the time was of the nature of an executory contract, the final consummation of which was only a contingent possibility, the contingency being the possibility of my increasing my earnings to such an extent as to render consummation possible. My uncle John McEachern, with whom I lived, became engaged about the same time, and proposed that we both get married in the fall. He married early in the fall, and my income having risen to about sixty dollars a month, I decided to take a gambler's chance; and finding my affianced willing to join in the desperate enterprise, with the help of the Rev. Dr. David Sullins, the partnership of Queen Bess and Sir Walter was formed on Thanksgiving Day, November 26, 1896; and this logically closes this chapter in the life of the hero of these chronicles.

XI

Queen Bess
and Home

Our honeymoon trip began at Powder Springs immediately after the marriage ceremony, and ended at a modest but neat five-room cottage which I had rented and partially furnished at 560 Woodward Avenue in Atlanta. Arriving in Atlanta about noon, we dined with my uncle.

Our cottage was comparatively new, and we were able, by scheming, to get the utmost value for every cent expended to furnish it—cheaply, to be sure, but neatly and comfortably—and we were very proud of it.

The serious problem was to support ourselves in it, and to pay the rent. The country had not recovered from the panic of 1893; and even those lawyers who had practiced long enough to have an established clientele were having a hard time. I had practically no established business, and such business as I was able to get was of a minor character. I had borrowed sixty dollars to get married on; and my wife had three hundred dollars with which to complete the furnishing of the house, and to supply casual deficiencies of revenue necessary to pay household expenses.

Under these circumstances our marriage was certainly a reckless and desperate adventure; and the first two years of our married life were years of desperate struggle, and often of heart-rending anxiety on my part; but they were happy years. I was occasionally employed to make an abstract of title, for which I received an average fee of ten dollars, made an occasional collection, tried a few justice court cases, and managed during the first year of our married life to earn about four hundred dollars. My wife, who had been a teacher of music in Centenary College at Cleveland, Tennessee, for two or three days of each week walked two miles to the neighborhood of North Boulevard and Jackson Street where she had secured a few music pupils, from whose tuition fees she supplemented our meager income. Without her aid we could not have supported ourselves during those trying years. But goods were cheap at that time—a quarter sack of flour costing sixty-five cents, and a good, fat hen could be bought for a quarter. We bought for cash and practiced the strictest economy; but despite our utmost effort to make every dime count, the larder sometimes came dangerously near to emptiness. At such times I would pick out a number of delinquent grocery bills which A. J. Thomason, a grocer at 700 Marietta Street, had given me for collection, and would tramp, sometimes for miles, presenting them until I would eventually make a small collection, and with the commission earned, stop on my way home and buy a twenty-four-pound sack of flour and a quarter's worth of steak.

My brother, Emmett, who had graduated in law at the University of Georgia, came to Atlanta in the fall of 1896, a few months before our marriage, and entered the practice of law with me as a partner, the firm name being McElreath & McElreath. Upon our marriage, he came to live with us.

My brother and I applied ourselves to the practice with all the earnestness and diligence possible, and soon acquired a few clients who retained us on yearly contracts, but usually upon outrageously small retainers. The first client who employed us on an annual retainer was the West Lumber Company, which we contracted to represent for a retainer of fifty dollars a year. We were also retained by two or three small loan companies at the same yearly rate.

During these first years our practice was largely confined to the justice courts, an institution now fortunately abolished. The story of their abolition and the writer's part in it will be told in a later chapter. We despised the character of the business in which we had to engage; but "beggars cannot be choosers," and consequently we took what practice we could get, and tried so to handle every case that came to us, however small the amount involved, as to win the confidence of our clients and the respect of the courts in which we tried cases. Although our practice was of this poor character, we did not resort to barratry or any form of sharp practice, and soon had the confidence of the judges of the courts before whom we practiced.

Young lawyers in Atlanta still have a hard time in getting established, but not as hard as those who were struggling for a foothold in 1896. The tremendous increase in population and the more than corresponding increase in business have brought about the organization of great firms in which juniors are necessary, and there are many openings for diligent and capable young men. In 1896 most of the young lawyers were compelled to go it alone, and to eat the crumbs that fell from some large firms that had business too unprofitable for them to handle, which they transferred to younger members of the bar. During this time many young men struggled for a while and then fell out of the race. When I now think of the young men who were practicing in Atlanta at that time, or came to the bar in the next few years, it is sad to realize how few were successful. Among those who began the practice at about the time I came to the bar and who have made conspicuous successes, I think of John D. Humphries and Edgar E. Pomeroy, now judges of the Superior Court; William Schley Howard, who came to the bar two or three years later, and who in addition to representing the Fifth District in Congress, has become a noted criminal lawyer; Eugene and Harry Dodd; William A. Fuller; Hugh M. Dorsey, for two years Governor of the State and now one of the judges of the Superior Court; Wharton O. Wilson, Harvey Hatcher, Shepard Bryan, and W. W. Gaines. There are several others who preceded me by only a few years, and many others who came to the bar

within a short time afterwards, who have been eminently successful, but who are not strictly my contemporaries as entrants to the
profession, and therefore are not here mentioned.

While mentioning my early associates in the practice, I cannot
forebear to mention O. E. Horton and his brother Millard. As
stated before, they were my officemates in the Temple Court Building in 1896 and for a year or two later. These brothers were not universally popular, but it was never my good fortune to be associated
with men of finer character. They were scrupulously honest, fair
and correct in all of their dealings, and until the death of O. E. Horton in 1934, I had no truer or more trusted friend.

One of the first cases of real importance I handled was a case
for a blind Negro named D. Brinkley. For several years before this
time, William C. Hale, a promoter, had operated in Atlanta and had
organized a number of allied companies—a so-called building and
loan association, an insurance company, a bank—the State Savings
Bank—and he was also largely engaged in real estate operations.
Finally the whole scheme of his operations collapsed, and he ab-
sconded. Brinkley had bought a small house and lot on Old Wheat
Street, and was paying for it on the installment plan. He was a de-
positor in the State Savings Bank, and there was a question
whether his deposits had been properly applied to the notes on his
real estate which were held by the bank. Foreclosure was threat-
ened, and I filed a bill in equity and enjoined the foreclosure. I finally secured an adjustment of the payments and negotiated a new
loan for him to take up the payments justly due, and thus saved the
old Negro's home.

Brinkley was a most remarkable character. He made his living
buying and selling old bottles, which he collected by training a
small Negro boy to go about with him singing in the quaint style
peculiar to the Negro race. Into the byways of the city he would go,
and wherever he stopped a crowd would collect about him. Brinkley would then offer to buy all of the bottles the Negroes had about
their houses, giving a few pennies for a dozen bottles which he sold
to junk dealers at a higher price, in this way making a few dollars a
week. After I had secured the loan necessary to save his home, he
came to me and asked me to take his money and save it for him. I
gave him a passbook, and each week he brought me his earnings,

which I took and entered on his passbook, giving him money when he required it, and thus acted as his private banker as long as he lived. He paid off the loan on his home when it was due, and owned it at the time of his death. Of all the clients I have ever had, I never felt towards any other of them the same degree of responsibility I felt to this old Negro who, in his state of total blindness, in the cold of winter and the heat of summer, plied his simple trade, collecting and saving nickels, dimes, and pennies and bringing them to me as his trusted friend to take care of for him; and I have no professional satisfaction greater than the service I rendered him, practically without reward.

D. Brinkley's case brought me into contact with one of the most celebrated trials which has occurred in Georgia in the past forty-five years. When I had prepared the bill in the Brinkley case, I found that the judge of the Superior Court of the Atlanta Circuit was not in the circuit, and I therefore took the bill to Decatur to present it to Judge John S. Candler, then judge of the Stone Mountain Circuit. At that time DeKalb County did not have its present magnificent courthouse, the old courthouse being an ancient and dilapidated brick structure with a stairway on the outside of the building, which stood on the site of the present courthouse. When I reached Decatur I found the courthouse surrounded with a cordon of state militia who would not let anybody pass without a permit. In the courtroom upstairs Flannigan was being tried for an atrocious murder committed a few months before in the town of East Lake. It was in this case that W. C. Glenn, an extraordinarily brilliant attorney of the Atlanta Bar, won his great fame as a criminal lawyer. I finally persuaded the commanding officer of the militia to admit me; and after securing an order on my bill, I spent the rest of the afternoon listening to the legal duel between Mr. Glenn and the Honorable Hal G. Lewis, later a justice of the Supreme Court of Georgia.

About the time of which I am writing, I formed one of the most valuable friendships of my life in forming the acquaintance of Colonel John C. Reed, who was the most scholarly lawyer I ever knew. He was reared at Lexington, Georgia, came to the bar just after the close of the War Between the States, and practiced in the same circuits with Robert Toombs and Alexander H. Stephens. He was a graduate of Princeton University, and was extraordinarily versed in the classics and in modern literature, and was one of the best Shakespearean scholars I ever knew. His *American Law Studies* was a monumental but not successful book. His *Conduct of Law Suits* is a legal classic. The publisher's note to the last edition says: "When an author has reached such a point of excellence that his work is beyond criticism and is accorded universal praise, it would seem eminently wise to leave his book unmarred by further effort to improve it." Professor Wigmore in his introduction to the second edition says: "This is the kind of book whose substance every young lawyer should commit to memory. I mean that statement literally — when a book is as good as this on every page, the pains are worth the bestowing." His book *The Brother's War* is a very profound study of the causes of the War Between the States. The chapter on Robert Toombs could hardly be excelled. Himself a leader of the old Ku Klux Klan and a participant in the postbellum fight to preserve the social and political rights of the South, Colonel Reed speaks in this book with authority. Trained as he was in the fundamental science of the law, on account of his profound legal studies and natural abilities, he was that rare thing — a real lawyer.

Excepting genius, which is exceptional and subject to no fixed rule, the legal mind is the highest form of mentality. It must be able to conceive an abstract principle clearly, and to exactly relate it to a set of practical facts. No two sets of facts are exactly alike in their combination and relation; but the perfect legal mind (if there is any) will clearly see the underlying fundamental principle and deduce the right result from a tangled skein of facts. The legal mind must be an impartial mind, honest, and just. The mere case lawyer is never a great lawyer, for the reason that each decision is based on a certain combination of facts and, as stated before, no two cases present exactly the same combination and relation of facts.

Colonel Reed had all of the qualities of a great lawyer, except that he was slightly pedantic and too theoretical from having studied abstract law so intensely. He knew underlying principles of law accurately, his mind was quick, active, and penetrating, and he was intellectually honest; but he could not quite bend down to the ordinary juror, and, it might be said, the ordinary judge, at all times. He had a good library of old English law books and the great American textbooks. These, with the *Georgia Reports* and the *Reports of the Supreme Court of the United States*, with which he had a remarkable familiarity, were his only authorities.

Soon after I came to the bar Colonel Reed removed his office to one adjoining mine, and I soon began to discuss my cases with him. If I was on the wrong track, he would immediately convince me of the fact and set my feet in the right path. Under his guidance, I began to dig back to first principles in every case that came to me, and to gain what seemed to me a facility of discrimination in distinguishing cases, not only useful, but delightful, as well; and I came to love the law as I have never loved any other literature or science. I have always felt that association with Colonel Reed was the equivalent to me of a regular course of study at a good law school.

The first few years of a lawyer's experience are made up of about ten percent practical business and ninety percent waiting. His ultimate success depends quite as much on how he spends the waiting portion of his time as what he does with the other portion. If he studies incessantly, reads the reports of the appellate courts as they come out, and is forever on the alert to observe the methods of the successful, experienced members of the profession, keenly watches the mistakes of the inefficient to avoid them, studies law every spare moment, particularly procedure and the quick and accurate drafting of legal documents, opportunity will sooner or later knock at his door, and at the most unexpected time.

When I came to Atlanta I knew only a few people, and at the time of my marriage my acquaintance was still very limited; but the few people my wife and I knew were people of high character and good standing. We joined and regularly attended Trinity Methodist Church, and through social and professional contacts and relatives we soon had quite a nice circle of friends.

One of the methods adopted for increasing my acquaintance was the organization of a Cobb County Club. The people of my old county have always had, and at that time had more than now, an unusually strong pride and a sort of clannish spirit. There were a very large number of former Cobb County people in Atlanta, some of them prominent in business and politics. Among these were the Honorable John B. Goodwin, who had for several terms been Mayor of Atlanta and was regarded as the Warwick of city politics;

James G. Woodward, who was at that time a member of the City Council, and later Mayor of the City; John Tyler Cooper, a former mayor; and Captain W. R. Joyner, Chief of the Atlanta Fire Department. Among the prominent professional men were Dr. T. V. Hubbard, Dr. J. W. Hurt, and Dr. N. W. Gober. Among the prominent businessmen were W. S. Duncan, Milt and Coleman Camp, cousins of my wife, James Warren, J. Bulow Campbell, and Collins M. Frazer. Besides those mentioned there were Cobb County men in the city in all walks of life.

The club did not survive very long; but through its organization and meetings, I became well known to the members of the club and to many old Cobb County residents who did not join the club. Years later in canvassing as a candidate for the legislature, whenever I met a man from Cobb County, he would immediately say—"I am a Cobb County man too, and I am for you." So far as I know I received the vote of every old Cobb County man in the county.

Notwithstanding the fact that my wife and I walked everywhere we went to save carfare, and Emmett and I usually carried our lunches to the office, by the fall of 1898 I had become ninety dollars in arrears in rent, and was expecting to be put out of the house. My landlord was W. A. Vernoy, who operated a large whiskey saloon on North Pryor Street, where the Ten Pryor Street Building now stands. One day when I was in a state of desperate anxiety about my rent, I went to Mr. Vernoy's place of business and told him that I had come to find out what he was going to do about my indebtedness. Without replying directly to my question, he asked me if I could make an abstract of title. When I told him that I could, he gave me the papers on a piece of real estate he had bargained for, and I set to work immediately and finished the abstract in two or three days. He gave me a credit for fifteen dollars, and when I carried the final papers to him, he stated that he had bargained for another tract. When I examined the title to this tract, I found an outstanding interest in one Sarah Holroyd, which I reported to him, and told him that the title was defective without the signature of the party in whose name the outstanding interest stood. In a few days he sent for me, and told me that the old lady who held the outstanding interest lived somewhere in Augusta, Georgia, and that he was informed that she would sign a quit-claim deed for a nominal sum. He opened the cash register and took out a twenty dollar bill, handed it to me, and asked me to go to Augusta and see the old lady, telling me that he understood that I could find her through Platt, the undertaker, and stating that if I would make the trip and get the quit-claim, he would pay me seventy-five dollars. I took the train that night; and when I arrived in Augusta the next morning I called on Mr. Platt, who kindly took me in his carriage to an obscure street on the banks of the Augusta Canal, where I found a very old English woman who readily signed the deed which I had prepared. So when I arrived back in Atlanta and reported my success, my rent was paid. I have had the experience many times in life — often in the vastly larger matters, when adverse circumstances seem like an insurmountable wall — that at the very moment when everything seems hopeless, something will suddenly happen which solves all of the difficulty in a seemingly providential manner.

While our two years on Woodward Avenue (1897-1898) were years of desperate anxiety, and what now seems privation, they were not dull years by any means, but were years in which happiness predominated over hardship. We had youth, good health and hope, and more than all, they were the years when the great adventure of marriage was fresh. On Sundays we would walk through the paths of the primeval forest, which then extended unbroken from Woodward Avenue to Grant Park, and frequently we took a weekend trip to Powder Springs to visit my wife's mother, and to Lost Mountain to visit my father's family. We attended Trinity Methodist Church for Sunday services, went to all of the lectures of the Atlanta Lecture Association we could afford, and an occasional musical concert. When I look back on those years, even their hardships seem pleasant; and I understand the meaning of the poet, who, describing Aeneas in the storm into which he had been driven by the scorn of jilted Dido, makes his hero say — *"Forsan et haec olim forsitan meminisse juvabit"* — ("sometimes perhaps it may be pleasant to remember these things").

Our relatives paid us frequent visits. They did not come so often as to be unwelcome, and did not stay so long as to be tiresome and expensive, and we were always pleased to see them, particularly my wife's mother, who was one of the gentlest and sweetest women who ever lived.

The year 1898 was replete with interest. In February the *Maine* was blown up in the Havana harbor, and from that day until the declaration of war on April 25th, the daily papers were awaited with tense and expectant interest. I shall never forget the thrill that shot through me when Mrs. McElreath, who arose before I did, brought me the *Atlanta Constitution* carrying the story of Dewey's victory over the Spanish fleet in Manila Bay on May 1, 1898. Soon after the declaration of war, the trains began to pass through the city loaded with troops bound for Cuba; long freight trains carrying "embalmed" beef jammed the railroad yards; companies of local volunteers were organized, some of which got as far as Griffin, Georgia. The hotel lobbies were resplendent with officers dressed in gaudy uniforms of those pre-khaki days; distinguished generals stopped on their way south and were feted; William J. Bryan rode the streets in the full panoply of war as the colonel of a regiment. Extras came out as fast as the newspapers could gather or manufacture any news to print. But the sorry little war which then appeared great to the American people was soon over. By the 17th of July the battles of El Caney and San Juan Hill had been fought, the naval battle of Santiago Bay had resulted in the destruction of the Spanish navy, the city of Santiago had surrendered. On August 12, a peace protocol was signed.

In July, 1898, just after the victories of the Spanish-American War, and while the martial spirit of the people was at its height, a Confederate reunion was held in Atlanta. For two or three days before the reunion opened, people poured into the city from all parts of the South. When the day for the opening of the reunion came, there was probably not a vacant room in the city. Tents had to be erected at Piedmont Park. The churches and the public buildings were opened for visitors to occupy and sleep in them, as best they could. The private homes were crowded with visitors.

On the last day of the reunion a monstrous parade was held under the command of General John B. Gordon. The parade formed somewhere out near Piedmont Park, and marched down Peachtree and Broad streets to where General Gordon sat on his horse reviewing the old grey lines as they passed him. Before the parade was half over a terrific rainstorm set in which lasted until after the parade was over, but this did not in the slightest degree interfere with the parade; in fact, the old soldier seemed to enjoy it.

Although General Gordon had been in ill health a short time before the reunion, he sat on his horse at the corner of Broad and Marietta streets with the superb martial spirit which made him the idol of his old comrades, his hat in his hand, and streams of water running down his grey locks. Mrs. McElreath and I had secured a place at a window on the second floor of a building near General Gordon's station, and we watched the old veterans salute and yell as they passed the General, who was taking the rain like themselves.

In the fall of 1898 a great peach jubilee was held in Atlanta which was attended by President McKinley. There was an immense crowd in the city on that occasion, but not so great a crowd as at the Confederate reunion. The President held a public reception at the state capitol, standing at the foot of the stairs in front of the Supreme Court room to shake hands with those who filed past him. My wife and I were in the crowd, and I was particularly anxious to shake hands with the President on account of the fact that he was a distant relative; but the crowd was so dense and the press so great that we could not reach him.

In the fall of 1898 I was employed by a client about some matter, the nature of which I do not now recall, and when I had concluded it, he stated that he owned a cottage at 66 East Avenue which he would be glad to have me rent. This cottage was located in the community where my wife's music pupils lived, and was a community of some more dignity than Woodward Avenue, the scale of social prestige then, as now, tipping to the north side. We accepted this offer and moved into our second home.

XII

My First Home
on the North Side

Our second home was a five-room frame cottage at 66 East Avenue which had been built during the days of the boom which struck that part of the city in the later 1880s, and which had been arrested by the panic of 1893. At the time of our removal to that section there were many large, handsome and, for that day, expensive homes on North Boulevard and Jackson Street, and on that part of Houston Street between Jackson Street and North Boulevard. These houses stood far apart, only one or two to the block, with vacant lots between evidencing the fact of arrested development. North of North Avenue and south of Ponce de Leon Avenue there was no house east of Jackson Street. All of that area was unbroken forest, except that on the south side of Ponce de Leon Avenue between Glen Iris and the Southern Railroad, and extending back south so as to comprise a tract of about ten acres, was an amusement park known as Ponce de Leon Springs. Ponce de Leon Springs was about where the east end of the present Sears-Roebuck Building now stands. This park was a popular resort for the population of Atlanta in those days before the automobile had made the whole wide country an accessible pleasure ground, and it was a favorite place for lovers to hold their trysts.

Ponce de Leon Avenue ended at the Southern Railroad, and east of it the country was all farm lands and forest. Druid Hills existed only in the imagination of that farseeing promoter, Joel Hurt.

The homes on Houston and Jackson streets and North Boulevard were occupied by some of the most prominent and well-to-do people of the city, not the nouveau riche and social strugglers, the latter of which lived on Peachtree. Captain John A. Miller, head of the Brady-Miller Stables, lived in opulent style at the northwest corner of Houston and Jackson streets; Captain John C. Hendrix, on the northeast corner of Houston Street and the Boulevard; and W. M. Terry, on the west side of the Boulevard between Cain Street and Highland Avenue. Levi B. Nelson lived in a great brick house located in the center of the block where the Georgia Baptist Hospital now stands. The large home of Judge John L. Hopkins was at the northeast corner of the Boulevard and Angier Avenue; and the smaller home of his son, Charles T. Hopkins, was next door to his father's. Colonel William S. Thomson's home was about two blocks further north on the Boulevard. The block bounded by the Boulevard, Angier Avenue and extending back south to about where Forrest Avenue is now located, consisting of about four acres, was occupied by the old A. M. Reinhart home. At the corner of Angier Avenue and Jackson Street there was a very large, handsome and costly home, then owned and occupied by J. B. Redwine, at that time the principal money shark of the city. When the fortune built upon loans at 10 percent a month slipped from him, as fortunes so gained usually do, his home was bought and occupied by Dr. Charles E. Murphy, one of the city's most prominent and best-loved physicians. The less prominent people and those of smaller means lived on Johnson Avenue, Randolph Street, Highland Avenue, east of Boulevard, East Avenue, Rice Street, Angler Avenue, Morgan Street, and Pine Street, which at that time were very respectable streets.

East Avenue, at the time we moved upon it, was unpaved, and in dry weather consisted of gulleys and dust, and in wet weather, of gulleys and mud; and the mud was so deep that the grocery wagons frequently had to stop at the Boulevard, from which their drivers had to carry their goods down the avenue in their arms.

Our house stood up on brick pillars, on a bleak lot, and was heated by small grates. On February 8, 1899, the ground was covered with several inches of snow and the thermometer dropped to eight degrees below zero. The cold welled up through the thin flooring and crawled through the cracks around the doors and windows, so that the little basket grates, which were our only means of heating, did not seem to affect the temperature beyond a few feet from the fire. Thousands of homes in the city were less comfortable than ours, and the suffering of thousands of people was intense.

Our home had no electric lights, but was lighted by gas. We had a tin bath tub, with no way to heat the water except to heat enough water on a stove and pour in enough to make the bath at least warm enough to bear in cold weather.

But as ill-equipped as our home then was, without the comforts and conveniences which are now common, it was well-planned, well-built with tight ceilings and large rooms, and was perhaps equal to the average habitation of the people of moderate means in the city of Atlanta at that time. This description and these details are given to illustrate both the improvement of my personal circumstances and the general improvement in domestic comfort in the past forty years. This is a story which the people of this discontented age should know, and upon which they should carefully reflect when inclined to carp at present conditions.

When we first moved to East Avenue, I rented the house at seventeen dollars a month, and continued to pay rent at that rate until I bought the house on January 4, 1904, for twenty-three hundred dollars, paying three hundred dollars cash, and giving notes for the balance, which I succeeded in paying in three or four years. After I had bought the house I began to improve it and, from time to time, as I could spare the money, I continued to make improvements on it, until it was finally made into a very attractive and comfortable cottage. Whenever we could spare the money we bought new furniture, a piece at a time, and my wife bought pictures out of the money which she earned in giving music lessons. One of the pictures which we acquired at this time (if it may be properly classed as a picture) was the exquisite intaglio by Orrion Frazer which is now in my present home.

Before we removed from East Avenue our little home was the subject of complimentary remarks by everyone who visited it. Nothing else that I ever did—no success at the bar or in politics— ever gave me a pleasure equal to that which I experienced when I could provide the means for my wife to buy a new rug or piece of furniture and observe the joy that it gave her. I doubt that if we had had a fortune when we married and could have immediately gone into a mansion on Peachtree, we would have been as happy as we were in earning the things we longed for, gradually, and by our own efforts.

Somebody who may read these lines may think my recital of the making of our home trivial, but I do not think so. The home and the woman and the children in it are the most important things in a man's life.

> *To make a happy fireside clime*
> *For weans and wife,*
> *Is the true pathos and sublime*
> *Of human life.*

When the Spanish-American War was over and the treaty of peace signed on December 10, 1898, the country began to emerge from the panic of 1893 and the severe depression which had followed. Depressions often come with a sudden crash—like that which ushered in the short but severe panic of 1907, and the depression which began with the collapse of the stock market in 1929— but they pass away, by a slow and, at first, imperceptible movement which gradually gains momentum. The population of Atlanta in 1900 was 89,872. In 1898 the first major revival of operations in the city, after the passing of the depression following the panic of 1893, was the construction of what was first known as the Prudential Building, now known as the Grant Building. It was soon followed by the Flatiron Building at the junction of Peachtree and Broad streets; and then came in quick succession, about 1902, the Candler Building, the Atlanta National Bank Building, the Peters Building, the Whitehall Viaduct, and the Austell Building. With the beginning of this new era, new homes began to be built in the Fourth Ward, and in a very few years practically every vacant lot in the ward was built upon; and the Jackson Hill community, as the section in which we lived was known, became one of the best and most delightful communities in the city. The people on Jackson Hill were fine, prosperous, churchgoing people, cordial, friendly, and all of about the same social grade, who associated with each other on terms of the most delightful social equality and friendliness. So high was the moral tone of the community that when any moral issue was involved in any city election, it was a foregone conclusion that the Fourth Ward would be on the moral side of the issue.

When we moved to East Avenue, the only white church in the ward was Grace Methodist Church, located on Boulevard, between Houston and Cain streets, whose pastor, at that time, was Dr. W. F. Quillian. My wife and I began to attend Grace Methodist Church as soon as we moved to the north side, but we kept our membership at Trinity Church until some time in the fall of 1899, when we transferred our membership to Grace. Although I was by this time more than thirty years old, I took no part for some time in the activities of the church. My wife, who was naturally as timid and shy of strangers as I, but who had better religious training and a deeper religious sense, joined the Epworth League, the missionary society, and soon became a member of the choir. After a year or two I began to take some part in the activities of the church, and in 1902 or 1903, to my surprise, I was appointed to membership on the Board of Stewards, of which I have been a member from that day to this, and for nineteen years I was its chairman.

In 1906 Grace Church abandoned its old location and erected a very handsome brick church at the corner of Highland Avenue and Boulevard. About this time Jackson Hill Baptist Church was built at the corner of East Avenue and Jackson Street, and Westminister Presbyterian Church at the corner of Boulevard and Forrest Avenue. All of these churches were within a block of our home. These churches were built about the time of the filling up of the vacant spaces of the Fourth Ward with new homes, the people moving in being almost entirely of the churchgoing class, and the social life of the ward was largely organized around these fine churches. The Woman's Missionary Society of Grace Church held an annual missionary testimony, which was always largely attended and was the great social event of the year. Soon after the new Grace Church was built I was made teacher of the Philathea Class, consisting of about thirty of the finest young women I ever knew. We gave many parties to the class in our home. Mrs. McElreath frequently entertained the Grace Church choir, and many musical parties were held at our house, attended by Charles E. Sheldon, whose great reputation as an organist was rapidly budding, Dave Silverman, a very accomplished violinist, and many fine vocalists. We were members of a Story Tellers' Club and a Domino Club, and with these entertainments in our home, the church receptions, and other social activities of the community, we had a simple, wholesome, but delightful social life.

In _____ we suffered a great sorrow in the death of Mrs. McElreath's mother who died on _____ of that year. Her death was almost as great a sorrow to me as to my wife. No sweeter, purer, gentler woman ever lived. She seemed to love me almost as greatly as she loved her own children, and I was always happy at the benediction of her visits to our home. On December 4, 1905, we suffered another great sorrow in the death of my father, account of which is given in a later chapter.

In _____ we took our first real vacation—a week's visit to Cumberland Island.* During this visit I acquired the name of "Alligator Mc," from shooting alligators in the marshes. One bright day we drove with Mr. and Mrs. W. A. Albright down the beach about twenty miles to Dungeness, and back through the island to the hotel over a road lined with great live oaks whose branches arched the way festooned with Spanish moss. Surely there are no more beautiful islands on earth than the "Golden Isles of Georgia."

In July or August, 1906, we took the trip of our lives, not that it was the most interesting trip we ever took, but because it was our first sea trip and our first visit to New York. We sailed from Savannah on the *Kansas City* at six o'clock in the morning, but long before

---

* These three blanks appear in Mr. McElreath's original manuscript. He clearly intended to ascertain the correct dates and insert them in the manuscript, but he never did so.

day, we, and many of the other passengers, were on deck seeing the
wonderful sights of the harbor and the great city on the Island. Mr.
and Mrs. E. A. White, old Cobb County friends of ours, had preceded us to New York and had secured a suite of rooms for themselves and another for us in the Caledonia Apartments located on
Twenty-Sixth Street, just west of Broadway and opposite Madison
Square Garden. The Caledonia Apartments, at that time, had at
least one famous tenant, O. Henry, who had a room there where he
was spinning the short stories which made him famous in American
literature. For the next week we certainly saw the sights — Coney
Island, the Eden Museum, the Metropolitan Museum, the Aquar-
ium, the Museum of Natural History, Central Park, Chinatown, —
[and took] a rubberneck trip over the city and, most delightful of
all, a trip up the Hudson to West Point.

In September, 1908, we made our first visit to Richmond and
Washington City.

When we moved into the Fourth Ward, we had no idea that we
should ever leave it. We hoped we might sometime be able to have
a better house and live on a more prominent street than East Avenue, but the Boulevard was the limit of our ambition. But we did
not take into consideration the transient habit which has character-
ized the Atlanta population from the earliest days of the city. In the
early days, some of the most prominent people of the city lived on
Decatur and Gartrell streets. When I came to Atlanta in 1895,
Capitol Avenue and Washington Street wagged their heads at the
new rich of Peachtree Street. We have told how the Boulevard and
Jackson had attracted a few prominent citizens and how, in the next
few years, the Fourth Ward filled up with a fine population. But by
1911 and 1912, Ponce de Leon Avenue and Druid Hills were in the
process of fine development, and many of the best people began to
move away from the Fourth Ward; that is, just as soon as the community in which we lived was finished, its citizens began to abandon it. In 1912 several very attractive houses were built on Ponce
de Leon, and Mrs. McElreath and I frequently went on Sunday
afternoon to admire them and long for one of them. I was particularly attracted by a home being built at 578 (now 838) Ponce de
Leon Avenue, on the north side of the avenue between Bonaventure
and Barnett streets. I had just bought my first automobile, a little

Hupp coupé, and had hired a boy to teach me to drive it. Nearly every time he drove me out, I stopped and looked over the house which was about completed. We finally bought this house and moved into it on February 1, 1913.

XIII

Participation
in Public Affairs

When I came to Atlanta I had no idea of ever entering politics and drifted into them almost unconsciously.

The question most intensely agitated in Atlanta municipal politics in 1901 was the fight between the Atlanta Consolidated Street Railway Company and the Atlanta Rapid Transit Company, the first headed by Joel Hurt and the latter by Harry M. Atkinson. The company headed by Mr. Hurt had, for some years, a practical monopoly on street railway transportation in the city; but in 1901 the company headed by Mr. Atkinson decided to enter the field in competition with the old company, and began to apply for franchises over competing routes, and sought to condemn certain strategic portions of the lines of the old company. This brought on a bitter fight in the courts, before the city council, and before the Railroad Commission of the state. Both sides employed counsel from among the best legal talent in the city and, in minor capacities, some lawyers not so conspicuous, among the latter class of which I was employed by the Hurt interests. This brought me to the notice of all of the local city politicians.

Every member of the City Council was known either as a Hurt man or an Atkinson man. The Hurt interests had a slight majority, and matters drifted in this condition until the next municipal election when each side put up a candidate in every ward and for each seat in the Aldermanic Board. James G. Woodward was the Atkinson candidate for one of the aldermanic posts, and A. C. Minhinnett was the Hurt candidate. I was employed as campaign manager for Minhinnett in the Fourth Ward; and although I had had no experience either in running a campaign or in managing one, I did the best I could, organizing meetings, hiring heelers, and getting out handbills and other publicity. My candidate was defeated in the election, along with most of the other candidates of the Hurt faction, but Minhinnett carried the Fourth Ward by a small majority, which to the best of my recollection, was the only ward he carried.

On September 12, 1902, without solicitation on my part, I was elected President of the Young Men's Democratic League of Fulton County. This organization had existed for many years, and its presidency was eagerly sought by aspiring politicians, though what they thought they ever did after their election is not a matter of record. The only thing I did was to entertain the Cook County Democratic Marching Club, an aggregation of "Hinky Dink's" Chicago hoodlums, on their visit to Atlanta on a swing round the country. After this I was usually put on some committee in political campaigns and, as is usually the case with an aspiring young lawyer, I got the bee in my own bonnet.

On September 25, 1907, I announced my candidacy for the legislature from Fulton County. My announcement was followed by the announcements of ten others: Henry A. Alexander, Charles W. Bernhart, Dr. George Brown, Joseph L. Cobb, Edward Crusselle, A. W. Farlinger, Henry W. Grady, Edgar Latham, Walter A. Sims, and Alex W. Stephens; and a hectic campaign followed. I noticed that the other candidates were working the lodges and secret orders in the city, to none of which I belonged, and handing out cards on the street corners.

I decided to open my campaign in the country districts and to get the country vote tied up before the others got to them. I hired a carriage and got Judge Spencer A. Atkinson, W. H. Abbott, and R. A. Broyles to go with me, and held my first rally at Sandy Springs. This meeting was a howling success, and I followed it with others in different parts of the county. In the primary election held on June 4, 1908, I was nominated, as were Dr. George Brown and Mr. Harry A. Alexander. The election of the nominees in the general election in November followed as a matter of course.

The period of which I am writing was a period of great political agitation in Georgia. The high waters of prejudice of the earlier years of Bryan and Watson had somewhat ebbed, and were succeeded by the era of LaFollette; but there were a great prejudice in Georgia against corporations, banks and railroad companies, particularly about freight rates which were considered discriminatory.

In 1906 the gubernatorial race was between Hoke Smith, who ran on a Progressive platform with the sympathy of the followers of Tom Watson, and Clarke Howell, who represented, or was thought to represent, the corporate interests. During this campaign, the question of freight rates was a leading issue, with Mr. Smith advocating "port rates." Joseph M. Brown was at the time a member of the State Railroad Commission and wrote and published a number of cards controverting the position of Mr. Smith. After Smith's election, when he tried to have his views enacted into law, Mr. Brown continued his opposition until the Governor became exasperated and removed him from office. During this time S. Guyt McLendon was publishing articles supporting Mr. Smith's views on port rates, and he was appointed to the vacancy created by the removal of Brown. This created many enemies for the Governor, and numerous other enemies were created for him by the abolition of the convict lease system and by the passage of the state prohibition law of 1907.

In 1908 in the Governor's campaign for reelection the faction which had opposed him in 1906, with the new enemies which he had made, brought out against him Joseph M. Brown, popularly referred to as "Little Joe." The campaign which followed was, perhaps, the bitterest gubernatorial campaign which has been waged in Georgia since the Norwood-Colquitt campaign in 1880, and the Governor was defeated. It was my misfortune to make my race for the legislature under circumstances of such political turmoil. I announced my candidacy independently of either faction, and maintained this position throughout the race. Towards the close of the campaign, both sides in the gubernatorial races tried to line up the local candidates for the legislature on the side of their respective candidates.

While I abhorred the extreme radicalism of the Watson philosophy, I leaned to the candidacy of Governor Smith, whose administration, I thought, had been excellent and in the public interest, and whose platform measures I heartily approved, though, in my campaign, I followed the maxim of Alex Stephens and "toted my own skillet." Notwithstanding my leaning towards the Hoke Smith side, I had many friends in the Joe Brown column and had their active support, and until about two weeks before the election it looked certain that I would be the leading legislative candidate and win by a majority of at least two thousand over any other candidate. About this time Henry A. Alexander came out in a card supporting the candidacy of "Little Joe." It was then demanded by both sides that I choose my candidate for Governor and publicly advertise my choice. This I refused to do, and my supporters in the Joe Brown faction began to desert me. Brown carried the county by a majority of two thousand and thirty-two; and I won by a majority of one hundred, and counted myself lucky at that.

In the fall of 1908 there occurred in Atlanta one of the most hotly contested races for Mayor ever known in the city's history. James G. Woodward, who had for years been a power in city politics, and had already served as Mayor for one or more terms, was again nominated for that office in the city primary. A few weeks before the regular election he was charged with certain conduct which in the opinion of thousands of the voters demanded his defeat. A mass meeting was called at which Robert F. Maddox was chosen to run against the nominee. On account of my success in running my own campaign, I was selected to manage the Maddox campaign in the Fourth Ward. I gave the city its first and most scientific lesson in carrying a municipal election. I took a map of the ward and cut it into sections containing as nearly as possible two hundred registered voters; appointed ten captains in each section, and had them see and talk to every voter in their respective sections; and on lists kept in the headquarters, made a memorandum opposite each name showing how he would vote. Two or three days before the election a street parade of the voters from all of the wards in the city was held, and on the banner carried by the voters of the Fourth Ward the words "Seven Hundred and Fifty Majority for Maddox" were printed. The general manager of the campaign told me that it would be impossible for the majority to be more than three hundred. Mr. Maddox's majority in the election was seven hundred and fifty-five in the Fourth Ward.

The session of the General Assembly to which I had been elected met the fourth Wednesday in June, 1909; and the Honorable John N. Holder of Jackson County was elected Speaker of the House and the Honorable John M. Slaton, of Fulton, President of the Senate. In the appointment of committees of the House, I fared exceptionally well for a new member. I was appointed to membership on the Committee on Amendments to the Constitution; Corporations; Excuses of Members; General Judiciary; Insurance; Labor and Labor Statistics; Military Affairs; Mines and Mining; Penitentiary; Special Judiciary; W. & A. Railroad; and vice-chairman of the Committee on Ways and Means, which made me an *ex-officio* member of the Committee on Appropriations.

After the defeat of Governor Smith for reelection, Mr. McLendon began to change his attitude with respect to freight rates, and there was a strong suspicion that he was making a personal profit from dealing in railroad bonds issued under the permission of the Railroad Commission of which he was a member. Acting under the authority given the Governor under the act creating the railroad commission, the Governor suspended Mr. McLendon from office and reported his suspension to the legislative session of 1909, with his reasons for the suspension, under which procedure it was the duty of the General Assembly to either confirm the suspension or restore the commissioner to office.

When I entered the legislature I had no idea that during its first session I would take any conspicuous part in its deliberations, but would follow the traditional custom of leaving the management of legislative affairs to the older and more experienced members; but when the message of the Governor came before the House for consideration, a joint committee of the House and Senate was appointed to investigate the charges contained in the Governor's

message and to report back to the House and Senate the committee's recommendation for final action, and, to my surprise, I was
appointed a member of the committee and made secretary of it.

This was the first time a suspension under the act had ever come
before the General Assembly, and there was doubt on the part of
some of the members of the right of the Governor to suspend and
of the right of the General Assembly to remove a railroad commissioner from office, their contention being that removal could be
made only by impeachment. Before the debate on the resolution for
the appointment of the committee opened, a caucus of those favoring the resolution requested that I open the debate with a legal argument on the right of suspension. On the day when the debate
opened the members of the Senate crowded into the hall of the
House of Representatives and the galleries were filled to capacity.
My speech was well received and highly recommended, and the
substance of it is contained in the opinion of the Supreme Court of
Georgia in the case of *Gray v. McLendon*, 134 Ga. 224 (1910).

The hearings before the investigating committee continued for
several weeks, during which time the legislative work of the House
went on. A few days before the committee made its report, James
B. Nevin, one of the newspaper correspondents reporting legislative proceedings, published an article on the Fulton delegation in
which he said:

> Without disparaging in any sense the other members of the House from
> Fulton, it can well be said that Mr. McElreath particularly is one of the
> strong leaders of that body. He has shown a capacity for hard and intel-
> ligent work that has resulted in his being used as a member of special
> committees as well as the regular committees of the House on which he
> has a particularly strong and important assignment. He has justified the
> faith and confidence of the Speaker and has shown his strength and read-
> iness in rendering much service in them all.
>
> He is a member of the General and Special Judiciary Committees, is
> Vice-Chairman of the Ways and Means Committee, and has presided
> over its meetings very often during its deliberations. He is also *ex-officio*
> member of the Committee on Appropriations, and has been able to assist
> in the important work of that committee. He is also a member of the Con-
> stitutional Amendments, the Western and Atlantic Railroad, Corpora-

tions, and Military Affairs, on all of which he has frequently rendered valuable service.

In addition to the general committees named, he is on several others. He is also a member of the special committee to investigate the charge against Railroad Commissioner McLendon, and was chairman of the subcommittee which prepared and sifted the evidence taken before the general committee. It is expected that he will be one of the leaders in this matter when the report is taken up for consideration by the whole House. On the general judiciary committee, he served as Chairman of the special committee which considered the question of the new code for the state.

The willingness shown by this representative from the State's Capital to discharge every duty which confronts him, his capacity to understand his work and facilitate it, has proven him to be one of the most useful members of the House and reflects credit upon both himself and his constituents.

•

I was never in doubt upon the abstract question of the right of the suspension of a member of the Railroad Commission under the statute; but I was in doubt about the sufficiency of the facts in the particular case before us to authorize the exercise of the right, and I made up my mind that if the investigation showed no more than a difference in policy between the Governor and the suspended commissioner, I would not vote to confirm the suspension. When the hearing before the committee had been concluded, it clearly appeared that the commissioner had, after authorizing an issue of bonds, in two instances, bought the bonds himself and resold them at a personal profit. This removed all of my doubts, and I voted with a majority of the committee to recommend the dismissal of the suspended commissioner from office. After a long and acrimonious debate, the resolution was adopted and the commissioner removed from office.

My successful participation in the proceedings above recounted having given me standing among the members of the House, I decided to push through at that session some legislation for the benefit of my local constituency in which I felt a deep interest. The School of Technology, although its student body had been increasing and, under the able direction of its president, Dr. Kenneth G. Matheson, had been rapidly growing in prestige, was operating under an inadequate appropriation of sixty thousand dollars, which had not been increased for years. I thought that this school had been discriminated against, and I introduced an amendment to the General Appropriations Bill raising the appropriation to seventy thousand dollars. This amendment was strenuously opposed by the Honorable Joseph Heard of Dooly County, but was passed. In 1911 I succeeded in having the appropriation raised to seventy-five thousand dollars. At the session in 1910 I introduced and secured the passage of a special bill appropriating the sum of thirty-five thousand dollars for building a new shop building at the school, conditioned on the raising of the additional sum of fifteen thousand dollars by private donation. This sum was contributed by the citizens of Fulton County, and the new shop building was erected. The increased maintenance by the state and the building and equipping of the new shop qualified the school to receive donations from one or more of the great foundations of the country of which Dr. Matheson was able to take advantage. In a public speech made a few years later Dr. Matheson stated that the school took on new life from the appropriations which I secured, and the credit for the greater Tech which the school was rapidly becoming was due to my efforts more than to any other cause.

Among the other bills introduced by me and passed at the session of 1909 was the bill for an additional judge for the Atlanta Judicial Circuit (introduced jointly by the Fulton delegation); the bill regulating the date of the adjournment of the superior courts in certain circuits; the bill to create a commission to examine the Code of Georgia (prepared by Judge John L. Hopkins and later adopted as the Code of 1910); the bill creating a lien in favor of laundrymen (written and introduced by me in the House and a copy introduced by Senator McIntyre in the Senate, the Senate bill being first reached, it became a law); the act fixing the amount of the assets required to be owned by mutual aid, benefit, and industrial insurance companies; and the resolution for the repair and refurnishing of the legislative halls in the capitol, the furnishings of which had fallen into a disgraceful state of dilapidation.

In the period between the legislative sessions of 1909 and 1910 I was again called upon to take a hand in municipal affairs. The administration of Robert F. Maddox as Mayor of Atlanta came up to all expectations. When he took office vast sections of the city were without sewers; many of the schoolhouses of the city were old, dilapidated, and insufficient to accommodate the fast-growing population; there was no sanatorium for tubercular patients, and the Grady Hospital was then, as now, insufficient. Under the Mayor's influence a bond issue of three million dollars was authorized by the council for the building of twelve additional schools, modern sewage disposal plants, a crematory for garbage, the elimination of eleven thousand surface closets, extension of the waterworks system, the establishment of the Battle Hill Sanatorium for the treatment of tuberculosis, and the erection of an addition to Grady Hospital. The election to ratify this bond issue was set for February 15, 1910, and a committee of leading men, of which I was made chairman, was appointed to manage the campaign for the ratification of the bonds. When the campaign opened there was considerable opposition, led by ex-Mayor Woodward. As it was necessary that there should be a total vote of a majority of the registered voters, and that two-thirds of those voting should vote in favor of the bonds, it was thought that the ratification of the issue would be difficult. The whole city was organized almost as completely as the Fourth Ward was organized in the Mayor's race; the newspapers, the Chamber of Commerce, the city school teachers, the telephone company, and practically all of the civic organizations in the city lent their help. In order to keep toll on the voting on the day of election, two checkers were posted at each polling place to count the vote and report to the central office exactly on the hour how many votes had been cast for bonds and how many against. The color of the ballots for bonds was slightly different from those against bonds, so that the watchers could keep an accurate count as the votes were cast. So accurately did the watchers count and so promptly did they report that within less than five minutes after polls closed we knew the result, which was more than six thousand for bonds and sixty-six against bonds. This was a campaign which has never been equalled in Atlanta, and it is safe to say that it will never again be equalled.

I offered for reelection in 1910, the other candidates being Harry A. Alexander, Dr. George Brown, and George Westmoreland. Fulton County has three representatives, and in the primary election I received 8,791 votes, Dr. Brown, 8,145, Mr. Westmoreland, 7,964, and Mr. Alexander 5,907. I received the largest vote in every ward in the city and in every country district but three, in one of which I tied with Mr. Westmoreland.

In the gubernatorial race Governor Brown was opposed by ex-Governor Hoke Smith, who won, wiping out his defeat of two years before. In 1911 he returned to his former office.

Upon the organization of the House for the sessions of 1911 and 1912, John N. Holder was reelected Speaker and I was appointed to the following committees: Amendments to the Constitution; Conservation; General Judiciary No. 1; Insurance; Mines and Mining; Municipal Government; Rules; and chairman of the Committee on Appropriations.

It was a complete but agreeable surprise when the Speaker informed me of his intention to appoint me to the chairmanship of the most important committee of the House. Under the constitution all appropriations must originate in the House, and it was true that he who holds the key to the treasury wields a commanding influence in the legislative body.

With no particular training in large financial affairs, the task of making up a budget for the state was a rather appalling task; but the responsibility having been placed upon me, I determined to meet it competently. Accordingly, I went about gaining the necessary information, and made a study of the income of the state from each source of its revenue for several of the preceding years. I ascertained the rate of increase or decrease from each source, the amounts appropriated to each department, and the amounts appropriated to each of the institutions supported by the state. After hearings were held before the committee (at which all the state departments and institutions presented their claims) a general appropriations bill was made up and reported to the House.

Before these hearings began I advocated and the committee agreed upon the policy of not appropriating one cent more than the carefully estimated income of the state during the two years for which the budget was being made up. There were some institutions which greatly needed increased support, and some increases were made; but the total sum appropriated was held within the income of the state for the period covered. This was not done without a bitter fight. Those members who were from the counties in which state institutions were located fought strenuously for increases to their institutions; and a faction led by Hon. Joe Hill Hall (of Bibb) and by Hon. Hooper Alexander (of DeKalb) fought with equal vigor for a reduction of all appropriations.

I was particularly impressed by my own investigation and by the information gained that better support of the higher institutions of learning should be made, that better provision should be made for care of the inmates of the sanatorium at Milledgeville, and for care of the old veterans at the Confederate Soldiers Home. In 1911 special appropriations were made to the State Normal School for furnishing the Carnegie Library located there; to the Georgia Normal and Industrial College for equipping its science hall; to establish at Valdosta an Agricultural-Industrial College as a branch of the State University; to build an annex to the hospital building of the Confederate Soldiers Home; and to manufacture hog cholera serum at the State College of Agriculture at Athens. In 1912 increased appropriations included five thousand dollars in the maintenance fund of the Georgia School of Technology; an equal increase to Georgia Normal and Industrial at Milledgeville and to State Normal School; twenty-five thousand dollars for the support of the Agricultural Normal and Industrial School at Valdosta; a special appropriation of twenty-five thousand dollars for the building of a new industrial building at the North Georgia Agricultural College at Dahlonega; ten thousand dollars for new equipment at the School for the Deaf at Cave Springs; seven thousand, five hundred dollars for the erection of an additional dormitory at First District Agriculture College at Statesboro; six thousand dollars for a new school building at the Third District Agriculture School at Americus; and six thousand dollars for a new school building at the Fourth District Agriculture School at Carrollton.

Notwithstanding these increases in appropriations for the years 1912 and 1913, the amount appropriated did not exceed the income of the state for that period. This does not mean, however, that the deplorable condition of the state's finances was relieved, or that the appropriations were promptly paid. The great bulk of the taxes for a given year are not collected until December. The expenses of the state, of course, begin to accrue at the first of the year, and the payment of the expense of running the schools and paying the teachers promptly as their salaries accrued was impossible as the treasury did not maintain a sufficient treasury balance to anticipate the collection of the taxes. The only financial glory I got out of the situation was in giving a little larger support to the institutions of the state and in not increasing the deficit.

In the session of 1911 a resolution was adopted for the appointment of a commission to review the insurance laws of the state, which had my active support. I was not appointed to this commission, but I collaborated with it to a certain extent, and, at my instance, a section was incorporated in the act prepared by the commission providing that any mutual, industrial, life, health or accident insurance company then existing or which might thereafter be organized under the laws of the state, might change itself into a stock company, and providing the method of making such change. The bill prepared by this commission was enacted into law at the session of 1912 and is known as the General Insurance Act. Under the provisions of this act, the Industrial Life and Health Insurance Company (of which I have been general counsel since its organization) was changed into a stock company and has become one of the most prosperous institutions of the state of Georgia and of the city of Atlanta. It now occupies a handsome office building, owned by the company, located at the corner of West Peachtree and Linden streets.

The most important legislation I promoted during my legislative service was the abolition of the justice courts in the city of Atlanta and the establishment in their stead of the Municipal Court of Atlanta.

Immediately prior to their abolition, eighteen justices of the peace and notaries public, as *ex-officio* justices of the peace, exercised jurisdiction over either the whole territory or parts of the territory of the city. In the month of April, 1909, there were 1,917 civil cases filed in these courts. The number of criminal cases filed in them during these months is not known except that there were 110 criminal warrants issued by one of the justices. At that rate there were, including the estimated number of criminal warrants, more than 25,000 cases filed in these courts annually. In a great city, which even at that time Atlanta was, where there were thousands of cases every month, and where innumerable incidents absorbed the attention, nobody except the parties directly interested in the cases gave any notice to what went on in these minor courts, which were often held in remote parts of the city, up obscure stairways. The rest of the public scarcely knew of the existence and location of these courts, except when they saw the streets choked with the cheap effects of a bailiff sale.

Some of the justices of the peace were honorable men and ran their courts on as high a plane as was possible under the system. Among these were J. G. Bloodworth, Edgar H. Orr, S. H. Landrum, and C. H. Girardeau, whose court rooms were in the center of the city, and who saw to it that their bailiffs kept within the law. But some of the justice courts were thought to be dens of extortion. One of the bailiffs of one of these courts was removed from office for that offense, and was later sent to the penitentiary for a more serious crime.

Having had to practice in these courts during the early years of my professional life, I became convinced that they were in many instances institutions of oppression to the ignorant, the poor, and the weak, and that some of them were dens of extortion. I determined, if possible, to abolish them, and to create in their place a system of courts better suited to the needs of a great city. At the session of the legislature in 1909 I introduced a resolution for the submission of a constitutional amendment authorizing the legislature to abolish the office of justice of the peace and of notary public *ex-officio* justice of the peace in cities of one hundred thousand population, and to establish other courts in their stead with a larger jurisdiction. This resolution failed in the session of 1909 and 1910.

At the session of the Georgia Bar Association held in Athens in June, 1910, at the invitation of the program committee, I delivered an address on "Justice Courts: Their Constitution, Jurisdiction, and Procedure." This address received the enthusiastic commendation of those attending the meeting, Judge Joseph R. Lamar and Judge Joel Branham being especially outspoken in their approval. Judge Branham was elected president of the association at that meeting, and in his address at its next meeting commended the legislation which I had attempted.

In several of their presentments, the grand juries of Fulton County condemned the malpractice in the justice courts of the city of Atlanta; the newspapers, in frequent and strong editorials, called attention to the evils of the system, and called for a remedy; the *Savannah Morning News* joined in the crusade; and public sentiment was so crystalized that when I again introduced the bill for a constitutional amendment in 1911, it passed at the session of 1912 and was ratified in the general election of that year. After ratification of the amendment, the Atlanta Bar Association appointed a committee, of which I was chairman, to draft a bill for the abolition of the justice courts of Atlanta and the creation of a new court in their stead. The bill drafted by the committee creating the Municipal Court of Atlanta was passed at the legislative session in 1913. It provided for a court having jurisdiction over all of the territory of the city lying in Fulton County, with five judges, a clerk, and a marshal, and with a central office at the county court house, with jurisdiction of suits in which the amount did not exceed five hundred dollars. A separate section for that portion of the city lying within DeKalb County was created, with jurisdiction in the same amount as that which had obtained as to justice courts.

Upon the organization of the court, I was tendered appointment as Chief Judge but declined it. The constitutional amendment first adopted limited the application of the act to those cities having a population of as much as one hundred thousand, but the Municipal Court of Atlanta proved so satisfactory that later amendments were adopted reducing the requisite population so that it included several other cities of the state. Similar courts were created in Macon, Columbus and Savannah. By successive legislative acts the jurisdiction of the Municipal Court of Atlanta has been extended over the whole of Fulton County, the jurisdictional amount has been increased to twenty-five thousand dollars, and the name of the court has been changed to the Civil Court of Fulton County. The court has been ably conducted, and it is now a court of dignity and usefulness.

My legislative experience was not entirely a bed of roses. For ways that are dark and tricks that are vain, municipal politics take the prize. In 1911 a coterie of men of professional and business ability, but with a total lack of political acumen, got together and drew

up a commission government charter for the city of Atlanta for submission to the legislature. According to legislative custom, the local
representatives have the sole approval of purely local registration,
the other representatives following their recommendation. In order
to preserve local self-government, it had been the custom of the representatives of Fulton County to introduce no bill for the amendment of the charter of the city of Atlanta until it had been submitted
to the City Council, and had received its approval. The new charter
prepared by this committee of citizens was submitted to the City
Council of Atlanta, which declined to approve it. The proponents
of the charter then sent out cards to the registered voters seeking
their signatures to a request for the introduction and passage of the
bill creating the new charter, and then presented the bill to the Fulton County representatives for introduction. The representatives
were then confronted with the proposition of introducing a bill
which had been disapproved by the City Council. After consultation, they decided to introduce the bill if twenty percent of the registered voters of the city requested it. In the meantime, violent
agitation had sprung up between those opposing the new charter —
led by the city politicians — and those favoring it. The faction favoring the new charter demanded that it be introduced and passed
without a referendum, and those opposing the new charter demanded that the bill be killed outright. The *Atlanta Journal* and the
Atlanta News favored the new charter and began to publish daily, vi-
tuperative editorials against the local representatives, accusing
them of delaying the introduction and passage of the bill. At the
hearing before the Committee on Municipal Government, the hall
of the House of Representatives was crowded to the last seat in the
galleries, and the feeling between the two factions was intense.

At this point Mr. Clarke Howell, Editor of the *Atlanta Constitution*, in order to allay, if possible, the local strife, called a meeting
of the local legislative representatives and the leaders of both factions, and proposed that a compromise charter be drafted containing the best features of both the councilmanic and the commission
government forms of municipal government. The other two representatives took a sort of negative, or neutral, attitude on the proposition; but I followed the lead of Hon. Courtland S. Winn, then
Mayor, who favored a compromise charter. Mr. Winn was one of

the purest and most honorable men who had ever been connected with the city government of Atlanta, and I had been active in the campaign in which he was elected. Having studied many of the new municipal charters in other large cities of the country, I agreed with his views. With the Mayor's help, a compromise charter was prepared and introduced as a substitute for the original compromise charter. This infuriated the proponents of the commission government charter. With malignant venom, I was lambasted daily in editorials in the *Atlanta Journal*, and caricatured as standing behind a column of the capitol with a dagger in my hand, stabbing the City of Atlanta in the back.

The new charter was introduced and passed (*Ga. Laws* of 1911, 566) with a referendum to the registered voters of the city of Atlanta. The advocates of commission government cooled down, and the *Journal* apologized editorially for its previous editorials concerning my actions in the matter. The campaign which ensued on the adoption of the charter was one of intense bitterness, and the charter was defeated. The opponents of the charter contended that it was drawn to suit the interests of the aristocracy of the "North Side," and they raised the cry "Try it on, Buckhead" and the charter was defeated.

I thought then, and I think now, that it was one of the best city charters ever proposed for a city of the size of Atlanta.

Naturally I did not make any political friends and I lost many on account of the city charter fight. I also aroused political opposition over the fight on the "near beer" saloons and "locket clubs" which the prohibition law of 1907 had left in existence. I had always been opposed to the liquor traffic and in favor of prohibition, but I was not fanatic enough to please all of the prohibitionists and, of course, no prohibitionist would please the liquor element.

I announced for reelection in 1912, but made no canvass for reelection. The legislature adjourned five days before the primary, and I had been so busy that I could not campaign. A five-day campaign would have done little good, so I made none. In fact, I cared little about further legislative service. Notwithstanding all of these handicaps, I would have been reelected but for the conditions under which I was required to run. A campaign amply financed was organized to defeat me. The adoption of a rule by the Democratic executive committee was secured under which no vote would be valid unless the voter voted for three representatives. The opposition put out three candidates upon which they centered. There were, at first, two other candidates running with me, but the day before the closing of entries one of these withdrew from the race. I was left where every person voting for me had to vote for at least one of my opponents. The handicap was too great, and I was defeated. Thus ended my career as a public office holder.

During my service in the legislature (and especially as a member of the committee on Amendments to the Constitution, General Judiciary, and Appropriations) many constitutional questions arose, and I became deeply interested in the Constitution of Georgia. I found that the constitutional provisions which had from time to time been in force in the state could only be found by tracing them through the scattered and rare volumes of digests, codes and sessions laws, and that it was impossible without great labor to determine what the constitutional law of the state was on any given date. To remedy this difficulty, and to lessen this inconvenience, it seemed to me that some permanent work should be prepared and published for the use of the lawyers and judges of the state. While this thought was running through my mind, I learned that Judge Joseph R. Lamar had intended to prepare such a work, but on account of his appointment to the Supreme Court of the United States he had had to abandon his proposed work. It was suggested that I prepare a work on that subject. Accordingly some time in 1911 I set about the task. The book was published in 1912 under the title *McElreath on the Constitution of Georgia*. It met with favor from the legal profession in the state, has been used in several of the law schools and by the profession generally, and has been cited on several occasions by the Supreme Court.

XIV

The Next Fifteen Years

On the first day of February, 1913, we moved into our third home, a brand new eight-room house on Ponce de Leon Avenue, having all the conveniences then common in the better homes of Atlanta. Elegant houses were then building on Ponce de Leon, and it was regarded as one of the most prominent residential streets in the city, then just in the beginning of its development. At that time there were probably less than a dozen houses on the avenue from the Southern Railroad to Moreland Avenue. According to my best recollections, there was but one home on Ponce de Leon Avenue in Druid Hills—the home of Judge John S. Candler, at the corner of Moreland Avenue. All the space south of Ponce de Leon Avenue and in sight of our home was vacant. The lands of the Clark Estate, consisting of some fifty or sixty acres, were virgin woodland. New streets were being opened in Druid Hills, and new buildings were going up in Druid Hills and on Ponce de Leon Avenue as fast as they could be erected. There was a general feeling of prosperity in the air. For the first time in my life I was enjoying a little prosperity.

There was, perhaps, no more desirable place in Atlanta in which to live than Ponce de Leon Avenue during the first few years we lived there. We had the finest neighbors that could have been found anywhere in the world. Our next-door neighbors on one side were W. Chester Smith and his family. Mr. Smith was a man of a high and noble character, genial and friendly, devoted to his charming family, and with all the qualities that go to make a good neighbor. His wife was one of the finest and most beautiful women I ever knew. They had a young daughter, Lillian, then about ten years old, who became my pet. But they had a little niece who affected my heart as no other child has ever affected it. She was at this time about four and a half years old and was the most beautiful child, and one of the most precious children, I ever knew. I spent my Saturday afternoons working with my flowers. Little Lollie's mother would dress her up in a dainty white dress and white shoes; and the little girl, with a precocity I never saw in any other child of her age, would beg me to show her the petal, the pistil, and the stamen of a flower. Late in the afternoon I would take her for an automobile ride. She always called me her best friend, and the little child wound herself into the tendrils of my heart. I could not have loved her much better if she had been my own child. One afternoon on coming home from the office, I was told that my little friend had been suddenly attacked by diphtheria the night before and was dead. I went immediately to the child's mother and asked her if there was anything I could do for her. She replied that there was; she wished me to go with the family to the burial at Conyers and to take the child's coffin and put it in the grave. She said that the little child always called me her "best friend," and that she wanted me to be the last person to handle her little body. With a sore heart, I performed this melancholy duty.

Others of our immediate neighbors were the family of Mr. and Mrs. Thomas L. Thrower, and the family of Mr. and Mrs. J. V. Wellborn; and a few years later, the family of Mr. and Mrs. B. H. Hill. Mrs. Hill was a beautiful and talented woman — a hostess of real merit.

The hectic days of politics being past and my book finished and published, I devoted myself during the day assiduously to the duties of a growing practice; and the evenings were devoted to reading or to social intercourse with our neighbors and friends. During these years I was Chairman of the Board of Stewards of Grace Church, a member of the City Club (which was influential in the city at that time), and I was one of the organizers and an active member of the Atlanta Writers Club. I was one of those who promoted the building of the Atlanta Burns Cottage, being one of those who purchased bonds for the raising of the money to buy the tract of property upon which the cottage was built, and was a constant attendant upon the meetings of the club. Mrs. McElreath was deeply interested in the Woman's Missionary Society of Grace Church, a member of the Wednesday Morning Study Club, and a constant attendant upon all of the higher-class musical concerts of the city. Thus, we led an exceedingly agreeable life.

The wave of comparative prosperity on which I was riding when I bought my new home in February, 1913, and which I counted on to last until I could pay for it, was destined to be short-lived. When Germany declared war on August 1, 1914, and England on the fourth of that month, it shook the fabric of American prosperity to its very foundations. Times began to grow worse and worse until America entered the war in 1917; and then until after the armistice, the law business became practically non-existent. A moratorium on the collection of debts was practically declared. Building and the trading in real estate stopped.

My partner, Mr. Thomas H. Scott, went into the army. I was left alone with office rent and the salary of a stenographer to pay, and with practically no practice. I spent weeks during which I did not have a client, filling out questionnaires, for which I could make no charge, for soldiers caught in the draft.

When war broke out I had not finished paying for my home. To pay the expenses of my office, I borrowed money at whatever rate it could be obtained, and contributed largely to the usurers. The memory of those years is like a nightmare. But the horror of those years was not confined entirely to the personal difficulties and the privations which the people of America suffered. The sympathies of this country were then as now with France and England. On the Sunday when the issue of the Battle of the Marne hung in the balance, none of my neighbors could sit quietly at home. We stood in clumps on the lawns feeling emotions of apprehension which must have been like those felt by the people of Rome when awaiting the news of the battle with Hannibal at the Battle of Cannae. The radio had not then been developed to its present perfection, and we had to wait for the Extras. Late in the afternoon when we could bear the suspense no longer, I drove uptown and met a newsboy with an Extra which had just come out. It brought the news that Joffre had turned the tide of battle. When I got back with it, we all had some of the feelings which the people of Athens must have had when the messenger arrived with the news of the victory at Marathon.

On the twenty-first day of May, 1917, one of the greatest disasters which ever came to the city occurred in the great fire which swept over the greater portion of the Fourth Ward. During the forenoon, a stubborn fire had raged in the western portion of the city. This had kept a large part of the fire equipment busy. When I returned from lunch, I saw from the window of my office that a fire had broken out in some Negro shacks south of Edgewood Avenue. I turned to the preparation of some papers for Dr. Milton N. Armstrong, who lived on Ponce de Leon Avenue where the Standard Club now stands, at a distance of a mile and a half from the place where the fire was then raging. I was engaged in this task for about an hour. During this time I was very apprehensive, and I expressed my uneasiness to him; but he was impatient with my nervousness, and would not go out and look to see whether the fire had spread or not. After perhaps an hour, I finished the matter I was working on for him, and we then went up to the roof of the Silvey Building where my office was then located. As soon as we reached the roof, we found that the fire had gotten out of control of the fire department, had crossed Edgewood Avenue, had reached Houston Street, and was rushing northward at a tremendous rate. The day was clear and dry, and there was a strong wind blowing. Most of the houses in the area where the fire was already raging and those ahead of it were built of wood with shingle roofs. Flaming shingles would rise in the ascending column of air caused by the terrific heat. The wind would blow them on ahead of the conflagration; and when they fell on a shingle roof, a new fire was started. Dr. Armstrong and I rushed down to the street. As soon as possible, we got into his car and drove out to his home. When we got there, flaming shingles were falling on Ponce de Leon Avenue, and in his front yard. A scene of pandemonium had already begun. Cars loaded with household goods were rushing out of the area south of Ponce de Leon Avenue, and hundreds of other cars were rushing in to be of help. I rushed back uptown to where my car was parked in a garage. The garage keeper did not take time to get out my car, but told me to take the first car I could find belonging to the garage. I jumped into a car and rushed back; but when I got to Argonne Street, I found that the police had stopped traffic at that point. I then went down to Piedmont Park and out Virginia Avenue to Highland Avenue. Finally I reached the hill on which the Forrest Avenue School is located. There the scene beggared all description. The whole ward west of us was one seething cauldron. The firemen and the police were blowing up houses ahead of the fire with dynamite. The hill around the Forrest Avenue School was covered with perhaps a thousand people, who had carried a few household effects away with them. There they sat and watched their homes, their household effects, and their heirlooms—the accumulations of their lives—being destroyed.

At that time there were three splendid churches in the Fourth Ward, Grace Methodist, Jackson Hill Baptist, and Westminister Presbyterian—all comparatively new, built at great sacrifice by their members, and just about paid for. All of these, with the homes of perhaps eighty percent of their members, were completely destroyed. The fire swept on northward, crossed Ponce de Leon Avenue, until it was finally checked about two blocks north of Ponce de Leon Avenue. If the wind had not shifted to the west, the city would have been completely destroyed. After the fire, the area which had been covered with lovely homes was a scene of the most complete desolation.

Grace Church being destroyed and its members scattered, it was questionable whether it should ever attempt to rebuild. Services were resumed in the Forrest Avenue School building. Having devoted some of the best years of my life to the church, I finally decided that the church ought not be allowed to die, and after a few months, I called a meeting at my home of a few of the leading members, to meet and canvass the situation. At this conference it was decided to rebuild, and the trustees set about finding a new location. After considering several locations, the present site of the church was bought. In a few months the Sunday school plant was erected—perhaps the best Sunday school plant in the city. In 1922 it was decided to begin the erection of the main church auditorium. I had served on the building committee of the Sunday school plant and was made chairman of the building committee of the main church. The firm of Pringle & Smith was selected as architects. I consulted with Mr. Smith and told him that the committee wished a pure Gothic-type church in every detail. How well they carried out the instructions of the committee may be seen in the church as it was completed. Every window frame, the pew ends, the carving on the rostrum, and all of the chairs, the lighting fixtures, the hammered hinges on the doors, are all true to type. Indeed, the church is acknowledged to be the purest type of Gothic architecture in the city. During all of the time of these building operations, I was chairman of the Board of Stewards; in fact, I served in that capacity for seventeen years continuously, and had the heavy responsibility of raising the finances for operating the church and for paying the large outlay in building its plant. At length, thinking I had served perhaps too long, I retired from the chairmanship of the Board for about six years, when I was again elected and served one year. During that last service, the church, for the first time in many years, paid out its budget in full without a "hide and tallow" meeting, which it has not since done.

In 1921 my wife and I took our first long automobile trip, covering approximately fifteen hundred miles. This trip illustrates the remarkable development which has been made in the road system of the country since that date. On this trip we traveled not over one hundred miles on paved roads. By starting early and driving hard, on the first day we reached Knoxville, Tennessee. We gloated over the fact, although we had traveled only two hundred miles. The next day, between Knoxville and Greenville, Tennessee, we dropped into a chuck hole and broke a spring. We limped along to Greenville, spending the afternoon in having the spring rewelded. This was done at a blacksmith shop, next door to Andrew Johnson's tailor shop, and we spent the night in Greenville. By hard driving over rough roads and detours, the next day we reached Wytheville, Virginia. The next day we got as far as the Natural Bridge, and the next morning we drove into Lexington, Virginia, where we spent several days attending the commencement exercises. From Lexington, we drove to Frederick, Maryland, and spent the night. The next day we drove to Gettysburg, Pennsylvania, and over the battlefields, and then back to Washington, D.C. From Washington we came back though Richmond, Virginia, and through the Carolinas, and back to Atlanta. This year [1940] I traveled over much of the same route at approximately the rate of four hundred miles a day in ease and comfort.

Our next trip, taken in 1925, was one of the most interesting we ever took, and one which was the fulfillment of a lifelong dream. As a little boy I somehow got hold of a copy of Longfellow's poems. I did not, at that time, greatly appreciate "The Belfrey Bruges," or "The Skeleton in Armor"; but I read and reread *Evangeline*, and cried over the final scene when, after her long search, Evangeline found her dying lover. All through the years I had dreamed of going to the village of Grand Pré. We went by boat from Savannah to Boston, and from there by another boat to Yarmouth, Nova Scotia. When we landed at Yarmouth, we were out of the United States for the first time. After spending a few hours there, we boarded the "Blue Nose Special" on the Evangeline route, and went to Digby on the Annapolis basin where we spent two days. While there we drove to old Annapolis Royal, and west through the old fort built by Champlain and Liscarbot. We drove through the gorgeous forests of fir and spruce along Bear River. We then went to Wolfeville and stopped at the Acadia Inn. We drove out to the beautiful Gasperean Valley, and to the village of Grand Pré. We saw the Evangeline Chapel, built on the site of the church into which the Acadians were herded for deportation; the ancient willow trees which are still standing from that time; the dikes which the incessant labors of the farmers had built; the forests all bearded with grey moss; the white mists standing on Blomidon; and the wonderful statue by Hebert of Evangeline standing back for a last look at the village from which she was being torn. At night I went out and saw the stars come out like forget-me-nots in the sky.

From Wolfeville we went to Halifax where we spent several days visiting the points of interest, the most marvelous of which were the incomparable public gardens.

After the terrific strain of the years of the great war was over, life became easier and we were very happy; but early in 1928 it became necessary for Mrs. McElreath to undergo a serious operation from which she happily recovered. The strain of long and hard application to work and the anxiety which I underwent during my wife's illness affected my nerves, and I came near to having a breakdown. By this time Ponce de Leon Avenue had been completely built up and was becoming decadent. A number of large apartment houses had been built in the immediate vicinity of our home. From their chimneys immense volumes of smoke and soot were constantly emitted. The traffic on the avenue had become so congested and the noise so great that we could not sit in comfort on the front porch. I became dissatisfied with the location and longed for a home with a quieter location. After discussing the subject for a short time, we bought a lot on Piedmont Road, built my present home, and moved into it on the first day of September, 1928.

XV

Braebiggin

We named our new home "Braebiggin," a name coined from the two Scottish words "brae," meaning a hillside, and "biggin," a Scottish cabin. It was dedicated at a housewarming party, attended by a few of our intimate friends. Annie Bass Hill, one of our most devoted friends, read the following poem:

BRAEBIGGIN

I

The Scottish words for home and hill!
The breath of heather bloom
On craggy mountains old and grey
And bluebells, in the gloom
Of Scottish dells, is in the names
That fill the minstrel's lay,
And a hint of Scotia's in the name
O' the biggin on the brae.

II

The blood of him who named the house
    And her the hearth stone tends
From ancient clans of Scottish hills
    Through worthy sires descends.
No mansion proud or stately name
    For pride's ornate display
But just a modest home they made,
    A biggin on the brae.

III

Braebiggin boasts no mouldy past,
    No grey ghost weird and tall
Like those that fill the oft-read tales
    Of old Moultrassie Hall,
Or told how brothers fought by night
    At ill-starred Ballantrae —
No shades like these can wander near
    The biggin on the brae.

IV

His gruesome majesty would flee
    The sunset's amethyst;
The pink azaleas that seek
    Their pal moon — lovers' tryst
Would catch him in a silver mist
    And spirit him away,
For nature guards with jealous care
    The biggin on the brae.

V

Conceived by those who love of friends
    Hold sacred in their breasts,
It stands where pine-boughs whisper "Come,"
    And proud oaks echo "Rest";
The city's harsh, discordant noise
    Is far enough away —
A home of quiet peacefulness —
    This biggin on the brae.

VI

And, best of all, within its walls
    Are hearts both leal and true

And kindly greetings in the halls
With cordial hand clasps, too;
You'll find when summer days are hot,
Or nights are chill and grey,
A hearty welcome in this home —
This biggin on the brae.

A few nights later the home received a second dedication at a surprise party given by the members of the Bonehead Club, of which, by preeminent qualification, I was a member.

Ours was a modern home in every particular, equipped with every convenience then known to domestic comfort. Mrs. McElreath (whose health had apparently been completely restored) was a perfect housekeeper, a good musician, and a gracious hostess, popular with her neighbors. She had a tender heart, an exceedingly kindly disposition, and was never satisfied when not doing some kindly deed. She soon began to take an interest in the community library at Buckhead, which had been founded by Miss Ida Williams, who (after her retirement from the principalship of the R. E. Hope School) organized the North Side Library for the primary purpose of providing good reading matter for her former pupils. Mrs. McElreath was soon elected President of the North Side Library Association, which sponsored the library. Under her leadership and largely on account of the impetus of her devoted services, the library grew rapidly, and it has now grown into a valuable community institution. During all of the years after she became interested in the work, she spent her Friday afternoons at the library dealing out books to the eager young people of the community. On those afternoons I would drive by and pick her up in the car to bring her home, but I always had to go by the home of an old and very poor lady, shut in by an infirmity, for the purpose of leaving with her a number of books from the library. My wife saw that she was supplied each week with books to while away her lonely hours.

As my wife grew older, her tenderness and works of charity increased. She spent a large portion of her time in attentions to sick friends and in attentions to the old women at the County Alms House. She was especially kind to a very dear old lady who had lost her fortune and had survived relatives and friends, and was an inmate of the Home for Old Women. The building of Braebiggin for my wife was the one act of my life which gives me most satisfaction. She loved every tree and flower and blade of grass which grew about it. Reared tenderly and in plenty, she married me when I was as poor as a church mouse. She went with me to the humble and poorly furnished cottage on Woodward Avenue; she helped me earn the money on which we lived during the first years of our married life. Through poverty and weariness and ill health, she never complained. She was my inspiration, my guide, my friend and helpmate. As I climbed from poverty to competence, and from obscurity to public notice, I had her encouragement and help; but I knew that if I had failed she would have shared the failure without a murmur. A good home in which to spend her last years was an infinitesimal compensation for the devotion of a woman to whom I owe thirty-nine years of happiness, and all of the success of my life.

I shall never leave Braebiggin until I go where she is.

Why I Did Not
Go to Congress

To use a phrase universally adopted by office seekers, in 1932 I yielded to "the solicitation of many friends" who thought that the Fifth District was not being competently represented, and announced my candidacy for Congress. The use of this phrase happened for once to be true, and my entrance fee was paid for me by friends who raised it, and then came to me and urged my announcement. I consented with the usual reluctance, and was defeated.

As a candidate for Congress at that particular time, I was especially vulnerable. I had been a lifelong Democrat, and from the time of my first vote (for Grover Cleveland in 1888) I had consistently voted the Democratic ticket. But in 1928 I voted for Herbert Hoover, whom I considered to be better qualified for the office of President than his opponent, Alfred E. Smith. I did not vote against the Democratic nominee in 1928 because he was a Catholic. I have never had any prejudice against that church, and hold, and highly prize, a certificate of honorary membership in the Catholic Layman's Confraternity of Georgia. The certificate was signed by

Bishop O'Hara, and issued to me on account of contributions to Catholic charities. I voted against Al Smith because I considered him to be a regulation East Side Tammany politician, and on account of his record on the liquor question. I did not approve of the Democratic platform of 1932 on this question, but on account of its specific promises (a) to prevent the return of the saloon with its attendant evils, (b) to protect the dry states (hoping that a solution of the liquor question might be worked out that would solve some of the recognized evils of prohibition resulting in some of the states from an insincere and lax enforcement of the law), (c) to curb the growth of the bureaus of the federal government, and (d) to balance the budget, I voted for Mr. Roosevelt. In the congressional election of 1932, the repeal of the Eighteenth Amendment was an issue. While there was no open issue between me and my opponent, my lifelong stand and my record in the Georgia legislature on the liquor question was held against me. My vote for Mr. Hoover in 1928 and the federal patronage in the hands of my opponent were handicaps impossible to overcome.

My failure to be elected to Congress was one of the most fortunate things that ever happened. I had been a lifelong Democrat, not only by tradition and environment, but from conscientious conviction. I profoundly agree with the political philosophy of Thomas Jefferson that the interests of the republic are in safer hands when the average, common man (the farmers and the free-laboring classes, not led by selfish agitators) and the average business and professional men (unbribed and free) effectively rule the country. I believe in the preservation of local self-government and states' rights, insofar as the same can be done in justice to all sections of the country, and in a low tariff. This I understand to be the traditional gospel of the Democratic party.

I am, and always have been, opposed to too great a concentration of power in the federal government, privilege to special classes, and a high tariff. This I understand to be the traditional gospel of the Republican party. If I had been elected to Congress, I would have favored some of the expedients of the Roosevelt administration, as temporary expedients; but I could not, and would not, have supported the "New Deal," falsely so called, which is, in fact, an "Old Deal," as hoary with age as recorded history. In times of overproduction, Joseph bought up the surplus crops and stored them in public granaries. In times of scarcity, he made "seed loans" to the farmers, and took crop mortgages. He constituted the Egyptian government into a Federal Land Bank, and took mortgages on the farmers' lands. This reduced the fellahin of Egypt to a peonage which has lasted for thirty-five hundred years.

When the soldiers came home from the wars during the pacification in the time of Augustus, they demanded the soldiers' bonus, and got it. The dole which had been inaugurated in the time of Julius Caesar was continued, and wheat imported from Corsica and Egypt was freely distributed to the unemployed. A "back to the farm" movement was promoted by the free-grant-of-lands to any ex-soldier who would leave the city of Rome and live upon it. A stupendous "W.P.A." programme was undertaken. Paved roads were built all over the empire, the longest stretching from the walls of the Antonines in England, interrupted only by the Strait of Dover, through the city of Rome, and on through Tarsus to Jerusalem, a distance of thirty-seven hundred and fifty miles. Colosseums, temples, and great aqueducts were built in the Roman cities all over the empire—in Europe, Asia, and Africa. These "temporary" expedients were continued for two centuries; but when these were finished and temporary expedients were ended, Rome fell and the empire disintegrated. The ruins of these great works stand as a silent testimony of the futility of temporary expedients which divert the energies of the people, to a too great extent, from their normal needs.

To a man of deep perception and of far sight, the troubles of the world lie in a selfish racialism, and a too intense nationalism. Witness the Aryanism and the persecution of the Jews by the Nazis. To secure abnormal profits for its manufacturers and those dealing in its products, and high wages for its laborers (not too high in relation to the subsidized cost of necessary commodities), this country has built up a tariff wall which has, to a large extent, destroyed our foreign commerce, reduced production, and created unemployment. The people of Japan, living in their tight little islands, are compelled to work and sell the products of their labor in order to live. In order to get their goods over our tariff wall, and to buy products which they do not produce in their country, they are compelled to lower their wages to the limit of a bare existence. Thus pent up and starved, they have resorted to a war of conquest to wrest from us our market in China, and to appropriate it for themselves. This selfish nationalism is at the root of all the wars which are now afflicting the world, and which threaten to destroy the order of civilization which has been built during the long centuries of this historic era.

No country capable of producing more goods than it can consume can long enjoy the favor of God and man. Such a country looks across its borders, or across the seas which separate it from other nations, and sees hungry multitudes lifting their emaciated hands, and hears them crying, "We are without sufficient clothing and are cold; we are without sufficient food and are starving. With these hands we wish to work and make things which you need. We will send them to you in our ships and exchange them for the cotton and food which you do not need." It then shuts the door to immigration, plows up its cotton and wheat and corn, kills its pigs, and lops off the extra hours its people might work without injury to their health.

The lessons of history are all against racial animosity and selfish nationalism. The Hebrews tried it in the conquest of Palestine and the extermination of the Canaanites. When the Great Teacher came, he was proclaimed as the messenger of peace and goodwill to all men — not to one race and nation, but to *all* men. If, instead of pursuing a policy of national selfishness, this country would, even to a small degree, lower its tariffs, Japan could sell more of its goods here, increase wages somewhat in its own country, and buy more of our goods; and as each country would naturally buy from the other more of the goods of which it produced least, there would be an increase, instead of a decrease, in employment. Finally, there would come about the free interchange of goods among all of the peoples of the world.

Freedom of trade should lead to freedom of residence. No part of the world was created by any race of man; all men have equal rights in all parts of it. Why should any honest, peaceable, and harmless man need a passport to sail upon any sea, or live in any land? If he is a menace to society, he should be locked up, and not allowed to live freely anywhere. There are enough resources, in soil and mine and sea, to support every man in the world in comfort and in abundance. It is only man's inhumanity to man that makes the earth's countless millions mourn and fight. There is no reason why the different races of men may not live harmoniously in the same country without mixing their blood. The Jews have lived in every civilized country for centuries. They have preserved their racial integrity; and in highly civilized countries like England and America, they have lived in amity with the other races residing in those countries.

There is not as much inherent difference in the abilities of the races of man as is commonly assumed. These differences, to a great extent, disappear from the less-developed race by contact with a more advanced race. The fact that two races can live together in the same country without amalgamation, and to their mutual advantage, is illustrated by the existence of the white and Negro races in America.

The conception of the natural brotherhood of man has been held in some degree of esteem by the wise of all generations. This has not been attained because not enough men have believed in it, and because most men prefer an immediate advantage to a better condition considered too remote. This conception has burned in the hearts of the seers, like a flame upon an altar. Isaiah foretold the time when the lion and the lamb should lie down together, and when men "shall beat their swords into plowshares and their spears into pruning hooks, and nation shall not lift up sword against nation; neither shall they learn of war any more."

Robert Burns was no less a prophet when he sang:

> It's coming yet for a' that,
> That man to man the warld o'er
> Shall brothers be for a' that.

Nor was Tennyson less inspired when he "dipped into the future, far as human eye could see," and

> Heard the Heavens fill with shouting, and there rained a ghostly dew
> From the nations' airy navies grappling in the central blue . . .

And then Tennyson saw further into the future:

> *Till the war drum throbbed no longer, and the battle flags were furled*
> *In the Parliament of man, the Federation of the world.*

Woodrow Wilson tried to realize something of this in the League of Nations; but the intense nationalism of Clemenceau and Henry Cabot Lodge and the paganism and egocentric nationality of Germany deferred it, perhaps for a thousand years. But it may not be so far distant after all, and as much of it as human nature is now capable of may come out of the war now raging. Cowper says, "God moves in a mysterious way his wonders to perform."

At this point I hear the reader ask: What has all this to do with service in Congress, or with the New Deal? Well, this is the story of "Me," and it illustrates what I think. It also illustrates the fact that if I had been in Congress, I might have favored temporary relief for the unfortunate victims of an emergency; but I am not a Communist. I do not believe that it is possible to cure the ills of a false economic system by dividing up the wealth of the country, however unequally distributed. The remedy is in the creation of more wealth. With Abraham Lincoln I believe that you should not tear down my house in order to give the lumber to another man to build him a home — but you should help him to build a house for himself. I believe that laws should be passed limiting the hours of labor in certain employments where the hours are so long as to be oppressive and injurious to the health of the laborer. Laws for that purpose are not new. Such laws existed in Georgia before the New Deal was ever thought of. But I would not have favored laws whose object was not to preserve the health, but to divide up the work, and to give a more abundant life in the form of leisure not necessary to serve that purpose. No man is entitled to any more leisure than is necessary to enable him to do better work when he returns to the job. A man who does not find more pleasure in work (up to his reasonable capacity) than in idleness is not fit to have a job; and he should be subjected to the consequences of the strict application of the philosophy "root hog or die." In Congress I could not have cooperated with this administration. It has attacked no question fundamentally; it is grossly material; it has so nearly destroyed our

foreign trade that it has been necessary to bolster it up with outright subsidies (and camouflaged subsidies under the guise of dollar devaluation and gold and silver purchases beyond the value of
the gold and silver purchases); and it has fostered a quasi-Com-
munism which it did not have the intestinal fortitude to call by its
right name. I put the good of the republic above servility to party
organization, and in the year in which this is written [1940] I voted
for Wendell Wilkie.

I suppose anyone who reads this will infer from it that if I had
gone to Congress, I would have been an impractical and idealistic
crank. I do not think that this conclusion is justified when my record in the Georgia legislature and the practical nature of my professional and business life are considered. Any man (not a cynic and
grossly sensual and materialistic) has ideals beyond his reach
which, to some degree, veer the compass which directs his course
along his path through the practical affairs of life. I believe with
Lord Juesumuir that "Someday and somehow the peoples must
discover a way to brigade themselves for peace." This cannot be
done unless somebody believes it can be done and tries to bring it
about.

Thousands of men hold the same views I have expressed; but
on account of the futility of any effort to immediately realize them,
they merely ponder them in their hearts.

In Congress I could not have worked a world revolution and
brought the Golden Age, but I would have tried to contribute my
mite—and certainly would not have frittered my time away in pet-
ting rural mail carriers for their votes, and in promoting the dev-
astating financial policies of the New Deal.

XVII

Cleaning the Augean Stables

In 1929 suspicions of irregularities and graft in the administration of the municipal government of the city of Atlanta grew so strong and definite that a public investigation was demanded. The Solicitor General, John A. Boykin, became convinced by evidence too definite to be disregarded, but not definite enough to secure convictions, that graft and bribery were running rampant through the city administration. He tried for months to bring about a thorough probe of city affairs, but, naturally, found it difficult to organize such an investigation. Finally, I was requested to organize a committee of citizens to finance and prosecute such an investigation. I made up a list of twenty of the city's most prominent and influential men and laid the proposition before them. They gave their enthusiastic support, and then the committee was enlarged to one hundred. A meeting was called at a dinner at the Capital Club, at which I was elected Chairman of the "City Graft Campaign." Several thousand dollars were raised for the employment of investigators to assist the Solicitor General and to pay the other incidental

expenses of the investigation. The grand jury, under the foreman-
ship of Rawson Collier, subpoenaed and examined hundreds of
witnesses, with the result that the City Clerk, several councilmen,
and others were convicted and sent to the chaingang, with highly
beneficial and continuing results in the administration of city
affairs.

For several years I served as Chairman of the Grievance Committee of the Atlanta Bar Association. At the end of that service, I
was appointed Chairman of the Committee on Legal Ethics and
Grievances of the Georgia Bar Association.

A few years before this time, the "fake damage" claim racket
(which had been operated in some of the other cities of the country)
began to be operated in Atlanta. Under this racket, when certain
lawyers could not get enough actual damage claims, even by the
employment of ambulance chasers, they faked claims; and by the
help of perjured witnesses, with whom they divided the profits of
the business, they reaped a rich harvest out of the businessmen of
the city, out of the utility companies, and out of the casualty insurance companies doing business in the city. On account of the fact
that I was at that time Chairman of the Committee on Legal Ethics
and Grievances of the Georgia Bar Association, and on account of
my success in organizing the "City Graft Campaign," I was employed by an association of casualty insurance companies, utility
corporations, and businessmen operating through an organization
known as the Index Bureau to break up this nefarious racket in Atlanta and to bring the perpetrators of the frauds to justice. The
campaign which resulted attracted such countrywide attention that
the *Saturday Evening Post* sent one of its special writers, Paul W.
Kearney, to Atlanta to investigate the methods used in the campaign
and to write a special article concerning it. His article appeared in
the April 11, 1936, issue of the *Post*, from which the following is
quoted:

> The spark plug of the campaign was Walter McElreath, member of the
> Grievance Committee of the Georgia Bar Association, and one of the
> city's foremost lawyers; the twelve-cylinder engine of the drive was the
> Hon. John Boykin, State Solicitor General of the district, who carried on
> the prosecution with a master hand.

Stripped of many incidental details, the procedure was this: A secret committee of adjusters familiar with the situation went to Mr. McElreath, who had accomplished wonders in a local graft clean-up a year before, and presented him with the facts as summarized by the Index Bureau's records.

Mr. McElreath was deeply impressed by the gravity of the situation and its potentialities, and promptly called a meeting of twenty leading citizens, gave them a picture of the problem which confronted them, and asked if they were willing to fight it to a finish. They agreed that they were, and each one was asked to invite five other influential men to attend a second meeting, at which a plan of action would be discussed.

At the meeting referred to above, several thousand dollars were raised. This money was spent to employ special investigators to investigate the court records, to run down clues, to interview witnesses, and to employ special attorneys to assist the solicitor in preparing cases for presentation to the grand jury and in the trial of those indicted. As a result of this campaign, about thirty persons were convicted and sent to the chaingang, among them several lawyers who, upon conviction and sentence, were disbarred.

The results of this campaign were most salutary. The local bar association became more alert. Damage claims in the local courts fell off several thousand dollars a year, and the juries became more careful in rendering verdicts in damage cases.

During the progress of this campaign, upon the invitation of a committee from the city of Birmingham, I addressed a large meeting held at the Chamber of Commerce Building in that city, called for the purpose of organizing a similar campaign. Following this meeting, a campaign was organized which operated on lines similar to the Atlanta campaign, and which had results in that city as salutary as the results in Atlanta.

In May, 1937, at the invitation of its programme committee, I addressed a conference of the Grievance Committees of the American Bar Association at the Mayflower Hotel in Washington City.

XVIII

Our Wedding Trip

In 1930 we took our wedding trip, deferred for thirty-four years, because when our wedding trip should have been taken we did not have the means to take it. For a description of this trip, I quote the account of it written by Mrs. McElreath on our return.

1496 Bishop Street
Montreal, Canada
August 21st, 1930

This is where we landed at the end of our trip which began at 6:30 Saturday night, August 16th. What an uncomfortable night that was — but there was newness, something different, and pleasurable anticipations. Sunday was a long and interminable day. But no matter — there was adventure ahead. Ohio is a beautiful state, full of big, fine cities. We changed cars at Cleveland, and reached Buffalo, N.Y., Sunday night at 9:30. We were bound for Niagara Falls, Canada; so, after spending the night at the Ford Hotel, on Monday morning we took a bus for that destination. We crossed Peace Bridge, and then the custom officers boarded the bus, asked us a few questions, pretended to examine our bags, and let us by. They questioned at length an old foreign woman who could just manage to make her English intelligible, and she created quite a bit of interest and diversion.

The next person to attract the attention and cause a laugh from everybody on the bus was one "Walter McElreath." When the custom officers were through with us, the conductor came for our tickets. We were the last ones in the bus. All other tickets were promptly presented, but ours could not be found. While the bus stood still and the conductor waited, every pocket was felt in—overcoat, coat, vest, pants. Over and over the process was repeated, while the conductor very patiently waited. But the owner of the lost tickets was not very patient; the "confounds" and "doggones" began to roll out; and everybody began to laugh. At last the creator of the mirth said, "All right, I'll just pay you. I'll get rid of this Canadian dollar I've carried around in my pocket for four years and couldn't get rid of." More laughter, and the bus started on. The pocket searching did not cease, however. At last the tickets turned up in the watch pocket, and the Canadian dollar was refunded.

The road was right beside the Niagara River, a river wide, swift, and green, unmarred by a single vessel. There were about twenty miles of this, and then, suddenly we saw the falls. We were going down the river; but the mist rose like a great cloud from the water, and we knew we were near the falls. With the first view came a feeling of disappointment. The mist obscured the bottom, and the height was far below your expectations; but as we gazed upon it from all heights and angles, illuminated at night, there was stamped upon our heart and mind an image of beauty, to remain changeless and indelible.

With the roar of the falls in my ears and a realization that a life-long desire had been fulfilled, that night as I laid me down to rest I thought what a pity that life is like that—days, months, years of commonplace happenings, and then in one day have enough thrills for a lifetime. For that day, August 18th, was one day of luck and continued surprises. Luck piloted us to the most beautiful hotel I was ever in, and not the most expensive. From our bedroom window there was a view of the falls, and the long bridge going over to the American side of Niagara. The first surprise was the rubber outfit with which we were presented as we entered the boat. The passengers all looked alike, and very much resembled Ku Klux whose robes had been dyed black. After the ascension from the ride, we wandered to and fro to see the cataract from different angles, and we ran into the greatest piece of luck that ever befell two wanderers. We came upon the building "The Refectory" in Queen Victoria Park. In it was being held a banquet, given by the Ontario Bar Association to the English, Scotch, Irish, and French bar members who had been invited to

attend the American Bar Association meeting in Chicago the following
Wednesday. I think I never saw "Sir Walter" so long at least to see, if he
could not participate. I persuaded myself to go to the door and look in,
and lo and behold, in a very short time we were seated at a table where
there were two place cards, not occupied. This is how it came about.
When Mr. McElreath told the young man at the door that he was a member of the American Bar Association, he said "you and your wife shall
have seats at the table if there is room." He darted in, and was soon back
with a London official of some kind, who simply made us go in. We pro-
tested, saying we only happened to be there, and offered to pay for our
seats. They said it was absolutely free; and before we knew it, we were
seated at a table for eight. On my right was this same London attorney.
Opposite us was a distinguished blind Frenchman and his wife. On my
left was a sweet-faced lady about my age, and thereby hangs another surprise and story. She was the wife of a Niagara Falls lawyer. She asked me
where we were from. When I said Atlanta, Georgia, she said she had a
niece in Atlanta, the wife of a Tech professor; she had visited her twice.

After a most delicious menu of many courses, and speeches by Lords
and Sirs and other dignitaries, we were invited to assemble in front of the
building with our backs to the falls to have our pictures made. Just after
the pictures were taken, we again saw the Niagara lady, Mrs. Fraser. She
introduced us to her husband. He immediately took us under his wing,
and introduced us to more thrills and surprises. Into his car we climbed.
In a few moments we stopped at "Table Rock House." Little did I dream
that in a few moments we would be a hundred feet below, going through
the Scenic Tunnel. Again we are garbed in rubber coats—and boots too
this time—and after walking long passageways, we are under the falls
with the spray blinding us, and the noise deafening us—an experience too
awe inspiring to be very enjoyable.

In the car again, we viewed more angles of the falls, and had a ride
that terminated at the home of our new friends. They emphasized their
hospitality with some now prohibited drinks, which I only sipped. Then
in the car again I was sure we were bound for our hotel, but no—in the
opposite direction to more thrills and surprises. Again we stopped at a
little house by the side of the gorge, and again we found ourselves shooting down an incline. Then we were ordered to seat ourselves with our
host and hostess and have our pictures made, the second time in one day.
Think of it! Then down the gorge, on a board walk by the raging rapids
of the river—quite as beautiful as the falls. When we returned the pictures were ready. Up the incline in the car, further down the gorge to another surprise, across the raging waters to the American side, and back

in an aero-car run by pulleys. I didn't choose this experience, you understand; but having been through so many experiences already, it was altogether bearable. This was *finis*. Our host drove us to the hotel as night approached, just in time for dinner. Was our host a typical Canadian? Then let me live in Canada.

After dinner we had a view of the illuminated falls from the observatory at the top of the hotel, and then we went to bed. Is it any wonder that sleep would not come, and that I would slip to the window again and again, to see if there was a new combination of colors—violet, indigo, blue, green, yellow, orange, red. And that reminds me. Twice during the day the sun came out, and we saw the rainbow over the falls. This was the end of a perfect day.

The next day, Tuesday, August 19th, we left dear Niagara by street car for Queenstown. There we took the boat for Toronto. In about two hours we were there. Having an hour on our hands before the boat to Montreal left, a taxi whisked us to the principal places of interest. We were amazed at the magnificence of the buildings, particularly the University of Ontario, which is more than a hundred years old. By five in the afternoon we were on the ship *Toronto*, which was to bear us over the waters of Lake Ontario into the beautiful St. Lawrence. We were on the ship that night, and the next day until 7:30 p.m., when we came to Montreal. If I only had a pen that would describe that trip; but somehow this one seems to be a very poor one and will not work.

I was out of my cabin by seven that morning, hoping not to miss any of the Thousand Islands. They say there are one thousand, six hundred and ninety-two. I saw a few thousand, I am sure. The only disappointment was the weather, cold as November, a driving wind, and fitful glimpses of the sun. We went darting in and out all day, staying out as long as we dared, then viewing from within. Fortunately, in the late afternoon, when we reached the most thrilling of the rapids, the weather had moderated and we could remain out. When I said the ship *Toronto* bore us to Montreal, I had forgotten that at Prescott we were transferred to a boat specially built to "shoot the rapids," as they call it. The bottom of the boat must be flat, for some of the rocks are not more than seven feet below the bottom of the boats. Some could be seen as we went perilously near them. It was near night when we reached this old city, and it was so crowded with tourists that we could not find hotel accomodations, hence we landed at this rooming house, a fine old residence. We were thankful to get a resting place of any kind after four days of excitement. I did not go out for supper, but stayed in and began to write this little sketch of our trip while it was fresh in my mind.

Braebiggin, August 26th: Back home, and it is already beginning to feel like a dream. Surely we could not have seen so much in eight short days. We spent two nights and a day in Montreal. The sight-seeing bus took us over the city, making three stops, and driving slowly through the old part of the city where the French still live. All the signs on the streets were printed in both French and English. To my sorrow, I found that we had to leave Montreal to return by rail instead of by boat. No boat can go up the rapids. At the rapids, boats go up the river by canal. They do not take passengers; hence we had to go by train till we reached Prescott, the point of transfer. Then again we passed through the Thousand Islands. This time the weather was fine, and we sat on deck far into the night and watched the sun go down, and the twinkling lights come out in the far distant shores. I thought when going up by the swift flowing green Niagara that there could not be a more beautiful river; but I had not then seen the quiet blue and silver waters of the St. Lawrence. To sit on the deck of the smooth running ship and watch the beautiful waters, with no land in sight at times, was the acme of happiness. At other times we passed very near the lovely homes on the islands — one home to an island, and often only a few feet left for the flowers. No quarrelling with neighbors over land lines!

Again we had good luck. We landed in Toronto during their great annual exposition. During the six hours between boats, we took in this really great exhibition. But for that I would not be the possessor of some green and white china, made in England: six square plates, six cups and saucers, and one large round plate.

The last boat ride from Toronto across the lake to the American side was fraught with sadness, for I knew I would never again ride its beautiful waters. Again we were in the hands of the custom officers, and my precious package had to be opened and examined. He seemed satisfied with unwrapping one cup, and I breathed a prayer of thankfulness that he did not disturb the carefully packed plates. Well, the thrills were not quite over. We had not been on the American side of the Falls at all. From the boat, we boarded the double-trolley car, which took us right beside the raging waters below the falls. We caught a new view of the falls, from below this time, and under the great bridge that spans the river just below the falls. I believe that the last glimpse was the most beautiful. It lingers with me. There was not a moment to stay when we reached the city. We ran with suitcase, bags, china, and wraps for a bus already leaving for Buffalo. The next morning — Sunday, August 20th — we boarded a train for Atlanta.

The thrills are gone, but the memories are indelible; and there is a feeling of thankfulness for a safe return from our adventures.

XIX

And Then Winter Came

In 1935 the Georgia Bar Association met at The Cloister on Sea Island on the last day in May. Mrs. McElreath accompanied me to the meeting. She was always eager to go to a new place and was very fond of the seashore. The prospect of this trip electrified her. She bought a beautiful soft blue silk dress, new shoes, and a new handbag. With her beautiful clothes, her beautiful grey hair, and her refined face, she was one of the most beautiful women who attended the meeting. At our first meal we had the good luck to have a table with Judge and Mrs. John B. Hutcheson. The two ladies fell in love with each other, and in driving over the island and visiting its historic spots, a very warm friendship matured between them.

In the early summer, after we returned from Sea Island, I realized that Mrs. McElreath was not well; but I thought, and she insisted, that her indisposition was due to the hot weather. I determined to get her away from Atlanta as soon as I could conveniently do so; but on account of the absence of my partner during the whole of August, and important work requiring my personal attention, we could not get away until September. In the climate of Atlanta the first weeks of September are almost always the hardest part of the summer to bear. I arranged to take her on a sea trip to New York where I hoped we might find a cooler climate, and where a change of scene might benefit her, intending to return about the third week in September, when the intense heat of the summer is past and the beginning of the long and delightful Indian summer is near at hand.

We did not go directly to Jacksonville where we intended to take the boat, but drove down to Thomasville so that she could pay a long-promised visit to one of her cousins. After spending a night and part of the next day in Thomasville, we drove to Tallahassee which, for some reason, she wished to see. We then drove to Jacksonville and took the *Shawnee* to New York. The boat was running late. We arrived in New York late in the afternoon and stopped at the Pennsylvania Hotel. In the evening we walked for awhile, amazed at the wonderful changes in that part of the city during the fifteen years since either of us had been in New York. After wandering around awhile on Broadway, glowing with the splendor of its bright lights, we went to Radio City and spent an hour on the roof of its highest building. It was a clear night, and the panorama which spread before us was one which is to be compared to nothing else in the world. The beauty of the scene and the exhilaration of it revived her spirits to such an extent that I thought the trip was just the thing she had needed.

The next morning after breakfast we started to walk over to the Empire State Building, only a short distance from our hotel, when I discovered that she was so weak that she could hardly walk, and that she hardly knew where she was. The questions she asked and the requests she made showed that her mind was completely confused. I became very uneasy and insisted that we return at once to the hotel. When we arrived there I immediately made arrangements for our return on the ship which sailed at noon on that day. On shipboard, she hardly left our stateroom and refused her meals.

On the last night before our arrival back in Jacksonville, after she had fallen asleep, I went to the upper deck and paced it until midnight. It was the clearest and most beautiful night I had ever seen. The stars were bright and seemed so near that it seemed as if

I were standing in the very vestibule of the celestial universe, and there came over me a strange premonitory sadness. It said to me as plainly as if the stars spoke — "This is the end."

When we arrived at Jacksonville, I took her to the Seminole Hotel and summoned a physician. After staying there two or three days, during which time she showed some improvement, one morning I awoke and found that she had arisen, had packed all of our baggage, and was sitting with her hat on. The first words she said when I awoke were, "Please, let's go home; I want to go home so bad." I called the doctor who advised me to bring her home that day. As soon as we had passed out of the city and were on the long road, she assumed towards me an attitude of ineffable tenderness, and after a long silence, said, "Mr. McElreath, if we could both have fallen off that boat and could have gone off together, wouldn't that have been the finest thing in the world?"

When we arrived back home, I secured a doctor and a nurse to stay with her day and night, and under their care she seemed to slowly improve. After some weeks she was so much improved that we somewhat relaxed our constant attentions. She would not allow the nurse to sleep in the room with her; so the nurse slept across the hall. I slept in the adjoining room, constituting (with her room and the open bathroom between) our private suite, where I could usually hear every move that she made.

The constant anxiety and watchfulness had almost completely exhausted me; and on the night following a day when she had appeared to be unusually well, I fell off into a profound sleep. When I awoke the next morning, the morning of November 20, 1935, I found that she had died in the night.

After my wife's death, my eldest sister came and made her home with me. For two years she showed me every kindness of an unselfish sister.

My very great friend, J. J. Haverty, who had had a similar sorrow, advised me that the only antidote to such a grief was to work absorbingly and unremittingly. I took his advice and followed it; but my recollections of the next few months are like the memory of a confused and frightful dream.

In 1926 I made the suggestion to a few friends that a historical society ought to be organized in Atlanta for the collection and preservation of the important, interesting, and neglected history of the city. This suggestion met with enthusiastic favor. After a canvass, a preliminary organization was formed, and on the 30th day of June, 1926, a charter was obtained from the Superior Court of Fulton County incorporating the Atlanta Historical Society. On permanent organization under the charter, I was elected President and Chairman of the Executive Committee. For seven years I held these offices, and for four years I acted as Editor of the *Bulletin* published by the Society. In 1933 I declined reelection as President, and Mr. Eugene M. Mitchell was elected President. I was made Honorary President for life and Chairman of the Executive Committee. Mr. Mitchell was succeeded as President in 1935 by Mr. Jack J. Spalding, one of the best citizens and ablest lawyers who ever lived in Atlanta.

Up to the fall of 1936, the Society had no paid officer or employee, and no headquarters of its own, its collections being stored in the Rhodes Memorial Hall, in which the state's archives were kept, in charge of Miss Ruth Blair, the State Historian, who acted as the Secretary of the Society and as custodian of its archives. In November, 1936, I suggested to Mr. Spalding that the Society should be endowed, at least for a term of five years, that a paid secretary should be employed, and that the Society should be established in quarters of its own. Mr. Spalding agreed with these suggestions, and with his influence and help, annual subscriptions for five years were obtained in a sufficient amount to accomplish this purpose. Temporary headquarters were secured in the Biltmore Hotel, to be occupied until a permanent home for the Society was secured, and Miss Blair retired as State Historian and accepted the position of Executive Secretary of the Society. Under her able direction, the Society has steadily increased in public favor and is now one of the more popular and important cultural institutions in the city.

The task of reorganizing the Historical Society having been accomplished, in order to renew my spirits in new scenes and to fulfill a cherished dream, I sailed from New York on January 30, 1937, on the *Roma*, a luxurious ship of the Italian Line, on a Mediterranean cruise. This was the first time I had ever crossed the Atlantic, and my first trip on a first-class ocean liner. The luxury of the ship, the elegance of the clothes worn at dinner and at the social affairs in the great Hall of Festivities, and the brilliant company made the voyage over an experience never to be forgotten. When I went on deck on the morning of the eighth day, there lay before me a sight of amazing beauty. The ship was anchored about a mile from the city of Funchal, on the island of Madeira. To the right was a sheer cliff, perhaps seven hundred feet high, and on the left another promontory of greater height. Between these, in a wide semicircle rising tier upon tier, and almost to the top of the mountains, rose the gleaming white houses of the city. Disembarking, we visited the famous wine houses. We drank the vintage, some nearly one hundred years old, rode in bullock sleds to the funicular which carried us to the top of the mountains behind the city through profuse gardens of flowers — poinsettias, flame vines, bougainvillea, camelia trees covered with red and white blooms — in fact, every flower that blooms in a tropical climate. After spending one hour gazing at the panorama of the city and the sea, we slid down the mountain in basket sleds guided by athletic Portugese, around hair-raising curves, along the road paved with smooth cobble stones. The afternoon was spent in driving over the island and in examining the incomparable needlework and laces.

In the early evening we sailed away to Gibraltar. We stopped there for a day and visited the town and all parts of the great rock to which the public is admitted. At this time the Spanish war was raging. From the heights of Gibraltar could be seen more than a dozen grim, grey British dreadnoughts lying about the sea. While we were on the streets, the shout went up that Malaga had just fallen.

From Gibraltar we sailed to Algiers where I received another great surprise. I had never made any particular study of Algiers, and only thought of it as the home of the Barbary pirates. I had supposed the city to be an old crumbling place of harems and dilapidated mosques. Imagine the surprise when we tied up at a modern quay before a waterfront along which there was a three-decked street, one of the notable works of modern engineering, and with an imposing and beautiful city rising from the sea, and up the heights beyond. We drove down the main street, lined with magnificent French shops, to the city park with its great banyan trees.

From there we went to a high eminence from which we could see
the Atlas Mountains sixty miles away, beyond which lies the Sahara. We visited the Kabala, the crowded Arab quarter with its
streets only a few feet wide and too narrow for anything but pe-
destrian travel; the Sultan's Palace, with its mosaics and ara-
besques and its abandoned harem; the New Mosque, at the prayer
hour; the Old Mosque; the Museum; and the Christian Church.
After a day in Algiers, we sailed late at night for Naples.

We arrived in Naples in the early morning two days later. We
were temporarily disappointed because Vesuvius was wrapped in
clouds, making that supreme object of interest invisible. We drove
down the magnificent strata through the heart of the city to Pom-
peii, the clouds having rolled away by the time of our arrival there.
After spending a couple of hours amid the excavated ruins of Pom-
peii, we drove along the famous Amalfi Drive to the Capuchin monastery at Amalfi. There we took dinner, after which we drove on
around the tip of the cape to Sorrento, one of the most famous small
cities of Italy. Afterwards we drove along the bay of Naples with the
island of Capri in sight, back to the city of Naples. The beauty of
the drive to Amalfi, along the road cut high in the side of the mountain, with the blue Mediterranean on the left, deserves its reputation as one of the world's most beautiful drives.

From Naples we sailed to Athens. On the morning of our arrival, I went out on deck and found that the ship was preparing to
anchor in a quiet bay surrounded by mountains with no city in
sight. I asked the captain why he was stopping there and told him
that I understood that we were to stop at Phaleron. He sent a thrill
down my spine by answering that the sea was too rough to anchor
at Phaleron, and that he had come up into the bay of Salamis. Pointing to the shore he said, "That is Mount Hymettus and beyond is
Mount Pentelicon." Disembarking, we drove to Phaleron; and from
there up the long avenue on the side of the ancient "long walls" five
and a half miles to the city of Athens. We visited the Temple of
Olympian Zeus, of which Hadrian said that it was the only temple
ever built that was worthy of its god, and of which fifteen columns
are still standing. From there we went across the Ilissus, to the ancient stadium which has been restored to its ancient condition.
From there we went to the museum in which in long rows of cases

are displayed the objects recovered from the ancient Mycenaean tombs of the age of Agamemnon and the Trojan War and, in addition, many ancient Greek statues. After lunch at the Grand Bretagne Hotel, we went to the Temple of Theseus, the Agora (which was being excavated), the Acropolis, the Parthenon (on the steps of which I had my photograph taken), and to Mars Hill. When we left just before sundown, the sea had so calmed that the *Roma* had come down to Phaleron. When I got aboard, I could see straight up the long avenue to the city of Athens, the Parthenon gleaming on the Acropolis, Mount Lycabettus just beyond, and the mountains of Attica stretching in the long distance towards the sunset. Henry Van Dyke says that the sight of Athens from the sea is the grandest prospect on earth to a man of literary culture.

From Athens we sailed to the Island of Rhodes, now called Rodi, and anchored near the site of the ancient Colossus of Rhodes, on the site of which now stands a tall column surmounted by the Roman Wolf. Rhodes is the site of the ancient castles of the Knights of St. John, of the days of the Crusades. It was also the site of the ancient school of rhetoric where Plato studied. We drove over the island from which the coasts of Anatolia are visible, and over the campus of the ancient school from which all the ancient buildings have disappeared.

From Rhodes we sailed along the coast of Asia to Beirut, and there took cars and drove across the Lebanon Mountains to Damascus where we visited the street called Straight, the House of Annanias where the scales fell from the eyes of St. Paul, the Mosque of the Omayyad, the tomb of Saladin, and the Mosque of Solyman.

From Beirut we sailed to Haifa, which lies along the sea, and along the slopes of Mount Carmel, on the top of which stands a monastery on the place where Elijah had his contest with the priests of Baal. At Haifa we took the train which runs down the Plains of Sharon, rich and as beautiful as when "Sharon's dewy rose" bloomed there in scriptural times, to the junction at Lud, the ancient Lydda, and thence through the barren hills of Judea to Jerusalem. I had a ticket to stop while at Jerusalem at the King David Hotel, one of the most magnificent hotels in the east; but when we arrived, we found that they lacked rooms to accommodate all of the guests. We were assigned to the Fast Hotel, which stands a short distance outside the walls near the Jaffa gate. In the afternoon we went down the Street of David, surely the most noisome, foul smelling upon the earth, to the Via Dolorosa and up it. We went past the Ecce Homo Arch, past the site of the point where Simon the Cyrenean took up the cross, past where St. Veronica spread the napkin over the face of Jesus, to the Church of the Holy Sepulchre. It is a great rambling building, with intricate mazes of aisles, covering the supposed site of Calvary. Over it is a great altar, covering the Stone of Anointing, and the supposed tomb of Joseph of Arimathea. We went into the antechamber of the tomb, and then stepped into the inner tomb where the body is supposed to have lain. From there we went back down the Via Dolorosa to Pilate's Judgment Hall, the location of which is certainly authentic. The pavement of the lower floor is said to be, and apparently is, the original stone floor of the Tower of Antonia in which the trial before Pilate was held.

The next morning we went to the temple enclosure on Mount Zion, a plaza of thirteen and a half acres, now known as the Sherif-al-Hassam. The center where the temple stood is now the site of the Mosque of Omar, the glory of Islam. We entered the mosque and saw the Dome of the Rock, upon which Abraham planned the sacrifice of Isaac. After visiting the Mosque of Omar and Al Aksar, we went to the Wailing Wall and to the Pool of Bethesda, which was at the bottom of a deep ravine which has been filled up with the debris from the successive destructions of the city. It is now reached by going down a long ladder in a deep well.

We then went to the Garden of Gethsemane. It is now almost covered by the Church of the Agony and other buildings. The old gnarled olive trees found there are said to be original trees which "were kind to Him" on the night of His arrest.

From Gethsemane we went to the Mount of Olives. From the roof of the Church of the Ascension we saw, to the west, a panorama of the city of Jerusalem; to the east, the Dead Sea, with the mountains of Horeb beyond; to the northwest, the mountains of Gilead, and Bethany sleeping on the shoulder of the Mount of Olives. From there we drove around north of the city, over the ground occupied by the armies of Sennacherib, and through Jerusalem without the walls, and along the road to Bethlehem. There we visited the Church of the Nativity. We saw the traditional manger, and the catacombs far beneath the church, in the seclusion of which St. Jerome translated the Hebrew scripture into the Vulgate—and in which his tomb lies. On the way back, we stopped at the tomb of Rachael which stands beside the Bethlehem road. From that place we could see the fields where the shepherds were tending their flocks by night when the angels sang the announcement of the birth of the Lord.

The *Roma* next anchored at Port Said, near the mouth of the Suez Canal, near the statue of De Lesseps. From there we went by train along the canal to the junction at Ismailia, and from there across the desert about thirty miles to the Land of Goshen, and across that land (irrigated by canals from which water is pumped up onto the bush farms by Archimides' screws, norias, and shadufs) to Cairo. Before reaching Cairo, we could see the tips of the pyramids in the distance. We remained at Cairo for five days, being registered at the famous Shephards Hotel. After I had registered and had come out and sat down upon the terrace, my first thought was that I cared nothing for a modern city of a million and half population. In the area in which the hotel is located, Cairo looked just like any other large city, but it was only a few hours until that mystic, mysterious lotus-laden feeling that creeps out of the "Garden of Allah," which has been felt by every visitor to Egypt, got hold of me. This feeling increased with every hour spent there. When we left on the fifth day, every one of our party heaved a sigh of regret that we had to leave at all.

On our first afternoon of sightseeing, we visited the Museum of Arab Art. This museum was of a fairly large size, having in it only objects of Arabian art; and while it was interesting for that reason, it was to me somewhat disappointing. The Arabs seem to have flowered in their genius in architecture, as illustrated by the Mosque of the Omayyad at Damascus, the Mosque of Omar at Jerusalem, the Mosque of Mohamet Ali at Cairo, the Mosque of Suleiman the Magnificent at Istanbul, the Sultan's Palace at Algiers, and the Alhambra at Granada. After the museum, we visited the Mosque of Al Hassan, the Mosque of Mohamet Ali, and the Citadel, the scene of the massacre of the Mamelukes. Embedded in its walls are some of the cannon balls fired at it by Napoleon's guns.

From one of the high terraces of the Citadel there is a fine panoramic view of the city of Cairo, the Pyramids, the Nile, and the desert.

After visiting the Citadel, we took a long drive through the streets of the Arab shops. It was a day or two before one of the great Mohammedan feasts, and the excitement of the Arabs was like that of Americans on Christmas Eve. Droves of lambs (with red paint daubed on their backs showing that they had been inspected for slaughter) were being driven about the streets. On the following night (which corresponded with Christmas Eve in America) I drove, with a lady who was one of the passengers on the *Roma*, through these same streets, filled with shouting Moslem celebrants.

However much one may read in guidebooks, or have talked with other travelers, one is not fully prepared for the experience of visiting the Pyramids and the Sphinx. They are situated about seven miles west of Cairo, at the end of the magnificent boulevard built by Ismail Pasha, Egypt's last "New Dealer." This grand avenue is at least one hundred feet wide, paved with cement, with a streetcar track down the center, and lined on each side with trees. The Pyramid of Cheops is so stupendous in size and height that no description of it can give any just idea of its dimensions and grandeur. When one thinks of its age, one is filled with awe. If Abraham saw it, as he perhaps did, it was then more than a thousand years old. Nearby is the Sphinx, still looking to the east, with that inscrutable smile with which it has greeted the morning sun for four thousand years. If one could know the secret of that inscrutable smile, one would know something of the mystery of that ancient world which, notwithstanding modern discoveries and research, is still a mystery.

On a Sunday afternoon I hired a car, and, with a companion, drove to Memphis and Sakkara, about twenty miles from Cairo. Memphis was the ancient capital of Egypt, and Sakkara the more ancient suburb of Memphis. There is now at Memphis practically nothing but the two prone statues of Rameses II, the pharaoh of the oppression and the alabaster sphinx. A short distance from the site of ancient Memphis, and about a mile within the desert, is Sakkara.

Here is the step pyramid, the oldest of the pyramids of Egypt; and about a mile further within the desert is the Serapeum, a vast underground series of passages and rooms cut out of the solid rock, in the crypts of which the sacred bulls were entombed. A short distance further in the desert is the tomb of Ti, the High Priest of the Second Dynasty; and, nearby, the Temple of Zozer. After spending an hour in the Serapeum, we went to the Tomb of Ti and spent quite a while examining its chambers. It was adorned with hieroglyphics and painted walls, on some of which the paint was still bright, notwithstanding the long centuries which have passed since the walls were decorated.

The highlight of our stay in Cairo was our visit to the Museum of Egyptian Antiquities. It is considered next in interest to the British Museum among all of the museums of the world. The museum occupies a vast building, choked with relics of all ages of Egypt's long history. The portion of the museum of most interest is the corridor in which the amazing contents of the tomb of Tutankhamen are displayed. The inner death mask of solid gold, the stone sarcophagus, and the seven wooden cases, all covered with gold leaf, with one fitted within the other, and the statuettes, the beds, the couches, the cots, the household implements, the jars of seeds to be planted when the mummied body came back to life—all made an exhibit of staggering magnificence.

But the greatest thing in Egypt is the Nile. It is older than the Pyramids. Without its waters, there would have been no Egypt. The first pharaoh sailed his ships upon it and worshiped its opulent, wealth-producing waters. Upon its bosom the barge of Cleopatra floated. On its waters Mark Anthony and Julius Caesar sailed. It runs through the city of Cairo in lazy majesty. Its waters, covered with feluccas and spreading out through the delta, gave sustenance to countless millions for thousands of years before Pharaoh's daughter found Moses floating upon its waters in his basket of bullrushes.

On the 22nd of February we left Port Said for Istanbul, sailing for two days among the Aegean Isles, passing in sight of Samos, and near the shores of Crete, Lemnos, and Tenedos. We passed through the Dardanelles at night and found ourselves in the morning in the beautiful Sea of Marmora. After a few hours we came in sight of

Constantinople, or Istanbul as it is now called, and anchored in the Golden Horn. This city, formerly the capital of the Roman Empire of the East, was at one time the most opulent city of the world. Built on the sides of a great and high headland, with the domes of its incomparable mosques and their tall and graceful minarets, it presents an imposing sight when seen from the sea.

Debarking and driving across the famous Galata Bridge, we spent an afternoon seeing the sights. We went first to the museum, which was large and full of very interesting exhibits, mostly the works of Turkish artisans and artists, but no pictures or statues. The object of most interest is the sarcophagus of Alexander the Great, discovered at Sidon in 1865. Whether this is the veritable sarcophagus of Alexander or not is not known; but it is a tradition that the body of Alexander was being carried from Babylon (where he died) to Alexandria for burial, and that for some reason the sarcophagus was abandoned at Sidon.

After the museum we next visited the Mosque of Suleiman the Magnificent, which is an immense building, richly ornamented, and with the largest dome in the world. From there we went to the Church of St. Sophia, said to be the glory of Byzantine art, and one of the most beautiful churches in the world. It was built in A.D. 525 by Justinian, and when I saw it, was fourteen hundred and twelve years old—yet in apparently perfect condition. Four of its great pillars are from Ephesus and four from Baghdad. The others had origins I cannot now recall. From St. Sophia we went to the Blue Mosque, a perfect gem of Saracen architecture. Its slender interior columns, its graceful minarets, and its exquisite mosaics make it one of the world's most beautiful buildings.

The *Roma* left Istanbul on the morning of February 25th, and at daylight was still in the Sea of Marmora, steaming towards the Hellespont. About eight we came to the narrow passage where the Straits begin. From there to the Aegean Sea are sixty miles of the most romantic scenery in the world, which Gibbon describes in one of his most glowing passages. Ancient Troy, seated on an eminence at the foot of Mount Ida, was about three miles from the Straits and from the Aegean; the site was plainly in sight, but not distinguishable, from our boat. On the east shore of the Straits, the Grecian camp (in the Trojan War) stretched for twelve miles from the Aegean to the Phaetean promontory. On the first of these, Achilles pitched his camp, and Ajax was upon the other. The flanks of the army were guarded by Agamemnon. On the western side of the Straits was Gallipoli, with its great monument and the vast cemetery where the ill-fated strategy of Winston Churchill sacrificed the lives of thousands of brave soldiers in the last great war. To sail those Straits on a warm clear morning was one of the high points of my life's experience.

In the early evening of February 26th, we came along the shores of Sicily, passed Mount Etna, and in a short time passed through the Straits of Messina, between Scylla and Charybdis, and on past Stromboli, in flaming eruption, and stopped again at Naples for a day. I took advantage of this stop to visit the crater of Vesuvius, with a lady who was leaving the cruise at Naples. She wished to visit the crater and had no one else to accompany her. When we reached the edge of the crater, it was quiescent, the smoke and gases coming out of a crevice on the other side of the mountain. The guides told us that it was perfectly safe to walk down into the shallow depression which was then the form of the crater. Soon after we arrived at the center, lava began to ooze out of some fissures on the side of the walls of the crater and to run down in narrow streams towards us. We stayed until the streams came to where we were standing, then, needless to say, we beat a hasty retreat. This all sounds daring, but it was perfectly safe. The scientists on duty at the observatory located near the crater, with their delicate instruments, were able to know when danger existed.

On Sunday, February 28th, in the early morning, we arrived at Genoa, built like Naples on the slopes of hills which rise from the sea. Its highest hills are crowned with old forts and other historic buildings. The city as described by Carducci, is "a marble amphitheater of palaces, mirrored in the bright Ligurian Sea." Genoa was the birthplace of Christopher Columbus. His statue stands on one of the principal streets; the house in which he is said to have been born is not far away. Space does not permit the enumeration of the many churches, statues, and places of interest in this beautiful city, except to mention the one sight that everybody sees at Genoa—the cemetery of Staglieno, universally held to the be the finest cemetery in the world. From Genoa we took a day's trip into the surrounding country, driving first through the finest parts of the city, and then to San Margharita and to Rappello, two of the finest little cities on the Italian Riviera. This drive rivaled, and some thought surpassed, the Amalfi Drive.

After a day and a half at Genoa, we left at one o'clock p.m. on March first for Villefranche, sailing the entire distance close to the shore. This afforded us a fine view of the Italian and French Rivieras. We only stayed at Villefranche for a few hours, for a visit to Nice and Monte Carlo. This was our last stop, except to pause at Gibraltar to take on passengers and mail.

On March 15th I was back in Atlanta. Refreshed, and my spirits revived, I immediately went back to work.

On January 9, 1938, I married Miss Mildred Dickey, the daughter of William Dickey of Toccoa, Georgia.

XX

Conclusion

It is a wise saying that no monument should be raised to a living man. With few exceptions, this wise rule should be applied to the writing of autobiographies. In my case, if anything I have done is worthy of recording at all, its proper title would be "A Saga of Small Things." I know many men, who started life under conditions no better than mine, who overcame greater difficulties and have achieved greater success. My excuse for writing this book is that if I had not written it, no one else would, and that I have wished to preserve the memory of my revered parents and grandparents, and to inspire any of their descendants who may see these pages to honor the worthy ancestors from whom they sprang. These people were not rich or distinguished, as the world measures distinction; but they worked hard, lived honestly, and died in peace with God and man. That is success; and distinction and glory for a good name is rather to be desired than great riches.

I have now reached an age when most men have passed from the state of human action, or have spent all of their energies. What a great age it is in which to have lived! In my lifetime, the electric light, the telephone, the radio, the automobile, the Linotype, the phonograph, the cinema, and artificial refrigeration have been invented; the Suez and Panama Canals have been opened, the Spanish-American and the Great War of 1914 have occurred, and now another world conflict is raging. I have seen the log schoolhouse replaced by magnificent school buildings to which the children, instead of tramping through rain and mud, now ride over cement roads in motor driven conveyances. Since I came to Atlanta, automatic heat, a tiled bathroom, and a garage have become standard equipment in every city home; and electric lights and city conveniences are coming into use in many country homes. During my life the social and political changes have been as great as the material changes. When I was born the Tsars still ruled Russia in medieval absolutism, Bismark was completing the consolidation of Germany under Prussian autocracy, and Garibaldi was forging Italy into a unified state. At this time Karl Marx was propagating his doctrines of socialism. For a time there seemed to be a growth of democracy in all countries. The institution of the Duma in Russia and the rising power of the Reichstag in Germany formed the hope of men the world over that free, popular government would supplement absolutism in the whole world. And then came the catastrophe of the Great War of 1914. When Germany was defeated, men hoped that it was the final overthrow of systems of government founded on force and conquest. How delusive these hopes were is shown by the subversion of the governments of Russia, Italy, and Germany to sovietism, fascism, and nazism; the dictatorships of Stalin, Mussolini, and Hitler; the conquest of Ethiopia, Albania, Austria, Czechoslovakia, Poland, Norway, the Netherlands, Belgium, and France; and the war which is now raging against the British Empire and Greece.

In the United States of America, until very recent years the powers of the federal government were limited, under the Constitution, as the framers of that instrument intended them to be. The federal government rarely touched the individual. But with the adoption of the amendment providing for the levy of a tax on incomes, by the natural growth of interstate commerce, and by fine-spun judicial interpretations of the federal power over commerce between the states, every individual taxpayer, employer, employee, farmer, manufacturer, and miner in the United States is personally under the supervision of the federal government. During the week in which this is written, the people of the United States have overthrown a tradition as old as the republic and elected a president for a third term. He is vested with normal and emergency powers, coupled with an influence over the legislative branches of the government through majorities belonging to the political party of which he is the leader, and over the judicial branch through the philosophic bent of a judiciary of his selection. This constitutes a condition so like dictatorship that the only hope of free, democratic life in this country is in the benevolence of the dictator.

In this situation, with the economic system of the country out of joint and thousands of people unemployed, many young men are perplexed, disoriented, and discouraged. In these times there is too often heard the statement that there are fewer opportunities for young men than in former times, that the professions are crowded, and that the machine age has taken the jobs away from willing hands. We may be going through a period of temporary adjustment where the old opportunities are less; but new opportunities will be made. The world is made up of men, and it will always take men to run it.

Insofar as I can speak through these pages to those who come after me, I admonish them to form a true concept of success. To get rich, have high social prestige, and hold office is not always a true criterion of real success. It is too often the result of craven selfishness. It is nobler to deserve success than to attain it unworthily. Any man with normal health and average brains can achieve reasonable success if he will use all of his energies to the limit. One of my friends, somewhat older than I, started in life as a blacksmith, with only the most meager education. After working all day at the forge and the anvil, he mended shoes at night. He saved his money, and soon was able to establish a small mercantile business at a country crossroads. At odd times he studied law, was admitted to the bar, was finally elected judge of the Superior Court of his circuit, and died worth a quarter of a million dollars.

The young men of this age are better educated than their fathers, and if this is not a satisfactory world, they can make a new and better world—if they have not lost the stamina and character of their fathers.

I admonish the young men of the present day and those who come after me not to yield to any defeatist philosophy. Tackle the problems of life with confidence. Do not tackle them with an over-confidence, for it breeds discouragement with the first defeat; and do not shirk problems from timidity. Above everything else, be self-reliant. Every success brings a larger one. When Hercules slew the Nemean lion, its hide furnished him a cloak which he wore to his other labors.

The best advice I can give a young man is to read Robert Burns's "Advice to a Young Friend." Commit it to memory and follow its sound philosophy.

Every sensible man who has reached my age is bound to have a certain sense of frustration. In his moments of retrospection he has more humiliation over his mistakes and shortcomings than pride in his accomplishments. I have lived long and worked hard, but I have not always worked wisely and well. I have dissipated my energies in too many directions. I have done some good work in law, but my professional life has not been an outstanding success. Lack of op-portunity prevented me from acquiring my academic education in the days of youth when the mind is plastic and when mental train-ing becomes part of the essential fiber of mentality; and it was im-possible to complete my higher education, even at the late period when it was undertaken. This handicap could have been overcome, if I had let politics and other side issues alone and concentrated all of my energies on my profession. I did not succeed in politics be-cause it was not my forte, because I was too stubborn in my own ideas and would not trim my sails to the winds of popular sentiment when they blew in a direction contrary to my own opinions and principles, and because politics was not really my ambition. As a lawyer, I have had quite an extensive practice, having tried cases in all parts of Georgia and in some of the other states, and in every kind of court, from the justice courts at Adamsville to the Supreme Court of the United States. I have won more cases than I have lost, but I think I can frankly say that the merit of my work has been in the quality of my work rather than in its extent. I have done my best in every case. I have never solicited a case, nor attended a funeral in the hope of representing the estate of the deceased. I have refused large fees because I could not conscientiously represent the causes in which I was sought to be employed. Nevertheless, I have made a living and something more.

I have always had a passion for reading, but my reading has been too desultory. Consequently, my general information has been too superficial. Reading can be a form of mental dissipation and become a mental narcotic. The best-read man I ever knew had an eyesight so defective that he had to read with one eye, through a magnifying glass. Consequently he read few books; but he remembered every word that he read, and its contents became part of the permanent furniture of his mind.

Success in the common connotation of the term is purchased at a terrible price, and while I cannot claim anything but a moderate approach to it, I am content. Cardinal Wolsey rightly said, "Ambition is a burthen too great for him who hopes for heaven." What a man closing his career regrets most is not the opportunities for self-advancement he has missed, but his deeds of neglect and selfishness. Real success consists of what a man makes of his inner self—and not of popularity, the offices he holds, or the money he accumulates. The unthinking neglect of acts of family affection, of social amenities, and of consideration for one's neighbors and friends is too often the price which a man who is too ambitious for personal success pays.

I naturally hope that those of future generations who bear my family name, and those in whose veins the blood of my ancestors shall flow, will be successful and stand above the common herd; but I hope they will attain such a position in life, not for vain glory, but as a reward for their industry and right living.

And so I conclude, as Robert Burns concluded his advice to his young friend,

> "And May you rock the rede,
> Better than ever did th' adviser."

INDEX

Walter McElreath: An Autobiography

Designed by Alesa Jones
Composition by MUP Composition Department
Production specifications:
    text paper—60 lb. Warren's Olde Style
    endpapers—Gainsborough Silver Text
    cover—(on .088 boards) Holliston Kingston 35448 Natural
    dust jacket—Gainsborough Silver Text Printed PMS 539
Printing (offset lithography) by Omnipress of Macon, Inc., Macon, Georgia
Binding by John H. Dekker and Sons, Inc., Grand Rapids, Michigan